RETURN TO *Glory*

THE INSIDE STORY OF THE GREEN BAY PACKERS' RETURN TO PROMINENCE

KEVIN ISAACSON
WITH TOM KESSENICH

Published by

 **krause
publications**

700 E. State Street • Iola, WI 54990-0001

Hugh McAloon, publisher, sports division

Please call or write for our free catalog of sports publications. Our toll-free number
to place an order or obtain a free catalog is 800-258-0929 or please use our regular business
telephone 715-445-2214 for editorial comment or further information.

Library of Congress Catalog Number: 96-77479
ISBN: 0-87341-488-8

Printed in the United States of America

To Ron Wolf, who will never get the credit he deserves
To Mike Holmgren, who deserves all of the credit he's given
To Bob Harlan, who scripted this story in his mind five years ago

Chapter summary

The right stuff

By effectively mixing tradition and change,
Bob Harlan, Ron Wolf and Mike Holmgren
have brought glory back to Packers football

Peer into a crowd anywhere in Wisconsin and you'll see Packers apparel, be it a cap, jacket, jersey or even one of those neat cheese hats.

It was different in 1991. Then, the average Packers fan would've sooner spent a summer in Illinois than wear green and gold outside of Lambeau Field. We might've loved the Packers then, too, but only in the privacy of our basements and rec rooms, away from the jeers of those whose affection for our team didn't extend through two decades without a playoff game.

For a very long time, it wasn't fun to be a Packers fan.

The optimism generated in 1989, when the Don Majkowski-led Packers finished just short of the playoffs at 10-6, was gone. In its place was anger over the holdout of Tim Harris, questions about the struggling "Majik Man," disbelief over the unprecedented failure of Tony Mandarich. Coach Lindy Infante, just two years earlier anointed a worthy successor to legendary Vince Lombardi, had won just three of his last 20 games.

Late in 1991, it was absolutely awful to be a Packers fan.

It is that perspective, the frustrated fan, that team president Bob Harlan considered as he contemplated the future of the Green Bay Packers.

"We can do better," Harlan said late that fall. "The fans deserve better."

Harlan, altering the tenor of the NFL's smallest city for the 1990s and beyond, convinced Ron Wolf, a 30-year NFL veteran with a rare appreciation for football history, to leave the Jets and become the first man to possess sole responsibility for Packers football decisions since Lombardi left in 1969. To label Wolf a perfect fit would be an understatement.

"He's got a lot of Lombardi in him," John Fabry, vice president of the team's executive committee, said of Wolf during the 1992 season. "I know how that sounds ... but it's a different atmosphere. We're coming back."

Wolf restructured the scouting staff, worked with Harlan to upgrade the team's practice facilities and began rebuilding the roster. He convinced Mike Holmgren, the most-sought head coaching prospect in an off-season in which eight NFL teams had vacancies, to come to Green Bay.

Harlan: "The prettiest girl at the dance, and we ended up with him."

Before their team played a game, Wolf and Holmgren made NFL history by hiring two minority coordinators, ex-49ers assistants Ray Rhodes and Sherman Lewis. A forlorn outpost since Lombardi's exit, Green Bay – NFL champions a record 11 times – was quickly returning to the spotlight.

Holmgren hoped for five wins in his first season, only because the 1991 team went 4-12. But he prepared himself and his family for much less.

"I thought 2-and-14," said Bob LaMonte, the coach's friend and agent. "Ask anybody in America to name a Packer player, and they would've said Mandarich. No offense to Sharpe, but they didn't have a lot of talent."

That ineptness, interestingly, drew Holmgren to the Packers. He saw a team with subpar talent, a losing mindset, the ultimate NFL fixer-upper.

Said Holmgren: "There's something about taking a team that had bottomed out, and building it and feeling that sense of accomplishment."

Even more special: Bringing good football back to Green Bay. Unlike previous leaders who either played under Lombardi (Starr and Gregg) or battled his considerable shadow (Devine and Infante), Wolf and Holmgren celebrate the Packers' incredible history. They decorated offices with vintage photos, named the new practice facility after legendary Don Hutson, talked glowingly about the Packers' glory years, and even introduced a former player as "honorary captain" before each home game.

It was an incredible double play: Infusing a new, improved version of Packers football while celebrating the franchise's rich tradition.

For the first time in a long time, the fans who favor Favre are cheering for the same team as those who still celebrate Starr. That sense of unity to the franchise, without any self-servitude from Wolf or Holmgren or their players, is the most critical factor in Green Bay's stunning return to glory.

Build on the tradition. Make it fun again. That was the plan all along.

"I knew that if this thing worked," Holmgren said, "Ron Wolf and I could kinda say, 'We've done it. This is ours.' I guess it's my ego talking."

Let it talk, Mike. Let it talk. ◈

Kevin Isaacson
Green Bay, Wis.
July 15, 1996

Return to Glory

A tough decision

Bob Harlan's stunning decision
to dismiss operations chief Tom Braatz was
the first step in the Packers' resurgence

It was shortly after 3:30 p.m. on a chilly November afternoon in 1991 when Bob Harlan snuck out a side door of the Green Bay Packers administration building.

He welcomed the breath of fresh air and the acceleration of his Buick as it pulled away from the stonefaced media members, reeling from Harlan's curt announcement that he had fired Tom Braatz, the team's operations chief for the past five seasons.

It was a new beginning ... exactly what Bob Harlan didn't want.

A Packers employee for more than two decades, he had suffered as only a long-time Wisconsin resident could through the tenures of Bengtson and Devine, Starr and Gregg. The breakthrough 10-6 season of 1989 instilled hope in Harlan and Packers fans that Braatz and his choice as head coach, Lindy Infante, had found whatever Green Bay lost when Vince Lombardi left more than 20 years earlier. Harlan so believed in Infante that after the 1989 season his first significant move as Packers president was finalizing a three-year extension – and removing Infante's carefully negotiated option to leave for any job in his home state (Tampa Bay Bucs?) in the process.

"We thought we had the right guy," Harlan said. "It was the right decision at the right time."

Less than two years later, it was very, very wrong. Green Bay had won just nine of 28 games since the contract extension. Three of Braatz's last four No. 1 draft picks – Tony Mandarich, Darrell Thompson and Vinnie Clark – were significant disappointments. Quarterback Don Majkowski, so sure of his future and so concerned about negotiating a multimillion-dollar contract that he bypassed a chance to play in the Pro Bowl, lost his "Majik." Playoff hopes, so prevalent after 1989, were gone and with them, Packers fans' patience.

"The bottom line is, you gotta win," the late Eugene Sladky of Kewaunee, Wis., a member of the team's board of directors, said at the time. "When you don't win, something's got to give."

Harlan, trained in public relations and administration, wanted no part of football decisions. Promoted in June 1989 to replace Judge Robert J. Parins as team president, he consciously kept his initial improvement efforts away from the playing field. He developed a marketing department and the Packer Pro Shop, both enormously successful ventures. "Everybody else in the state was selling the Packer logo," Harlan recalls. "I thought it was time for us to do it, too." He initiated an expansion of Lambeau Field that included private boxes and club seats and a replay board to provide fans with added entertainment. He hired ex-NFL star Mike Reinfeldt, a respected administrator at Southern Cal and with the Los Angeles Raiders, as chief financial officer, providing the franchise with a savvy negotiator and a Wisconsin native as the likely successor to Harlan as team president. Harlan made the Packers an NFL trend-setter by hiring a corporate security officer, former Green Bay police administrator Jerry Parins.

Bob Harlan
Replacing Tom Braatz
'was a decision I
had to make.'

In two years, Harlan had rebuilt the Packers into one of the NFL's leading franchises – except on the playing field.

When he assumed the team presidency, Harlan pledged the Packers would succeed on two key "bottom lines: One is winning football games and the other is keeping the organization financially solvent and strong so it can always remain in Green Bay and compete with the other clubs in this league."

Half the equation was complete. But the football side wasn't started.

"The franchise was floundering and everybody was frustrated," said John Fabry, a member of the team's executive committee since 1981.

"We had to make a bold move. Bob had the guts to make it."

Harlan, on the morning of Nov. 21, 1991, located Braatz in Indiana, where he was scouting, and told him to come home. Harlan told Infante before afternoon practice. He told the media in a 28-minute press conference. Then he walked out of 1265 Lombardi Ave., uncharacteristically early, more upset than any time in two decades of service to the Packers.

He could live with firing Braatz, essentially his second in command, because he or the handful of top NFL executives he had

Bob Harlan, pictured prior to the team's flight to Dallas for the NFC Championship game, knew the Packers could return to NFL prominence. The question: Would replacing Tom Braatz as football operations chief be an appropriate first step?

consulted saw little hope for significant improvement from the Braatz-Infante operation. What made Harlan queasy was his next decision, the summoning of a new football boss. Harlan knew the success or failure of that selection process would likely determine the fortunes of the Green Bay Packers' franchise for the 1990s and beyond.

"That's when you hope you've done your homework," Fabry said. "You consider it, you do it and you hope it's right. Then you live with it."

Could he find the right guy? Would that guy want to come to Green Bay? Would he find a way to bring the glory back to Packers football?

Those questions hounded Harlan as he stopped at Arby's for a couple roast beefs, then headed home. His wife, Madeline, was in Kansas City under the guise of a Thanksgiving visit with the grandchildren. In truth, she knew the turmoil in which her husband was immersed, and decided she had no interest in answering the questions, concerns and criticisms.

Harlan felt the same way.

He unplugged the phone, pulled the drapes, sat down on the couch, kicked off his shoes and clicked until he found a James Bond film festival on TBS. He poured a drink, waded into the sandwiches and tried to forget.

The next morning, he was still on the couch, still wondering if his analysis had been complete, if he really had done the right thing for the Green Bay Packers.

One week later, he got his answer.

Ron Wolf said yes. ◈

Five years too late?

Ron Wolf declined to pursue
a key job with the Packers in 1987,
before the team hired Tom Braatz

Imagine Ron Wolf saying yes ... five years earlier.

Wolf flew into Green Bay in 1987 to interview for the Packers' new job – vice president of football operations. Judge Robert J. Parins, then the team president, had made the creditable decision to break away from the Lombardi-generated concept of omnipotent coach. Parins knew that handling player personnel duties in the 1980s was dynamically more demanding than anything Lombardi experienced 20 years earlier, and determined Coach Forrest Gregg should focus on the practice field instead of the waiver wire.

But Gregg's powerful presence and his AFC title in Cincinnati five years before probably prevented Parins from infusing the new position with true "football boss" power. Instead, Parins decided Gregg would share personnel duties with the new VP and charged Harlan, then the Packers' executive vice president of administration, with developing a "short list" of top NFL executives. Wolf, then a Raiders personnel official, and then-Chicago Bears executive Bill Tobin were at the top.

The Packers were flatly denied permission to talk to Tobin. They convinced Wolf, one of the league's true "superscouts" and the architect of Tampa Bay's NFC runner-up team in 1979, to visit Green Bay. But Wolf quickly ended negotiations, expressing discomfort over the lack of definition between his potential role and Gregg's.

Braatz, who wasn't on the Packers' initial "short list," had been demoted by the Atlanta Falcons when he was courted by Green Bay. A state standout (Kenosha High School, Marquette University), he played defensive end for the Redskins and Cowboys for four seasons in the late 1950s. His start in scouting came in 1965, when he gave Vince Lombardi a ride from the airport to an interview with Falcons owner Rankin Smith. Smith liked

Braatz enough to hire him for the scouting position. Braatz became Atlanta's director of player personnel in 1969, and was appointed general manager 13 years later. Three years later, though, his title was reduced to director of college scouting when Rankin Smith, his sons and Coach Dan Henning became more involved in personnel matters.

Braatz in 1987 became the Packers' new vice president, and Wolf returned to scouting for the Raiders. Though Braatz's tenure in Green Bay featured several excellent mid-round draft picks, including Tim Harris,

Ron Wolf
"I was shocked, because I had been here before and said, 'No.'"

Chris Jacke and Bryce Paup, his teams combined to win just 27 of 74 games. Braatz pinned some of the team's shortcomings on the "50-50" relationship between the personnel chief and the head coach, the very reason Wolf wasn't interested in that job.

Wolf's brief visit to Lambeau Field wasn't for naught, however. He spent much of that evening visiting with Harlan, the clear second-in-command in Packers administration during Parins' tenure as president. "He struck me as a nice man, an honest, decent man," Wolf recalled.

Five years later, Harlan asked Wolf to visit again. This time, the "lack of definition" had been removed from the job description. Wolf would have full authority over Packers football decisions. He could hire and fire coaches, scouts, players ... anyone or anything involved with the football side of the operation. A bonus: A friend from their time with the Raiders, Mike Reinfeldt, had recently joined the Packers as negotiator and chief financial officer.

"I said, sure, we could talk about it again," Wolf said.

Harlan had compiled a list of eight candidates, but had no interest in moving past his top choice. Five days after Jets president Steve Gutman granted the Packers permission to negotiate and just one week after Braatz's dismissal, a contract had been signed and Wolf was meeting with the Wisconsin media, reveling in a second opportunity to direct an NFL franchise.

"I never imagined I would have this opportunity," Wolf said. "I was shocked because I had been here before and said, 'No.' "

The Packers, of course, are not the first franchise Wolf has directed.

In April 1975, after 11 years with Al Davis' Raiders, Wolf was hired as vice president of operations for the expansion Tampa Bay Buccaneers. At age 36 and already one of the NFL's most respected personnel experts, Wolf constructed a solid team – highlighted by defensive end Lee Roy Selmon, the first overall pick in the 1976 draft – that made the playoffs three times from 1979-82. But Wolf wasn't around to enjoy the success he'd helped create: He was dismissed by owner Hugh Culverhouse after the 1977 season. Of the 22 starters on the Bucs' playoff teams, more than 70 percent were acquired by Wolf. Those who are close to Wolf enjoy noting that Tampa Bay hasn't made the playoffs since 1982.

Ron Wolf's hiring was step No. 1 in the Green Bay Packers' rebuilding process.

"I think what it came down to is that (Coach John) McKay wanted more power," said Ken Herock, the personnel chief at Atlanta. Herock was Wolf's assistant at the time and then succeeded him with the Bucs. "Culverhouse sided with McKay, which in my mind at the time was a mistake."

Wolf returned to the Raiders, accepting his old job. Shortly thereafter, he turned down high-profile positions with the Jets and Lions.

"I probably wasn't mature enough to handle that because my confidence and psyche had been affected greatly by the termination ... more so than I would probably want to own up to and admit."

Yet Wolf says he'll never view Tampa Bay as a mistake. Despite all the losses (the Bucs lost 26 of their first 28 games) and the humiliation, Wolf left a winner: He met his wife, Edie.

"In that sense, it was the best thing that ever happened to me," Wolf said.

Wolf spent the next 13 years with the Raiders, earning Super Bowl rings in 1980 and 1983. But in 1990, after 25 years with the Raiders, he made an abrupt lateral move to the East Coast, accepting what he thought would be his final job: Director of player personnel for the New York Jets.

Wolf says he was eager to work under the late Dick Steinberg, the Jets' GM and one of the league's top personnel officials. "I learned a new system, something I probably needed to learn," Wolf said, while struggling to explain concisely why he left the Raiders.

Shortly before taking the Jets' job, on April 10, 1990, he suffered a mild heart attack and underwent angioplasty. He returned to work two weeks later to finalize preparations for the NFL Draft, a testament to the priority Wolf has always placed on the job at hand.

He says the heart attack did not directly impact his decision to leave L.A., but "it has made me appreciate life a heck of a lot more."

He would've been satisfied to complete his career with the Jets, and admits he would not have considered Green Bay had the job description been less defined. At the same time, he's sometimes amazed at the authority provided by the Packers' unique community ownership and Harlan's selfless approach to his presidency.

"You couldn't ask for a better person to be your boss," Wolf said. "(Head coach) Mike (Holmgren) and I talk about that a lot. If there's something we want or need, Bob says, 'OK, we'll get it done.' There's complete cooperation and no interference, which is what he said it would be."

Wolf admits it is interesting to consider what might have happened had he pursued the Packers' position in 1987, but believes his experiences with the Raiders and Jets in the interim left him better equipped to direct the Green Bay football franchise.

Given the results thus far, who's to argue? ◈

Lindy leaves

Ron Wolf dismisses the coach who, despite
a 24-40 record, was one of the most popular
figures in the Packers' recent history

Ron Wolf was wearing his comfortable shoes and his comfortable sweater, but he wasn't comfortable.

Miserable is more like it.

He had just told a good guy, then a good guy's friends, then the good guy's football team and eventually his legion of supporters that the good guy is no longer good enough to coach the Green Bay Packers.

To some, he knew, that made Ron Wolf a bad guy. But Lindy Infante, who knows what the numbers 24 and 40 mean better than anyone else, didn't see it that way.

"It's a bottom-line business," Infante said. "I knew from the very outset that when the man was hired, it would be just a matter of whether he decided to make a change or not."

For Wolf, it wasn't that easy. He had spent the last month of the season evaluating Infante, his staff and their players. They won just one of four games after Wolf's hiring, finishing with a 4-12 record. Despite no playoff appearances and just 24 victories in 64 regular-season games, the 10th coach in Packers history had fostered a following that ranked behind only Lombardi and Lambeau. In fact, a WFRV-TV (Channel 5, Green Bay) viewer poll during the "Majik" season of 1989 – a poll certainly not designed or endorsed by sports anchor Larry McCarren, a former Pro Bowl lineman – gave Infante a higher rating than both NFL legends.

Wolf knew how popular Infante and his wife, Stephanie, were among Packers fans, and, for that matter, among his own administrative staff. He admired the coach's charity, class, professionalism and work ethic. The Infantes were key contributors of time and resources to several area charities and had truly made Green Bay their home.

"He's represented this community about as well as any human being could ever represent any community," Wolf said.

Wolf's wife, Edie, said her husband agonized over his decision, to the point of not sleeping for nearly a week.

"I think he admires and likes Lindy as a person," Edie Wolf said. "It was very difficult for him to do this."

Yet Wolf decided to release Infante and swallow the coach's three-year, $1.65 million guaranteed contract. Infante spent his three paid seasons finishing a new home in his native Florida. Not long after receiving his last payment from the Packers, he signed on as offensive coordinator at Indianapolis and played a key role in an excellent Colts' season that, like the Packers', ended one game short of the Super Bowl. In early 1996, the Colts released head coach Ted Marchibroda and provided Infante with another chance as an NFL head coach. In a curious twist, Infante is now the head coach at Indianapolis, working under operations chief Bill Tobin, who would likely have been Harlan's choice as general manager had Wolf refused the Packers' offer.

Lindy Infante
"It's a bottom-line business," referring to his 24-40 record as Packers coach.

Wolf attributed his decision to release Infante to a "comfort level." Infante had shared responsibility for Packers' personnel decisions with Tom Braatz; Wolf had no intention of extending that arrangement, a role reduction with which Infante might've struggled. Infante often conducted practices and dealt with his players in what might be termed a relaxed manner; a perception existed in Packers administrative offices that star players such as Don Majkowski and Sterling Sharpe either didn't receive or didn't respond to Infante's direction.

Wolf believes in strong leadership in a head coach, often citing his admiration for the diverse but unquestionably dominant styles of Bill Walsh, Joe Gibbs, Mike Ditka and Bill Parcells. Infante brought a more subtle, sometimes sarcastic approach to player motivation. His wry, sometimes biting sense of humor found favor in dozens of interpersonal relationships, but often didn't serve to motivate a larger group of players. Infante's skills as an offensive coordinator were unquestionable, given his track record

16

with the Bengals and Browns. Under Infante's tutelage, Ken Anderson became the league's MVP in 1981 and led the Bengals into the Super Bowl for the only time during his illustrious career. An extremely young Bernie Kosar became one of the league's most efficient quarterbacks and the Browns advanced to two AFC championship games, a level the Browns, now the Baltimore Ravens, have achieved just once since Infante's departure. In both situations, however, Infante worked under a strong leader as head coach: Forrest Gregg with the Bengals and Marty Schottenheimer with the Browns.

Most critical in Wolf's decision process, though, was to immediately establish in Green Bay a confident, winning mindset.In the past two seasons, Infante had won 10 games.

The morning after a 27-7 season-ending victory at Minnesota – Packers players awarded Infante the game ball

Lindy Infante was well-liked in the community and organization, making Ron Wolf's first big decision very difficult.

– Wolf dismissed the 51-year-old coach and his entire staff.

Said Infante at an impromptu press briefing, his eyes red from a morning of farewells: "For them to go out and do what they did yesterday ... man, it looked like a mountain. But they made it a mole hill and I'm going to be forever grateful that I could walk away with that game ball."

Packers staff members, while not surprised by the decision, still reacted emotionally, a testament to the Infantes' immersion in the community.

"Everyone tried to work together like a family," said staff assistant John Johnson, acknowledging tears were being wiped in many offices at 1265 Lombardi Ave. "Well, Coach Infante was the head of that family."

Wolf, confident but clearly not the least bit pleased by his course of action, explained his decision as a need to "feel comfortable in doing what I know how to do, and who I can direct to do it with. I didn't particularly feel comfortable. That's the reason for the move."

It's worth noting that Wolf sat alone in front of the assembled media. In the Braatz era, other team officials took part in major Packers media events. Members of the executive committee, the six-person board of key stockholders who advise Harlan and other executives on the Packers' business operation, often attended. This day, executive committee members were conspicuous by their absence; in fact, they hadn't been consulted on the coaching change. Harlan, one of the most accessible executives in any sports league, chose not to answer his phone.

Between legends

The coaches who followed Vince Lombardi and preceded Mike Holmgren in Green Bay:

Coach	Years	Record	Pct.
Phil Bengtson	1968-70	20-21-1	.488
Dan Devine	1971-74	25-28-4	.474
Bart Starr	1975-83	53-77-3	.410
Forrest Gregg	1984-87	25-37-1	.405
Lindy Infante	1988-91	24-40-0	.375

Clearly, the Packers wanted to underscore the fact that Wolf – not Harlan, not the executive committee, not the former or future head coach – was in charge. The distinction didn't go unnoticed throughout the NFL.

"Rather than have people pulling from one direction or the other, you clearly say, 'This guy's our point man.' Bob has that personality in Ron Wolf," said Roger Headrick, Vikings president and CEO. "I think you can see that throughout the league. Without pointing fingers, some teams have the coach wanting this, the personnel wanting another and the financial people run the organization. Those teams aren't in the playoffs."

Neither were the Packers, yet. Wolf knew he needed a special individual to overcome the Lombardi mystique, the 20-year playoff drought (excluding the Super Bowl tournament of 1982) and the players' collective malaise regarding the NFL's smallest franchise. Remember Michael Irvin and his family chanting "No way, Green Bay" during the ESPN-televised first round of the 1988 NFL Draft? Wolf did, but he believed Green Bay's solid financial base, incredible fan support and excellent facilities could make it the destination of choice for every talented collegian ... provided the Packers hired the right head coach.

He dialed Bill Parcells' phone number. ◈

Hiring a head coach

With Bill Parcells on the inactive list,
the Packers pursued Mike Holmgren –
much to the 49ers' chagrin

Ron Wolf and Bill Parcells are friends.

In a fraternity as small as theirs, relationships develop enough to go one way or the other. Wolf and Parcells probably relate to each other better than most of the other 100 or so key figures in the National Football League, although one shouldn't confuse professional respect and shared experience with a regular Saturday tee time at a local country club.

People like Wolf and Parcells are focused on football. Subtract their families and perhaps an untended hobby and the NFL remains. They're both believers in ball-control offense and dominating defense, and they both know who Seattle drafted in the third round in 1986 (it was Patrick Hunter, if anybody else cares). Those are the kinds of topics that arise on the college campuses, at the scouting combines and at league meetings where football-focused folks like Wolf and Parcells spend the majority of their time. Given their similar experiences and joint interest in adding to their collection of Super Bowl rings, it's not surprising that Wolf and Parcells talked about the Packers' vacant head coaching job.

The truth: Wolf wanted to hire Parcells.

And why not. In January of 1991, Parcells had led the New York Giants to their second Super Bowl championship in five seasons. He was an excellent cold-weather coach, and his philosophy – hard-nosed defense, ball-control offense – mirrored Wolf's, and seemed to provide what was necessary to excel in Lambeau Field in November, December and January. His forceful personality, Wolf believed, would be an asset to Packers players, and his record (85-52, five playoff berths in eight seasons) was unassailable.

Parcells was the best coach available on Dec. 22, 1991, the day Wolf dismissed Infante.

The only problem: Parcells wasn't interested in coaching, at least not in Green Bay.

"That didn't come as a surprise to me," Wolf said later.

Wolf knew that Parcells, who worked the 1991 season as a studio analyst for NBC's NFL Live, had struggled with his mortality after undergoing angioplasty surgery. Wolf had the same experience one year earlier.

"It's just amazing how that knocks you in the rear end," Wolf said. "Suddenly, you realize that you're vulnerable, that you're a human being, that your life could be gone, just like that (he snaps his fingers for emphasis). It's a feeling you get, and it really gets hold of you. That's what happened to him. You know you can't do what you've always done, because you've been through the procedure. So before he even called me back, I knew what his answer would be."

Another factor that kept Parcells from coaching the Packers was his desire for a Lombardi-type role that controlled both the coaching and personnel operations. While Parcells might have enjoyed coaching with Wolf as general manager, it wouldn't have been an advancement from his position with the Giants. Wolf and Parcells talked at length during the last week of 1991 but never negotiated. Parcells, the center of a circus atmosphere given his contacts with Green Bay and Tampa Bay and the NFL's six other coaching vacancies, at one point accepted a GM/coach position with the Buccaneers, then declined just hours before a scheduled introductory press conference. He underwent a second angioplasty surgery and remained with NBC for another year before accepting the GM/coach role he sought with the New England Patriots.

Had Parcells wanted to talk further, "that would have been interesting," Wolf admits.

But he didn't, and Wolf officially began his search. It ended two days later, after 49ers assistant Mike Holmgren spent a day in Green Bay. Much like Harlan's search for a general manager, Wolf conducted a formal interview with only his top candidate. He did speak to Terry Robiskie, a Raiders assistant, but attributed that to their long friendship. Holmgren was clearly the only serious candidate for the job.

The entire process was clean, professional and positive, a significant departure from Green Bay's last coaching search. Packers execs still shudder at the recollection of Michigan State coach George Perles accepting, then declining, an offer to replace Forrest Gregg. Tom Braatz and the Green Bay management team, figurative egg on faces, had to approach

A turning point in Packers history – the hiring of Mike Holmgren.

Infante with a public admission he was Choice No. 2.

As Infante deadpanned at his introductory press conference, "I'd like to thank the man who made this all possible – George Perles."

Holmgren was clearly the Packers' No. 1 guy, from the moment they left their luncheon interview.

"Ron approached me after their lunch and said, in that understated way of his, 'I could work with that guy,'" Harlan recalled.

Said George Young, the Giants general manager: "Once Ron started interviewing, it was pretty obvious that Holmgren was his choice."

Even so, nearly two weeks passed between Holmgren's visit to Lambeau Field and his hiring as the team's 11th head coach. The wait began to wear on many Packers faithful, who were well aware that many of the seven other teams with head coaching vacancies wanted to talk to Holmgren. What fans didn't realize was that, while Holmgren and Wolf had an agreement, the Packers and the 49ers did not.

Normally, NFL coaches and executives can move freely from team to team regardless of their contract status, provided their new position is a promotion. Holmgren's contract was different. Two years before he interviewed with the Packers, he was the candidate of choice for both the New York Jets and Phoenix Cardinals. He declined both jobs, in great part due

Mike Holmgren keeps an eye on practice at the Oneida Street facility. Watching with him: Ted Thompson (left), who coordinates the Packers' pro personnel operation, and chief financial officer Mike Reinfeldt.

to his twin daughters' desire to finish high school in California. He signed a three-year contract for $900,000, easily the highest assistant coaching salary in the NFL, that mandated he remain with San Francisco through 1992. He could break the contract only if head coach George Siefert left and the 49ers promoted someone else.

Complicating matters was the 49ers' dismay over their trade for Packers linebacker Tim Harris four months earlier. Harris missed the first month of the '91 season due to a contract holdout and asked to be traded out of Green Bay. Braatz, then the operations chief, complied by sending Harris, one of the NFL's premier pass rushers, to the 49ers for a pair of second-round draft picks.

After consummating the trade, however, Braatz told a Green Bay booster club during a luncheon speaking engagement that Harris, who had a history of substance abuse during his four years in Green Bay, had been the subject of a possible Brown County (Wis.) drug investigation. The 49ers, after reading media reports of Braatz's comments, cried foul and filed a complaint with NFL commissioner Paul Tagliabue. While the league didn't take any action, the 49ers did when the Packers asked to pursue

Return to Glory

Holmgren.

49ers president Carmen Policy demanded compensation for releasing Holmgren, arguably the league's best offensive coordinator, from his unique contract. Policy was well aware that Holmgren hoped to hire fellow 49ers assistants Ray Rhodes and Sherman Lewis as his defensive and offensive coordinators, and the 49ers had no interest in losing three key assistants to the Packers, especially given the backdrop of the Harris trade. Said Policy: "I'd rather have a dissatisfied Mike Holmgren staying with us than a happy Mike Holmgren going to Green Bay."

Policy was posturing, of course. The Packers would've probably found an ally in Paul Tagliabue, had the dispute gone that far. During the dispute, the commissioner issued a memo to all 28 NFL teams, directing them to allow their assistant coaches to take head-coaching jobs regardless of the terms of their contracts. The memo carried an indirect message to the Packers and 49ers: Take care of business.

Wolf agreed that the Packers would return one of the two second-round draft picks involved in the Harris trade; San Francisco released Holmgren from his contract and agreed to allow him to negotiate with Lewis and Rhodes. The Packers weren't the least bit happy with the 49ers' ransom, especially since it was linked to a trade from the pre-Wolf era. At the same time, after two weeks of waiting, they now had Mike Holmgren as their head football coach.

"I probably can't tell you how glad we are to have this thing done," Wolf said.

The 49ers were happy, too. They were going to lose Holmgren anyway – several other teams were interested, and he had an interview scheduled in Pittsburgh had he not accepted the position in Green Bay. The 49ers knew that, even if Green Bay was the only team interested, they would have lost Holmgren had the league intervened, and they certainly wouldn't have wanted to prevent a key employee from advancement.

But their stubbornness did net a second-round draft pick.

"We put it to bed. It's over," said 49ers owner Eddie DeBartolo. "We didn't want to stand in the way of Mike furthering his career. ... We're pleased with the outcome."

It was one of the few times in NFL history that a team has traded a draft pick to acquire a head coach. In 1970, Miami gave the Baltimore Colts a No. 1 pick as compensation for hiring Don Shula, who retired after the 1995 season as the winningest coach in league history. Baltimore used the pick to select running back Don McCauley, who played 11 seasons for the Colts but never bettered 700 rushing yards in a season.

In an interesting twist of fate, the 49ers also used their pick on a running back, Amp Lee of Florida State. Lee was the featured back for FSU; his primary blocker was Edgar Bennett, who was selected in that same 1992 draft by the Packers, more than 50 picks later than Lee. Interestingly, Lee's career has mirrored McCauley's – some solid years as a third-down back for the 49ers and Minnesota, but certainly not the impact expected on draft day.

Wolf, a keen student of NFL history, would certainly appreciate the correlation of the ransomed draft picks, the underperforming running backs ... and the inevitable link between his new head coach and the legendary Don Shula. ◆

The trade

The Packers swapped a first-round draft pick
for a third-string quarterback who
had never completed an NFL pass

Brett Favre sat alone in a popular Green Bay sports bar.

It was overflowing with football fans, but no one talked to him. The fans were preoccupied with basketball anyway, as the UW-Green Bay men's basketball team was in line for a bid to the NCAA Tournament. The party was beginning, but Favre wasn't asked to join. Nobody knew him.

He'd been in Green Bay less than a month and, frankly, had spent most of that time wondering how a guy from southern Mississippi was going to survive a winter in Wisconsin.

He wasn't enjoying this. Then again, he hadn't enjoyed Atlanta, either.

The Falcons had selected him in the second round, 33rd overall, in the previous year's NFL draft. Coach Jerry Glanville activated him for just three games. He threw five passes as a rookie, completing two to the opposition and not one to his teammates. The NFL wasn't what he had hoped. Green Bay wasn't what he'd hoped. But, he reasoned, at least Green Bay wanted him.

Favre didn't have any idea how much.

Ron Wolf had envisioned Favre as the future quarterback of his team since early 1991, when he spent a day in Hattiesburg, Miss., watching game film of Southern Mississippi's 1990 football season. The majority of Wolf's career has been spent visiting college campuses and watching game film, building mental and physical databases on the college players available in future NFL drafts. When the Southern Miss film was complete, Wolf mentioned to a school administrator that, yes, Brett Favre certainly was a good football player. "If you think he's good as a senior, you should've seen him as a junior," the administrator replied.

Wolf, who was college scouting director for the New York Jets at the time, was intrigued. So he sat back down and watched Favre's game films from the previous year. That was the season before Favre was involved in a terrible off-season car accident that forced doctors to remove 30 inches of his intestine in mid-August 1990.

That junior year included a 30-26 victory against No. 3 Florida State.

"He was right," Wolf said of that administrator's comment. "(As a senior) he was coming off the stomach injury. As a junior, you could see all the athleticism, and everything you wanted to see was there."

How good was Favre? The best player in the entire draft, according to Wolf. Fortunately for both quarterback and general manager, the rest of the NFL didn't share Wolf's opinion. Quarterbacks Todd Marinovich and Dan McGwire, DE Huey Richardson, RB Jarrod Bunch, CB Bruce Pickens and T Stan Thomas were some of the notables who were selected before Favre in what is considered one of the weaker drafts in NFL history. The Packers, under Braatz, selected Ohio State defensive back Vinnie Clark; Wolf and his Jets didn't have a first-round pick, having spent it in the 1990 supplemental draft on wide receiver Rob Moore of Syracuse. When the second round began, Favre was still available.

"I was thinking, 'We're blowing this. We've got to get up there and get him,'" Wolf recalled.

The late Dick Steinberg, who was making the draft-day decision for the Jets, tried to swing a trade to select the quarterback but couldn't find any takers. Atlanta selected Favre with the 33rd pick; with the next choice, the Jets took Louisville quarterback Browning Nagle. Interestingly, the Falcons selected Favre against the wishes of Glanville and assistant head coach June Jones, who wanted Nagle. But Falcons VP/personnel Ken Herock, Wolf's former assistant in Tampa Bay, preferred Favre and made the final decision.

"I don't think (Glanville) liked him from the start because he wasn't his favorite in the draft," Herock recalled.

Favre did nothing to endear himself during that rookie season. As the No. 3 quarterback, he knew he wasn't going to play. In time, he became a fixture in the Atlanta nightclub scene. He once missed a team photo after a night on the town, pulling into the parking lot at the Falcons' practice facility just as Glanville was leaving. He was fined $1,500.

"He said, 'I got trapped behind a heck of a car wreck,' " Glanville told the *Green Bay Press-Gazette*. "I said, 'You are a car wreck.'"

Glanville, now a commentator for Fox's NFL telecasts, suggests he didn't want to trade Favre, but others in the organization remember differently.

(In Glanville's defense, his starting quarterback was Chris Miller, a Pro Bowl quarterback in 1991; the backup was Billy Joe Tolliver, who had started for the Chargers. The Falcons appeared set at QB for several seasons.) Glanville admits he thought Favre, who carried 10 or more pounds above his normal playing weight of 220 during most of his rookie season, wasn't committed to the Falcons or football.

"He was running wild," Glanville said. "But I couldn't take him home and sleep with him every night."

As much as the Falcons didn't think they needed Favre, Wolf did.

His first day on the job as Packers' general manager came in Atlanta, where Lindy Infante's team was playing the Falcons. Herock met Wolf during pre-game workouts and, recalling Wolf's appreciation of Favre and realizing the Packers probably needed to upgrade at quarterback, suggested he take another look at the young quarterback.

"But you'd better do it now," Herock laughed, "because you won't see him once the game starts."

Wolf's opinion hadn't changed during the six months since the draft. He saw in Favre, son of the football coach at Hancock North Central High School in Kiln, Miss., a natural leader, a player to whom other star athletes were unmistakably drawn. The Packers, strongly supportive of Majkowski in 1989, had lost confidence when he "went Hollywood" the next season, bleaching his hair and eschewing the weekly get-togethers that had won the admiration of his linemen.

Infante used journeymen Blair Kiel and Mike Tomczak to supplant the oft-injured Majkowski throughout 1991, and told Wolf and several others in the organization that his top recommendation for rejuvenating the Packers was investing in a quarterback other than the "Majik Man." (It's more than coincidence that after Infante became offensive coordinator at Indianapolis before the 1995 season, the Colts chose not to re-sign their popular backup QB, one Don Majkowski.) Wolf viewed Favre's approach to the game – playing without regard for money or marketing – as a rare throwback to the NFL's legendary quarterbacks. Others in the league compared the fun-loving Favre to Sonny Jurgensen, Bobby Layne and Billy Kilmer.

"You could tell there was something special about him, the way people responded to him in the huddle," Wolf said.

That intangible leadership, more than his size or his incredibly strong throwing arm, is what lifted Favre out of the ranks of recruit defensive

Packers' trades for QBs

✔ Jim Del Gaizo, No. 2 to Miami in '74 and '75
✔ John Hadl, No. 1, 2, 3 in '75, No. 1, 2 in '76 to LA Rams
✔ Jack Concannon, No. 5 in '75 to Dallas
✔ Lynn Dickey, No. 4 in '76 to Houston
✔ Randy Dean, No. 6 in '81 to NY Giants
✔ Scott Brunner, No. 6 in '86 to Denver
✔ Brett Favre, No. 1 in '92 to Atlanta
✔ Ken O'Brien, No. 5 in '93 to NY Jets

backs as a 17-year-old freshman at Southern Miss. He spent time at defensive back and quarterback that fall, rising from No. 7 to No. 3 on the offensive depth chart in a matter of weeks. He played during the second week, throwing two TD passes to beat Tulane, and on his 18th birthday started in a 61-10 loss to No. 1 Florida State.

As a sophomore, his 1.57 interception ratio was the lowest among the 50 most productive QBs in the nation. As a junior, he threw for 1,264 yards and 15 touchdowns, cementing his status as a first-round draft pick.

But on July 14, 1990, he flipped his Nissan Maxima and was nearly killed. His brother, Scott, following in another car, broke the front window with a golf club to pull him from the wreckage. Favre went to the hospital with a concussion and a cracked vertebra and, as it turned out, complications. Severe stomach pain three weeks after the accident prompted a return to the hospital, where doctors removed 30 inches of intestine.

He reported to school two weeks later as a shell of himself; his first visit to football practice left teammates stunned. When he didn't regain any strength at school, his mom, Bonita, had him return to Kiln, where home cooking put him on the road to recovery. Five weeks after the intestinal surgery he was back at Southern Miss, in uniform, 30 pounds underweight, leading the Golden Eagles to a 27-24 upset over Alabama.

"You can call it a miracle or a legend or whatever you want," Alabama Coach Gene Stallings told reporters afterward. "I just know that on that day, Brett Favre was larger than life."

Favre led Southern Miss to an 8-4 record that season and ended up in the East-West Shrine Game, earning MVP honors. Three months later, he was drafted by Atlanta – and found himself back on the bench, just like his freshman year in Hattiesburg. That's where he spent Dec. 1, 1991,

Why did the Packers trade for Brett Favre? A key factor is leadership. Mike Holmgren and Ron Wolf saw in the young quarterback, shown with running back Edgar Bennett, a player who has the rare talent to lead and inspire other supremely talented athletes.

watching the Falcons beat the Packers 35-31, never imagining the new Packers' general manager had every intention of trading for him.

Informal negotiations began almost immediately. The Packers weren't the only team interested, however. Denver and Kansas City also made offers, but when Wolf upped the ante to a first-round draft pick, the Falcons couldn't say no. Atlanta was coming off a playoff season and its executive and coaching staffs believed the team was just a few players from Super Bowl contention. When the Packers agreed to part with one of their two first-round draft picks – the 17th selection overall – in exchange for a third-string quarterback who had been the 34th selection a year earlier, the Falcons figured they couldn't lose.

"We would've loved to keep Brett, but we needed help in other areas," Jones said.

The Falcons, though, didn't find the help they sought. Running back Tony Smith, chosen with the No. 17 pick, never made an impact and is no longer with the team. At the time, though, Packers fans – unfamiliar with Wolf and just a month into Holmgren's tenure – wondered if their new regime had been duped by the Falcons. Many would've preferred a "name" acquisition at quarterback. The Packers did consider building around a veteran QB, and discussed the acquisition of one of the 49ers – Steve Young or Steve Bono, both behind Joe Montana on the depth chart – and several other "available" QBs. The prospects of negotiating another deal with the 49ers weren't favorable, though, and both Holmgren and Wolf had a special feeling about Favre. In fact, they were positively giddy at a Lambeau Field press conference announcing the acquisition.

"When you get a chance to get a quarterback that you think is a great one, you do it," Holmgren said. "So that's what we did."

Said Wolf: "The opportunity to acquire Brett Favre, in our opinion, easily outweighed the unknown quantity that might have been available to us in the 17th pick in the first round of this draft."

Jones, now the Falcons head coach, had grown close to Favre during their year together. He applauded the trade.

"The Packers knew what they were getting," Jones said a day after the deal was announced. "Mike (Holmgren) did such a great job at San Francisco, taking Steve Bono out of obscurity and by the end of the (1991) season making him look like Joe Montana. I think he could do the same for Brett."

Playing like Montana wasn't on Favre's mind, however, as he drank a beer and watched the UW-Green Bay fans gather around the TV.

He just wanted to play. ✪

Mandarich

He never played a game under
Mike Holmgren, yet his impact on
the new regime is unquestionable

Tony Mandarich popped in the dusty videotape, sat down in the basement of his rural Pulaski home and began laughing out loud.

"The outrageous things the guy was saying, I couldn't believe it," said Mandarich, chuckling at the memory.

The comedian's name: Tony Mandarich.

It was spring 1992, three years since Mandarich and his then-girlfriend, Amber Ligon, compiled videotapes from his almost-daily TV appearances, including visits with David Letterman, ESPN interviewer Roy Firestone and actor Judd Hirsch from the NBC sitcom "Dear John."

"My plan was to let people know who Tony Mandarich is, and to have Tony Mandarich as a household name," Mandarich said. "I think both of those were accomplished."

And then some.

Mandarich heard himself say that, as the second pick overall in the 1989 draft, he deserved more money than No. 1 selection Troy Aikman. That he was willing and able to defeat boxing heavyweight champion Mike Tyson. That he'd much prefer residing and playing football on the West Coast than in the "village" of Green Bay. That he would become the greatest tackle in NFL history.

Looking back, Mandarich couldn't help but laugh.

"There were some things that I said that I just can't believe. I thought, 'Oh, my god. What the hell did I do?' You talk about a cocky person. I could not believe it."

That's because the Tony Mandarich who playfully chased 15-month-old Holly Mandarich around his residence the summer before Mike Holmgren's first season as Packers head coach appeared to be nothing like the hard-rocking Guns N' Roses fanatic whose cutting comments shocked the Green Bay faithful early and often. He was satisfied with the financial security provided in his $4.4 million, four-year contract. He very much doubted he could have outpunched Mike Tyson. He reveled in Midwest living, especially his rural home just 15 minutes northwest of Lambeau Field, claiming he'd suffocate after more than a minute in L.A.

"I think if you were to show them to somebody, and then have them spend two or three weeks with me now, they'd have to think that guy was my evil twin brother," Mandarich said.

He imagined explaining his career to little Holly when she's older.

"Obviously I'm not going to talk to her about all the steroid allegations, all that stuff I was accused of," Mandarich said. "I don't want to tell her that, yeah, Dad had a really lousy rookie year. The second year he played but not real good, and the third year he started playing a little better. I'd skip over the bad stuff, just like any father would."

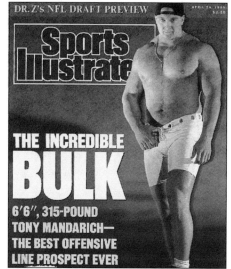

One hopes Amber, who turned 5 in April 1996, never asks the questions. If her dad excluded the "bad stuff," he wouldn't have any answers.

Mandarich is perhaps the biggest bust in the history of the NFL draft. He started 31 games for the Packers, never approaching the level of play exhibited during his pre-draft workouts and four years at Michigan State. Holmgren and offensive line coach Tom Lovat installed him as the starting right guard, but a series of ailments, including a parasitic infection incurred during a black-bear hunt in Canada, post-concussion syndrome and hypothyroidism prevented Mandarich from playing a down in 1992.

The Packers chose not to extend his contract, and Mandarich left pro football as humbled as any athlete in league history.

His exit was telling: He left for his off-season home in Traverse City, Mich., without arranging maintenance for the log home he owned near Green Bay. Water pipes froze, then ruptured, forcing repairs of more than $10,000 before the home could be sold the following summer.

The damage to the Packers, however, was much more costly.

That Wolf and Holmgren waited four years after Mandarich's departure to invest a high draft pick in an offensive tackle speaks volumes about the impact his failure has had on the franchise.

Certainly, the unfulfilled expectations of that No. 2 draft pick were a contributing factor to the dismissal of Tom Braatz and Lindy Infante. (Mandarich, after a three-year absence from the NFL, planned a comeback in 1996. His team of choice: Indianapolis, where he was reunited with Infante, now the Colts head coach, and position coach Charlie Davis.)

To be fair to Braatz and his scouting staff, few NFL executives disagreed with the Mandarich pick. Interestingly, one of the dissenters was Infante.

Mandarich, who had run a 4.65 40-yard dash and had bench-pressed 225 pounds an impressive 39 repetitions for NFL scouts, was the perfect choice for the offensive system Braatz preferred. Much like Ron Wolf four years later, the Packers operations chief sought a run-oriented coach after Forrest Gregg's departure for Southern Methodist University. But after George Perles spurned the Packers' offer just hours before a press conference announcing his hiring, Braatz summoned Infante. Little more than a year later, they drafted Mandarich, Perles' star lineman.

Even at his best, Mandarich wouldn't have fit well into Infante's offensive scheme. At Michigan State, his primary responsibility was drive blocking, smashing the defender in front of him and pushing him as far back as possible. The Spartans under Perles ran more than 80 percent of the time (despite having Andre Rison as a receiver), so Mandarich's pass-blocking techniques never developed.

Infante's offense was driven by the short passing game, which requires linemen who are quick and agile, who have the ability to fend off a pass rusher for a few seconds. Mandarich entered the league with incredible strength and speed, but agility wasn't one of his attributes. Even he admitted that, with coaching, he may have been only average as a pass blocker.

Infante wondered about Mandarich's limitations, especially after the 330-pounder declined to participate in any NFL scouts' testing except for the bench press and 40-yard dash, and the coach also realized that Oklahoma State running back Barry Sanders had incredible potential, especially as a single back in his three-receiver sets.

The Cowboys had already negotiated with UCLA quarterback Troy Aikman, cementing his status as the No. 1 pick in the 1989 draft. Braatz and the rest of the NFL viewed Mandarich as the obvious No. 2 choice, followed by Barry Sanders, Derrick Thomas and Deion Sanders in what was perceived to be one of the best "top fives" in NFL draft history. *Sports Illustrated* draft guru Paul Zimmerman, in his pre-draft commentary, rated Mandarich and Deion Sanders as possibly the best at their positions ever to come out of college. He also noted that the Bears would "love to strike a deal with Green Bay to get Mandarich with the second pick, but you don't give away a guy like him."

Infante would have.

In the final days before that fateful draft, Infante became enamored with Barry Sanders and began trying to convince Braatz and the Packers' scouts to reconsider their decision. Infante spent much of the week reviewing film of the Oklahoma State running back, even into the early morning hours on draft day. He entered the Packers' administration building convinced he wanted Sanders ... but Braatz, a veteran of the second-guessing and emotional upheaval the draft can create in NFL executive offices, counseled Infante to "be confident in the work we've done. Let's stay with our (draft) board." Infante grudgingly agreed.

Years later, Infante still wondered what might have happened had he, not Braatz, had the final say on that draft pick. Sanders' impact in the Green Bay backfield would have dwarfed that of Keith Woodside or Herman Fontenot or Vince Workman. Would Sanders have put the Packers in the playoffs in '89? Probably. Would he have saved the wear and tear on quarterback Don Majkowski that cost the Packers a shot at the playoffs in 1990? Certainly. Would Infante and Braatz have retained their jobs? Perhaps, though it's likely some issue other than the Mandarich pick would've exposed the flaw in their joint decision-making arrangement.

The impact of the Mandarich pick, however, carried far past Infante and Braatz. Has it affected the decisions made by Wolf and Holmgren? Certainly. In fact, the selection of Southern Cal tackle John Michels in the first round in 1996 – a full seven years after the Mandarich pick – can be considered the first step toward recovery from the Mandarich mishap.

To understand the enormity of the failure, one must first appreciate the value NFL teams place on quality left offensive tackles. Wolf, like most NFL general managers, believes a quality left offensive tackle is one of three critical positions for any football team: Quarterback and impact pass rusher (lineman or linebacker) are the others. The left tackle is critical because he protects the quarterback's blind side on passing plays. A quarterback with confidence that he won't be hit in the back is an infinitely better player than the alternative. Given the money teams invest in marquee quarterbacks (the average of the league's top 10 QBs is more than $5 million a season), it makes sense for any NFL coach or GM to ensure the investment with the best left tackle available. Bonita Favre, Brett's mother, underscored that point in the 1992 exhibition season, when the Packers were using a handful of retreads to replace holdout Ken Ruettgers. "If they don't get somebody to block over there," Mrs. Favre said, "they're not going to have much of a quarterback left."

There are perhaps 20 quality left tackles in the NFL, a handful who might be rated exceptional. Though players such as Willie Roaf of New Orleans and Gary Zimmerman of Denver don't draw the media attention of a receiver or running back, they often receive as much respect – and salary – from the NFL's decision-makers as the majority of so-called "skill" players. It's worth noting that Favre's worst game during his MVP season came in the opener against St. Louis, which Ruettgers missed with a back injury. The Rams' Sean Gilbert dominated Gary Brown and Joe Sims, forcing Favre into a state of disarray and indecisiveness that wasn't apparent the rest of the season. The lesson: You can't win without a good left tackle.

Mandarich, of course, was supposed to be that insurance policy for Green Bay through the 1990s. Despite his disappointing debut, he remained on the roster as Wolf prepared for his first draft as Packers general manager in April 1992. The No. 1 player on Wolf's list that April was an offensive lineman out of Stanford, Bob Whitfield. But Wolf decided against selecting a lineman with the Packers' pick, No. 5 overall, because the team needed help at other positions and because of the potential backlash that he felt might be generated by the selection of another lineman who probably wouldn't make an impact during his rookie season.

Instead, the Packers pursued receiver Desmond Howard (Holmgren's preference) and defensive back Terrell Buckley. When Washington traded up for the No. 4 pick and Howard, the Packers' decision was made. Wolf shakes his head when asked to assess the impacts of Whitfield and Buckley.

"I should've gone with my gut and taken Robert Whitfield," Wolf admits. "We went with the flow, which meant taking Howard or Buckley. We needed to add some spark to our team. Howard would've been a spark, and Buckley provided the same thing. You have to remember that Terrell did help us win three games that first year."

Whitfield was drafted with the No. 8 pick by the Atlanta Falcons and has developed into one of the NFL's better linemen, excelling as a pass blocker in Atlanta's run-and-shoot offense. In a draft filled with disappointments (Buckley, Howard, RB Tommy Vardell, QB David Klingler, RB Vaughn Dunbar, QB Tommy Maddox), Whitfield would've been an excellent selection at No. 5. Interestingly, the Falcons were concerned with Deion Sanders' interest in baseball and would have been more than willing to swap Whitfield for Buckley on draft day.

Whitfield wasn't the only tackle the post-Infante Packers coveted.

One year later, Ruettgers was in the middle of another holdout (his fifth in eight years) and the Packers were getting antsy for a replacement. Ruettgers, a fixture at left tackle from 1986-89, never quite reached the potential that prompted Forrest Gregg to trade up in the first round in 1985 (Buffalo got the 14th and 42nd picks in the draft for its first pick, No. 7 overall). Injuries caused him to miss parts of 1990, 1991 and 1992. Though the Braatz-Infante regime initially put Mandarich at right tackle, the intention was to replace Ruettgers as soon as possible.

Complicating matters was the NFL's new salary cap, which allowed each team to name two "transition" players and one "franchise player." The Packers chose to name Ruettgers a "transition" player, which under NFL free agency rules allowed them to match any contract he was offered by another team. During the negotiations with Ruettgers, however, the NFL altered its interpretation of the "transition player" rules. Ruettgers initially would have received the average of $1 million, which was 20 percent over his 1992 salary. The revised rule extended the deadline for salaries included in establishing the "transition" averages for each position, and since several linemen had been signed to high-dollar contracts in the interim, Ruettgers' transition designation was now worth at least $1.905 million per year – all without a word of negotiating from the veteran tackle.

Even that 130 percent raise couldn't compel Ruettgers to report to training camp, though teammates joked that Ruettgers' repeated holdouts were more attributable to his dislike for the exhibition season than for any pursuit of additional finances. The longer Ruettgers waited in his native

California, though, the more interested Wolf became in investing in a "franchise" left tackle.

The Vikings had one available in Gary Zimmerman, one of the best linemen in NFL history. Zimmerman was also involved in a salary dispute, and in August 1992 went public with a demand to be traded. Wolf had always thought highly of the seven-year veteran and quietly began negotiations with Minnesota. A few days later, Wolf believed he and the Vikings had agreed on a price: The Packers' No. 1 picks in 1993 and 1994 plus one player, possibly receiver Mark Clayton. The Packers had also reached a tentative agreement with Zimmerman's agent on a three-year contract. But Minnesota backed away, probably because its coaching staff didn't relish the thought of playing against Zimmerman twice a season for the next 6-8 years. For speculation's sake, the Packers would've traded Wayne Simmons and Aaron Taylor (the players they eventually selected with the No. 1 picks in question) plus Clayton for a franchise left tackle.

Said Wolf: "I would've done the deal. He would've been a heckuva player for us. But they didn't want the picks."

The Vikings traded Zimmerman to Denver for three draft picks (a No. 1, CB DeWayne Washington; a No. 2, safety Orlando Thomas; and a No. 6, TE Andrew Jordan). The Packers then signed Ruettgers at slightly above the "transition" player rate, hoping he'd remain healthy for the forseeable future, which he has, approaching Pro Bowl caliber while playing in all but one game during the last three seasons.

Even with Ruettgers under contract and playing well, Wolf couldn't avoid the temptation of an excellent offensive lineman when LSU's Willie Roaf was available early in the 1993 draft. Green Bay had the No. 15 pick in the first round, but when Roaf wasn't taken in the first handful of picks, Wolf took to the phones and tried to obtain a higher pick. He nearly had an agreement with the Bears, who had the No. 7 overall pick. At the same time, Mike Reinfeldt, the Packers' chief financial officer, was on another phone in the Packers' draft "war room" explaining Green Bay's interest to Roaf's agent. Then, to the dismay of Packers executives, Chicago changed course, deciding to keep the pick and selecting receiver Curtis Conway of Southern Cal. New Orleans selected Roaf with the next pick; he has quickly become one of the NFL's most dominating linemen. Finally, in the third year of the Wolf-Holmgren regime, the Packers invested a first-round draft pick in an offensive lineman: Aaron Taylor of Notre Dame, a guard whose promise has been dimmed slightly by knee injuries.

In spring 1996, the Packers drafted what they hope will be their offensive tackle of the future. Michels has been frequently compared to Ruettgers, for good reason: Both played in college at Southern Cal, both wore No. 77 for the Trojans, both won a Rose Bowl, both are stronger pass protectors than run blockers, both are devout Christians.

"I'm reading his book right now," Michels said on draft day. Ruettgers wrote *Home Field Advantage*, which discusses youths and role models.

Said Wolf: "When you see Michels, he will probably remind you of how Ruettgers looked when he first came in here."

Unlike Ruettgers, Michels won't be rushed into a starting job. He's expected to play a reserve role during the 1996 season, then be available to supplant Ruettgers, who is 34 and in the final year of his contract.

"For the first time, we could take a guy that wasn't necessarily an immediate player and afford the luxury of waiting for him to become available to play," Holmgren said. "That's really a good feeling when that happens."

Another Packers-Michels link: Holmgren also is a Southern Cal grad. The coach and player began building a relationship at the scouting combine in Indianapolis more than a month before the draft. "He told me old Trojan stories and I told him new Trojan stories," Michels recounts.

Clearly, Michels appears to be a perfect fit for the Packers' present and future. There is one nagging issue, however. The Packers have decided Michels should wear uniform No. 77. Assigning uniforms was a duty clearly enjoyed by long-time equipment man Bob Noel, who played a role in awarding No. 8 to Mark Brunell, a left-handed, scrambling quarterback that reminded some of Steve Young ... giving the No. 5 once worn by Paul Hornung to brash young quarterback Don Majkowski, whose blonde locks and good looks created fan fervor seldom seen in Green Bay since the original "Golden Boy's" exit in the late 1960s ... placing the No. 75 worn by the great Forrest Gregg on the shoulders of Ken Ruettgers, the young offensive tackle then-head coach Gregg was so eager to draft ... awarding the No. 24 of safety Willie Wood to a similar prospect, Johnnie Gray.

The significance of Michels and No. 77? Perhaps there isn't any. Noel retired in 1993, and with him went any game-playing with uniform numbers. Michels wore No. 77 in college, making it an obvious choice in Green Bay. A few observers will note, though, that No. 77 was worn prominently in Green Bay a few years back, by another rookie offensive tackle selected in the first round.

His name was Tony Mandarich. ◈

Transition

The joint personnel philosophies
of Mike Holmgren and Ron Wolf
are reflected in the rebuilt Packers

LeRoy Butler. Ken Ruettgers. Chris Jacke.

Of the 56 players Ron Wolf and Mike Holmgren inherited just four years ago, only those three remain.

Of the 11 assistant coaches Holmgren hired in spring 1992, only six still work in Green Bay.

Buffalo's Bryce Paup is the reigning NFL Defensive Player of the Year. Tony Bennett is a Pro Bowl linebacker for the Colts. Terrell Buckley won AFC Defensive Player of the Week honors for Miami last season. Ray Rhodes was NFL Coach of the Year in 1995, his first season with the Philadelphia Eagles. Dick Jauron is defensive coordinator at Jacksonville. Jon Gruden is offensive coordinator at Philadephia. Steve Mariucci is head coach at the University of California.

How do Wolf and Holmgren continue to improve the Packers despite the defections?

The answer starts with Wolf and Holmgren. Their relationship may be the most intriguing and critical element in the Packers' success story.

Early on, they seemed like a football odd couple.

Wolf spent most of his professional career in a Raiders system that embraced a power-running offense, spiced by an occasional long pass. He was convinced that a critical aspect of a winning Packers team would be a running game that would control the clock and advance the football in Wisconsin's inclement winter weather.

Holmgren, a talented high school quarterback who later played with O.J. Simpson at USC, loves the passing game. He is supremely confident in his ability to dissect a defense, to adjust formations and personnel faster than any defensive coordinator, to put points on the board. His teams have consistently passed more than they've run.

reconcilable differences?

"No," Wolf says. "The great thing we have going is a line of communication. There's no B.S. We shoot straight. I don't think either one of us lets our egos get in the way of what we're trying to do – and that's make the Packers a success."

Wolf and Holmgren say they made a commitment of sorts when Holmgren accepted the Packers' offer. Wolf offered Holmgren a five-year contract, the same length team president Bob Harlan had given him. The clear message: We're in this together. The Packers have subsequently extended Wolf's contract another three years, through 1999; Wolf and Holmgren agreed on a duplicate extension for the coach's contract as well.

"When we got together, we made some vows to each other," Wolf said. "Some have been tough to stick to. But if a guy's not good enough, we agreed to get rid of him, regardless of who he is, or what he might mean to one of us."

Clearly, there are defined areas. Holmgren calls the plays. Wolf picks the players. But Holmgren and his staff have significant input into player selection, and if Wolf has an opinion on a player or strategy, you can bet it's eventually heard by the coaching staff. Have there been conflicts? Apparently none worth reporting. Wolf has walked into several meetings thinking, " 'For sure, this is going to be it.' But we haven't had one of those. It's never gotten that far."

Holmgren and his staff generally aren't protective of players, or position areas. If the Packers are better served with just four running backs and nine defensive backs, the staff finds a way to make it work. Holmgren's leadership and team-building skills generally limit the territorial battles among his position coaches.

"It's a team, a best-for-the-group thing," Mariucci, the former quarterbacks coach, said. "Everybody understands they're working together for the ultimate goal."

A telling example of the Wolf-Holmgren relationship, from their first season in Green Bay: The Packers had to cut a running back to create a roster spot for Darrell Thompson, and the obvious choice was backup fullback Harry Sydney. Wolf was concerned about Holmgren's reaction, because Sydney was a former 49er who knew the offense, contributed on special teams and was well-liked in the locker room. The only alternative was dropping Buford McGee, the starting fullback, who was certainly a better runner than Sydney. Holmgren knew that Wolf's affection for the ground game made McGee a tough player to cut.

The result? Wolf argued to keep the ex-49er Sydney, and Holmgren argued to keep McGee. Eventually, they decided together that Sydney's versatility and familiarity with the offense were decisive factors and McGee – to the surprise of many, including McGee – was released. Sydney's understanding of the offensive system during that 9-7 debut season paid dividends for Holmgren and young runners like Edgar Bennett, a role Sydney continues to play today as a Packers assistant.

"The great thing about Mike is he's in this strictly for the good of the club, and in this game, that's not always the case," Wolf said.

Said Holmgren: "We have a check on each other, when we think one guy might be overcompensating. We've talked at length about having our backgrounds influence decisions we've made."

Said Harlan: "They disagree, but they do it in such a way that it turns out to be a plus for the organization. Egos don't get in the way here."

If Holmgren and Wolf ever reach an impasse, their agreement dictates bringing the dispute to Harlan.

Said Harlan: "I don't think we'll ever get to that situation, especially looking at where we've been already."

One of the most critical moments in the Wolf-Holmgren era occurred a few weeks after the Packers' first playoff appearance in 21 years. Ray Rhodes, coordinator of the NFL's second-ranked defense, told Holmgren his family was not happy in Green Bay and preferred to return to San Francisco. Rhodes' desire to leave, just as the Packers began to approach the success he, Holmgren and offensive coordinator Sherm Lewis envisioned when they came over from the 49ers in early 1992, stunned Packers executives.

"Everything was OK, or so we thought," Wolf said.

Holmgren and Rhodes were close friends, having worked together for nearly a decade. That friendship, and Holmgren's unwillingness to keep Rhodes in Green Bay against his will, were central in the Packers' decision to grant Rhodes' wish and tear up his contract. Within a month, San Francisco promoted Bill McPherson to assistant head coach and Rhodes installed as defensive coordinator, the job he had pursued unsuccessfully before agreeing to join Holmgren in Green Bay. Interestingly, Rhodes' family – his stated reason for leaving – did not move back to San Francisco for another four months, until the Green Bay school year had ended.

Says Wolf: "To this day, I'm not really sure what happened. When he came to see me, he said it was a family situation. I have to go with that."

Of course, Rhodes was making a lateral move. Under NFL guidelines, the Packers weren't compelled to release him, and they certainly had a precedent: Just two years before, the 49ers had extorted a second-round draft pick for Holmgren. Yet the Packers simply let Rhodes leave.

"You never want to keep someone against his will," Holmgren said. "I'll always support anyone who wants to improve himself."

Rhodes spent just one season in San Francisco, winning another Super Bowl ring before achieving his ultimate goal: Becoming an NFL head coach. The Philadelphia Eagles hired him to replace fired Rich Kotite, and he led the Eagles to a 10-6 record – and a convincing 58-37 victory over Detroit in an NFC first-round playoff game in his debut season.

The acrimonious relationship between the Packers and Rhodes hasn't ebbed in the two years since his departure. Wolf and Rhodes have sparred in the media regarding their roles in drafting Terrell Buckley.

"There's a lot there that is better left unsaid," Harlan said. "Obviously, there are some hard feelings."

The departure of Rhodes, who endeared himself to players with his interest in their personal lives, his willingness to hang out in the locker room and, most important, his aggressive defensive philosophy, could have been a huge setback for Wolf, Holmgren & Co. But less than a week after Rhodes' decision to leave, veteran Fritz Shurmur had agreed to join the Packers as defensive coordinator.

It was a profound addition, in many ways.

Shurmur, then 61, was familiar to the staff, having worked with Gil Haskell and Nolan Cromwell during a stint with the Rams and coached against Holmgren's 49ers offenses for half a decade. Despite the highs and lows involved in working for five teams during 20 seasons, Shurmur, author of three books on football coaching philosophy, never once was without a job when training camp rolled around. Released with the rest of Joe Bugel's staff after three years in Phoenix, Shurmur had offers from four other NFL teams when he agreed to direct the Packers defense.

"As soon as the option became available to me, it was my No. 1 choice," Shurmur said. "I look at this as my best opportunity and the one I'd be most comfortable with."

The unassuming Shurmur was the perfect replacement for Rhodes. He didn't attempt to compete with Rhodes, or challenge the popular assistant's strategy and obvious rapport with the players. Instead, he complimented Rhodes' accomplishments, pledged to adapt to the team's existing defensive approach and generally declined to make waves. He was the perfect solution to what could have been a divisive situation for Holmgren and the Packers.

"I'm not married to any particular scheme," Shurmur said upon joining the Packers. "I've always believed our job is to get the guys in the best position to make plays. The people come to watch the players play, not the coaches coach."

The seamless transition to Shurmur is only one example of the remarkable flexibility Holmgren and Wolf have displayed. The Packers' unexpected loss of talent, particularly at linebacker, would be enough to set most teams' excuse factories in motion. Yet they have managed to survive the departures of standouts Bryce Paup and Tony Bennett, veterans Brian Noble and Johnny Holland, prospects Mark D'Onofrio and James Willis.

"You just do the best with what you have," said Bob Valesente, linebackers coach for three of the past four seasons. "A lot of times, you're surprised at how the players you have step up and meet the challenge."

Certainly, the Packers won't argue that Wayne Simmons is better than Paup, or that recently acquired Ron Cox can outperform Bennett. Neither will they contend that Shurmur definitely is a better coach than Rhodes, or that Harry Sydney is a better offensive assistant than Gruden. But what team officials will contend is that, when one considers the money involved, the Packers have received as much or more value per dollar from the players they've kept – and the football operation as a whole continues to get better.

"We're still learning how to operate in this new free agency system," Wolf says. "I'm used to going out and getting the best possible player for whatever need you have. With free agency and the salary cap, you can't just go out and do something that you ordinarily would have done."

The NFL's free agency rules, implemented after the 1992 season as part of the league's collective bargaining agreement, placed a salary cap on each team. The intention: Preventing a major-market team from "buying" enough players to win a Super Bowl. Some franchises, including Dallas and San Francisco in their hiring of Deion Sanders, have worked around the fringes of the cap, delaying payments to top-dollar players for several years to provide a "fit" under the salary cap. The salary cap dictated significant change on the NFL's personnel directors, forcing them to be mindful of available dollars when pursuing additional talent. In Green Bay, Wolf works closely with chief negotiator Mike Reinfeldt and legal counsel Lance Lopes to ensure a prospect's talent is in line with his contract demands.

To prepare for the salary cap, the Packers in 1992 developed an "11-player wheel" philosophy. The concept: They'll pay 11 key veterans – five on offense, five on defense and one specialty player – significantly more than the rest of their roster. Salary cap limitations, combined with the rapidly increasing salaries paid to the league's most-sought free agents, made it no longer feasible, the Packers reasoned, to hope to employ a top-line player at every position. Thus, the 11-player wheel.

Through the four years of free agency, the Packers have altered the model slightly. As the salary cap has increased (the league determines the cap number – about $40.75 million in 1996 – based on a percentage of its gross revenues), they've expanded the "wheel" list to perhaps 13 players entering 1996. Another factor: Though Green Bay has signed many of its key players to extended contracts, only two – Favre and White – will make more than $2 million this year. Sean Jones was in the $2 million range, but accepted a $900,000 pay cut before the exhibition season.

Entering 1996, the key players on offense are: Favre, RB Edgar Bennett, WR Robert Brooks, TE Mark Chmura, TE Keith Jackson and T Ken Ruettgers. On defense, they're DEs Jones and White, DT Santana Dotson, S LeRoy Butler and perhaps CB Doug Evans and LB George Koonce. Kicker Chris Jacke fits the "special player" role.

In addition, the Packers' salary-cap formula includes significant contributions from their draft picks still playing under the terms of their rookie contracts. In the best case, they'll receive a few years of "key player" performance from individuals receiving draft-pick salaries. Some of the players in this category: G Aaron Taylor, T Earl Dotson, LB Wayne Simmons, WR Terry Mickens, CB Craig Newsome, RB William Henderson, DE Gabe Wilkins, RB Dorsey Levens, WR Antonio Freeman, G Adam Timmerman and DTs Darius Holland and Bob Kuberski, plus all of the team's selections in the 1996 college draft.

Perhaps the most critical area for Green Bay, though, has been its ability to develop serviceable players from the league's scrap heap. Koonce is a prime example; he came to the Packers from the virtual anonymity of the World League in 1992. Others: NT Gilbert Brown, a third-round pick dumped by the Vikings before the 1992 season; T Gary Brown, a 300-pound project waived by the Steelers in 1994; P Craig Hentrich, a versatile specialist originally drafted by the Jets who tried out for Green Bay in 1993 and returned a year later to win a roster spot.

A final category: Veterans in transition to or from the "wheel" level. Backup quarterback Jim McMahon is a good example. He no longer commands the salary of a top NFL quarterback, but the insurance he provides is a commodity the Packers must have to rank among the league's best teams. This category also includes veteran starters who don't rank among the league's elite players, but nonetheless play key roles – often in the locker room as well as on the field. They include: C Frank Winters, S Mike Prior, WR Anthony Morgan, plus free-agent acquisitions LB Ron Cox, LB Mike Johnson and WR Desmond Howard, as well as S Eugene Robinson, a former Pro Bowler for Seattle acquired for DE Matt LaBounty in June 1996.

Wolf and Holmgren have made creditable use of the "veteran" category, using the experience and winning attitude of players on the "south side" of their career to plug a hole for a few games or a season, as well as hone the skills of younger players. Vets like RB Harry Sydney, T Tootie Robbins, T Tunch Ilkin, LB Fred Strickland, WR Mark Clayton, WR Mark Ingram, NT Bill Maas, LB Joe Kelly, G Guy McIntyre, DT Steve McMichael didn't play as well in Green Bay as they had at the high points of their NFL careers, but their contributions to the Packers' development can't be discounted.

By maintaining players in all four segments – "wheel" players, free agents, veterans and youngsters still under rookie contracts – the Packers have been able to retain salary-cap flexibility as well as an acceptable balance between youth and experience.

Of course, the Packers haven't always made the right decisions. Most notable might be their inability to retain Paup, who had been a flexible, unpretentious performer for five seasons. Team executives argue that a salary-cap situation, caused by the unresolved contract status of waived/injured Sterling Sharpe, prevented the Packers from competing with salaries other teams offered the ex-Northern Iowa linebacker. But Wolf admits he undervalued Paup's ability, and should have made a greater effort to generate the finances to keep him in Green Bay.

"When you look at it, we've done a lot of dumb things," Wolf said. "I've always said we should feel good if one out of four turns out the way we hoped it would."

Packers fans and members of the organization, including Reggie White, admit to similar concerns. Early in the 1995 off-season, after Sharpe was released and Paup signed with Buffalo, White questioned the direction the team was heading. He believed the Packers would be better served by plucking established players from the free-agent pool. But Wolf, after pursuing a handful of high-profile free agents including receiver Andre Rison, decided the Packers had better talent – at least, better talent per dollar – on their bench than he could acquire in free agency. In time, White agreed that the lack of a high-dollar acquisition brought the existing squad closer together.

"I looked back and kind of re-evaluated Ron (Wolf's) decisions on going out and getting free agents," White said. "I thought maybe this would be good for the team to try and keep everybody together, one, and two, Brett is either going to step forward and be the leader he needs to be, or he's going to take a step backward.

"People looked to me to be that type of leader and that's good. But we need a quarterback to take that type of responsibility and Brett has. Around July, I felt that yes, something good could happen."

The Packers in four years have removed almost every vestige of the Infante regime. Only three proven performers – Ruettgers, Butler and Jacke – remain from the team Wolf inherited in November 1991. In reconfiguring the roster, Wolf and Holmgren have brought hundreds of players through Lambeau Field, some for a workout, some for a week, some for as long as possible. During that process, both the coach and the general manager have adjusted their perceptions on player personnel.

"We don't agree on everything, that's for sure," Holmgren said. "But the beauty of it is, I know where he's coming from, and he knows where I'm coming from."

Holmgren has gradually moved toward a bigger offensive line, a prime reason 260-pound Harry Galbreath wasn't retained after the 1995 season. The 49ers traditionally employed technique-oriented linemen for their passing-dominated offense, but Holmgren – allowing for the Wisconsin winters – has seen the need for more run blockers. Entering the 1996 season, four of the team's five projected starters – Gary Brown, Frank Winters, Earl Dotson and Aaron Taylor – carry more than 300 pounds.

"The 49ers used to believe you could win games by propping any guy up on the line," Wolf said. "In this weather up here, that doesn't work."

Meanwhile, Wolf has adapted to Holmgren's offense. His 25 years with the Raiders developed an affinity for speedy receivers, evidenced by the visits of Charles Jordan, Shawn Collins, Bill Schroeder and Corey Harris. The 1996 draft, though, shows Wolf's heightened appreciation of Holmgren's system: He was thrilled to find Derrick Mayes of Notre Dame, a possession receiver with suspect speed, in the second round.

What Wolf wanted in 1992 was a coach with a ball-control offense. What he didn't fully appreciate was the ability of Holmgren's scheme to win the possession game – without a dominant running attack.

"This is a ball-control offense, but with throwing, not running," Wolf said. "It's very interesting how that works. When we have the ball more minutes than the other team, we usually win. It's well-designed."

Early in the Holmgren Era, Wolf pursued players who fit into his vision of a ball-control offense. Notable were running backs John Stephens and Reggie Cobb. Both were former 1,000-yard rushers for the Patriots and Buccaneers, respectively. Both worked best out of a two-back set, lugging the ball 20 or more times per game. Holmgren's schemes call for his featured back to receive the ball in a variety of methods, including swing passes, screens and even as a wide receiver. Neither Stephens nor Cobb made the transition. Cobb lasted one year, Stephens even less than that (he was traded to Atlanta in October 1993 for Eric Dickerson, who couldn't pass the Packers' physical and subsequently retired).

Another mistake: Spending a fifth-round draft pick on ex-Jets quarterback Ken O'Brien. While O'Brien's track record made him a promising backup for Favre, the veteran was unable to adjust to the decision-making demands of Holmgren's offense.

"I should've known better," Wolf admits. "When we made the deal, I knew it wasn't going to work. But I did it anyway, and sure enough, it didn't work. I guess I had to prove to myself that it wouldn't work."

O'Brien fared so poorly during the 1993 exhibition season that Holmgren, after much deliberation, decided to release him and enter the regular season with backup quarterbacks Ty Detmer and Mark Brunell. Neither had played an NFL game, though neither Holmgren nor Wolf were bothered by that issue.

Wolf cites NFL history to illuminate his point: The 1955 Steelers didn't want to go without a veteran backup, so they kept quarterbacks Ted Marchibroda and Jim Finks along with rookie Vic Eaton.

"The guy they cut," says Wolf, pausing for emphasis, "was John Unitas. So much for needing the veteran backup quarterback."

A key component of the Packers' success is the willingness of everyone, including ultimate boss Wolf, to admit mistakes and move forward. While the Packers have certainly made some questionable moves – "sometimes I think for every thing we do right, we do 360 things wrong," Wolf says – the intent was improving the football team. Bryce Paup? The Packers had a salary cap issue that spring, before Sterling Sharpe's grievance against the team was resolved. At the time Paup was negotiating his three-year, $7.6 million contract with the Bills, the Packers weren't certain they'd have the salary-cap money to compete for his services. Of course, the Packers didn't see Paup as a $2.5 million/impact player, either. "We missed there," Wolf admits. Similarly, the team would've been helped had it not swapped free agents with Tampa Bay in 1994 (Cobb for TE Jackie Harris) or if it had retained LB Tony Bennett, despite his 102-day, six-game holdout in 1994. In each instance, Wolf said the Packers weren't willing to pay top dollar for what they perceived to be an "almost" Pro Bowler.

"For a guy to get to that level contractually, they have to prove it over the test of time," Wolf said. "I'm not saying there was anything wrong ... but you can't be the CEO if you've had only three years on the job."

Since the Bennett holdout, though, the Packers have made a priority of extending the contracts of their key young players. Brooks, Edgar Bennett, Chmura, Butler, Dotson and Evans are among the young talents committed to Green Bay beyond the scope of their rookie contracts.

Another indication of the Packers' desire to improve: During the first two years of the Wolf-Holmgren era, Green Bay led the league in free-agent visits (yes, the league tracks that statistic). Only a handful of those players, notably Koonce and Morgan, have become key contributors. But the effort indicates the depth of the Packers' pursuit of talent.

"I truly believe Ron Wolf spends every waking moment attempting to make the Packers a better football team," Harlan says.

Through their joint consideration of hundreds of players, Wolf, Holmgren & Co. believe they've melded to the extent they'll no longer expend time, money and draft picks on players like Stephens and Cobb.

"It took a couple of years for all of us (on the scouting staff) to understand what was needed," Wolf said. "I think we have it down now." ◈

The free agent

The Packers shocked the sports world by
convincing free agent Reggie White
to play in the NFL's smallest city

When the phone rang that morning in April 1993, Ron Wolf had been at work for the better part of two days. The caller was a prominent East Coast football writer, offering condolences for Green Bay's fruitless pursuit of free agent defensive end Reggie White.

"I know he's going to the 49ers today," the reporter told the Packers' GM. "It's unfortunate you guys came in second."

Wolf thanked the caller, hung up – and started laughing.

Minutes earlier, team financial officer Mike Reinfeldt had completed a landmark negotiation with White's agent, Jimmy Sexton. Their stunning agreement: White, the best defensive end in league annals, would receive $17 million, then the third-highest salary in NFL history, for playing the next four seasons with the Packers.

"I wished I could've told the guy," Wolf said later, "but maybe it was better he found out the way he did."

As the shock waves spread throughout Green Bay and the NFL, the smiles at 1265 Lombardi Ave. grew broader. Even in Packers meeting rooms, the excitement was building.

"It started out as a murmur between the players," lineman John Jurkovic told the *Green Bay Press-Gazette*. "It was like, 'I think we signed Reggie. I Think We Signed Reggie. HEY, WE SIGNED REGGIE.'"

In a quiet two-day negotiation, the Packers had addressed three critical issues: Small-market survival in the NFL's free agency system, the willingness of talented players to work in Green Bay, and the willingness of prominent black athletes to spend half the year in Northeast Wisconsin.

"It gives you credibility and it gives you a pass rush," Ken Herock, Atlanta's vice president of personnel, told the *Press-Gazette*. "White gives you everything you need."

The Packers gave White everything he needed as well.

He had spent more than a month touring the NFL, the unquestionable prize in the league's first year of free agency. More than a dozen teams expressed interest in his formidable pass-rushing and leadership skills; several bid seriously. In San Francisco, White went to dinner with Jerry Rice and Steve Young at a restaurant owned by 49ers exec Dwight Clark. In Cleveland, the Browns gave his wife, Sara, a $900 leather coat and a key to the city during a visit to her hometown. In other cities, the Whites were introduced to politicians and celebrities and provided extravagant celebrations and accommodations.

Reggie White
'I think every team was shocked that I picked Green Bay.'

Green Bay did none of that. When White agreed to visit – doing so only because he'd already committed to stop in Detroit, just an hour's plane ride away – the Packers designed a tour of the practice facilities, Lambeau Field and the Packer Hall of Fame. He met with the team's top executives. He went to lunch with Brett Favre. That was it.

"We just wanted to show him Green Bay was a great place to play football," coach Mike Holmgren said. "You can drive to work in five minutes. Our facility is the best. You can feel comfortable with your family here."

The simplicity of Green Bay's presentation certainly differentiated it from the more boisterous pitches from Washington, Cleveland, Detroit, Phoenix, the Jets, Atlanta, Seattle, Tampa Bay, the Raiders and the 49ers.

As one wag noted, "When it's August and it's hot out and you need a Gatorade, is the governor going to be the one to hand it to you?"

White's odyssey included two goals: A team committed to winning a championship, something he hadn't accomplished since he was a teenager; and a venue to extend his ministry to inner-city youth.

Many NFL executives assumed Green Bay's poor performance for more

Return to Glory

than two decades and lack of an inner city, or significant racial minorities, for that matter, would force an early exit from the Reggie Sweepstakes.

Holmgren understood the perception. In fact, while with the 49ers, he and other coaches sometimes threatened players with exile in Green Bay. "If you would've asked me then if I'd be in Green Bay, I would've said, 'I don't want to do that.' We used to threaten 49er players if they screwed up that we would trade them to Green Bay. From a coach's standpoint, that was a pretty good threat, too. But it's not like that."

White noted the commitment to winning so evident in Wolf, Holmgren and defensive coordinator Ray Rhodes. He admired Favre, who played the second half of the Packers' 27-24 victory over White's Eagles the previous season with a separated shoulder after a crunching hit from White.

He saw an opportunity to develop inner-city housing, financing and education programs in Milwaukee, just 90 minutes south of Green Bay.

Two weeks later, Holmgren and Rhodes underscored those positives in an unpublicized visit to White's home in Knoxville, Tenn. They attended White's speech to a local Kiwanis club, took a tour of the city and visited at his home a few hours. (The deeply religious Holmgren got a laugh from the All-Pro defensive end as well, having left this phone message: "Reggie, this is God. Go to Green Bay.") White was taken with the coaches' attention and commitment, something not nearly as evident in other bidders.

"I think there were certain teams that really thought they were going to get a break on this contract because they were proven winners over the last 10 years," Sexton said. "If you're the Redskins and 49ers, you may not think (the Packers) can win, but (White) thinks they can win, and he's the only one that matters."

White and Sexton settled on three finalists: Washington, San Francisco and Green Bay. The agent, sitting in a New Orleans hotel room and holding tickets to the NCAA basketball championship, took to the phones.

The Redskins offered $13.6 million over four years. The 49ers, hampered by rules in the new free agency system (they had advanced to the NFC Championship game and were thus limited in their free-agency spending), offered $19.5 million over five years. Green Bay had previously made a four-year offer for $16 million, the best on the table. When Washington didn't upgrade its offer and White indicated he'd be as happy in Green Bay as anywhere, the Packers were suddenly, surprisingly, in the driver's seat.

Sexton made another call to Reinfeldt, who indicated the Packers would be flexible in structuring the contract payments. (Reinfeldt and Sexton had built a solid relationship weeks before when they completed a three-year contract for guard Harry Galbreath, another Tennessee alum who was a close friend of White's. That successful negotiation and Galbreath's eagerness to join the Packers certainly were assets in constructing the White deal.) The agent and the negotiator shared a laugh at their predicament: Both are ardent college basketball fans, and Reinfeldt was as eager to watch the North Carolina/Michigan game as Sexton was to attend it. Yet they continued talking up to tipoff ... past halftime ... until 1 a.m.

Neither saw a basket – but they did manage to agree in principle on a $17 million contract that would pay White $9 million in the first year.

"When it was finished, there was almost a sense of disbelief – that, and a kind of a quiet satisfaction," Reinfeldt said. " Of course, we still had to get Reggie into Green Bay and have him officially sign the contract. For me, that was the worst part ... until his name was on the line."

As Reinfeldt and Sexton completed the negotiation the next morning, Green Bay radio stations reported White was signing with the 49ers. Margaret Meyers, one of the Packers' executive assistants, heard the radio reports. She was more than a little surprised when Reinfeldt placed a $17 million contract on her desk.

"He just dropped it off like he would with any other contract and said, 'We're going to do this.' He was pretty calm," Meyers said.

Not calm: The team's public relations staff. Lee Remmel, Mark Schiefelbein and Jeff Blumb were in Atlanta at a league meeting. Only long-time staff member Shirley Leonard and secretary Linda McCrossin were on duty for what Remmel later called "one of the most dramatic moves in the Packers' history. It's maybe not quite the magnitude of Lombardi winning the Super Bowl, but it's on that kind of scale."

While the rest of the public relations staff scrambled to arrange flights back to Green Bay, Leonard and McCrossin scheduled a press conference – the news of which initiated an almost immediate tidal wave of excited phone calls from media and fans hoping to confirm the Reggie Report.

"It was crazy – unlike any other day here, ever," McCrossin said.

An afternoon press conference brought in a horde of state and national media, plus team executives and several players. It was an event like no other in Packers history. Harlan rated it as the most momentous day in his more than 20 years with the franchise.

In an instant, the Packers had gained national respect. Their defense, which ranked 23rd in the league in 1992 and hadn't had a defensive lineman with more than five sacks since 1985, now possessed the best pass rusher in NFL history. As important: The Packers had a defensive leader to mirror the impending offensive greatness of quarterback Brett Favre.

White, during the celebratory press conference: "Me and Coach made an agreement. We're going (to the Super Bowl) this year, aren't we?"

Wolf: "I think we can compete for the NFC Central Division title. With Reggie in place, we're going to be considered a serious contender."

Holmgren: "It boils down to trust and respect and handshakes sometimes, even in this business. Personal guarantees, to me, are important, and I think we have some of those."

White admitted he'd at first dismissed the small-market Packers, but also admitted he had been wrong. "I've changed. I think every team was shocked that I picked Green Bay. I think I made the right decision."

Not everyone agreed.

White was criticized by media members for accepting the most lucrative offer, after indicating his search had a strong religious bearing.

Wrote Will McDonough in the Boston Globe: "White said from start to finish of his nationwide tour that God would 'speak' to him and tell him where to go. Tuesday, God apparently told White to go to Green Bay. ...

"Have you ever wondered why it is called 'Green' Bay when every time you see it on television it is covered with snow and ice, buffeted by wind and doesn't look like the kind of place most people would call heaven?

"We now know that God speaks in signs," a top executive with one of the bidding teams told McDonough. "Dollar signs."

Other believed the Packers spent too much for too little.

"The (Eagles) did not want to commit four years to Reggie White because they felt that he did not have four good years left, and they were right in the sense that his best days are behind him," wrote Bill Lyon in the Philadelphia Inquirer.

The Packers were unbowed. Wolf and his scouting staff had reviewed tape of Eagles games before Green Bay's initial contact with White. They were convinced the 31-year-old had at least four dominant seasons left.

Plus, they fully intended to supply him with as much help as possible. They had linebackers Tony Bennett and Bryce Paup under contract, and had recently signed veteran nose tackle Bill Maas. They'd make sure triple-teaming White wasn't a viable option for opposing offenses.

"He can do great things for us," Holmgren said. "The thing I want to emphasize – Reggie and I have talked about this on more than one occasion – while he is maybe the finest player that's ever played his position, no one man, no one player, can take you to the championship."

Yet Holmgren knew that, as the 6-foot-5, 300-pound NFL legend walked from Lambeau Field toward a return flight to Tennessee, his team had just moved closer to Super Bowl contention than he could have hoped.

Holmgren packed his briefcase, corralled the jubilant Wolf and headed toward the airport. Lost in the hoopla was an afternoon flight to Syracuse, where they were scheduled to evaluate NFL draft prospects the next morning. No problem – a prominent Packers shareholder, enthused with the White signing, loaned the team his Lear jet for the evening.

Within minutes, Holmgren and Wolf were climbing over the lights of Green Bay, relaxing in plush comfort, still grinning unabashedly at how fast their franchise had moved forward during the past 24 hours.

Holmgren suggested a toast.

They scoured the cabin, but found only a few cans of soda.

They shrugged shoulders, laughed again and tipped cans, knowing full well that the NFC playoffs were, in all likelihood, only 16 games away. ◆

The drafts

His No. 1 picks haven't made a huge impact,
but Ron Wolf's drafts still compare
favorably with the NFC's best teams

Terrell Buckley. Wayne Simmons. George Teague. Aaron Taylor. Craig Newsome. John Michels.

The names of Ron Wolf's six first-round draft picks don't strike fear in the hearts of anyone ... including Wolf.

Yet the Packers can argue successfully that the work of Wolf's college scouting staff has put the Packers among the NFL elite. How? Try these names.

Robert Brooks. Mark Chmura. Earl Dotson. Antonio Freeman. Edgar Bennett. Doug Evans.

Those six players – all selected in Rounds 3-6 of Wolf's drafts, have played huge roles in the Packers' ascension to Super Bowl contender. Despite the limited impacts of high picks such as Buckley and linebacker Mark D'Onofrio, and to a lesser extent Teague, Simmons and Taylor, the Packers have prospered through the draft.

"That's the only way I know how to do it," Wolf admits.

Wolf has assembled a scouting staff that features an appropriate mix of veterans (John Math and Red Cochran) and comparative youngsters (George Streeter and Shaun Herock, son of Falcons executive Ken Herock). Ted Thompson, formerly of the Houston Oilers, oversees pro scouting, and Bryan Broaddus coordinates the entire operation, which at any given time can send Wolf and his staff from their three small rooms in the Packers' administration building to a dozen college campuses throughout the country. The Packers take pride in their scouting prowess, and are more than willing to spare the expense of a flight into Green Bay and a night's stay at the Midway Motor Lodge to learn a little more about a potential acquisition.

Fans would be stunned at the number of "name" players who visit Green

Bay without ever appearing on the Packers' practice field. Suffice it to say that, even if you've never heard of a player, Wolf and his staff have a complete bio prepared for perusal in their voluminous files at 1265 Lombardi Ave.

That begins to explain how the Packers decided Doug Evans, a spindly safety at Louisiana Tech, had a decent chance to become an NFL corner-back. Few of the "draft-niks" included Evans on their "Top 25" lists at safety or corner. Many didn't know who he was when Green Bay chose him in the sixth round in 1993. But Evans' visit to Green Bay shortly after the draft wasn't his first. He'd stopped in town a month earlier, taking part in a private indoor workout at the team's Oneida Street practice facility.

1992 draft
at a glance

WR Robert Brooks, RB Edgar Bennett and TE Mark Chmura more than overcome the disappointment of Buckley and D'Onofrio. A bonus: Ty Detmer's selection in the ninth round. Worth noting: The Packers also traded a 1992 first-rounder for Brett Favre, and gave a second-round pick to the 49ers to release Mike Holmgren from his exclusive, three-year contract as the 49ers offensive coordinator.

"That's easily the best draft we've had," general manager Ron Wolf said. "It would've even been better had we not tried to pick an explosive type player with our first pick, if we'd just picked a solid player. D'Onofrio ... that (torn hamstring) was a rare injury. But still, to get Favre for a first-round pick and Mike Holmgren for a second ... we did well."

"He possesses such great speed and he's such a good hitter," Wolf said at the time. "Hopefully, we can train him and develop him into being a corner."

Three years later, Evans has become a strong performer in an outstanding young secondary. He finished third on the team in 1995 with 90 tackles, and set a team record with 27 pass breakups, surpassing LeRoy Butler's previous mark of 25 in 1993. The Packers view him as one of the better right cornerbacks in the NFL.

"We expect great things from him," Wolf said.

Evans is one of the Packers' draft successes. Another cornerback is among the most prominent failures.

Terrell Buckley, one of the nicest young men to spend time in Green Bay, left as one of the most disliked Packers in team history. His post-draft braggadocio turned the most loyal Packer Backers against him. Before he ever played a down, 60 percent of the respondents to a WFRV-TV telephone poll encouraged the Packers to trade him.

"He wasn't ready to be here," Wolf said.

Buckley's failure can likely be attributed to his applying for the NFL draft after his junior season at Florida State. Even Buckley admits he wasn't ready to leave the security and structure of a college campus, even factoring in the $3.2 million signing bonus Green Bay gave him. A healthy share of that bonus bought an extravagant house in Orlando, but during his rookie season in Green Bay, Buckley lived in a small apartment, most of the time with his mother or sister. They had jobs and lives back home in Georgia, but Buckley wanted them, needed them, so they kept him company.

Green Bay can be a lonely place for a 21-year-old black man who has alienated a state of Packers fans and many of his teammates with blatant self-promotion. In many ways, Buckley's demise patterned that of Tony Mandarich a mere four years earlier: Big talk, big money, big disappointment.

Edgar Bennett, a fourth-round pick in 1992, has been a workhorse at halfback and fullback for the Packers.

Once again, the Mandarich experience played a role in the Packers' strategy. Braatz had a string of drawn-out negotiations with the team's high-profile players, including Mandarich in '88, Majkowski in '90 and linebacker Tim Harris in '91. Each of the three missed training camp and at least one regular-season game. Buckley was the first "name" negotiation of the Wolf-Holmgren regime, and both coach and general manager were determined to get him on the field.

But agent Carl Poston realized the Packers' desire for a quick negotiation and used it to his client's advantage. He kept Buckley in Florida throughout training camp and, much like Mandarich toyed with Hollywood and boxing, Buckley made an embarrassing attempt at minor-league baseball. Much like Mandarich, Buckley took his negotiation to the public. Some of the 21-year-old's proclamations:

• "I'm a skilled defensive back. You have two kinds of defensive backs – you have defensive backs who cover receivers, and you have defensive backs like me. I have one other back that I could compare myself to, and that's Prime Time (Deion Sanders). We cannot only stop the receiver and make the tackle, we can intercept the ball and run it back with the grace of a running back. I can play wide receiver and I'm also a return man. The Packers are getting five players in one. They can't pay me like I play one position."

• "I hate for people to try my intelligence with chump change."

• "I'm not a Hollywood-type guy. I just want to smell good, keep my clothes up to date and have a nice haircut."

• "I honestly believe I could be an all-star in baseball."

Terrell Buckley
'Here I am, the best athlete of the second half-century.'

• "I'm a better baseball player than a football player. Football is a priority. You have to go with what will put a meal on your table. At the same time, I will be playing baseball."

• "Everyone knows that Jim Thorpe was the best athlete of the first half-century. Here I am, the best athlete of the second half-century. They (the Packers) are really insulting me."

Poston and the Packers, after a 48-day holdout, finally settled on a four-year contract one week into the 1992 season, but the eight-week delay in learning defensive coordinator Ray Rhodes' system and building relationships with his teammates likely cost Buckley much more than the $6.8 million the Packers paid him.

"We paid him too much money," Wolf says now. "He didn't have to work for anything."

Though he had 12 interceptions in his three-year Packers career, Buckley's blown coverages, missed tackles and fumbled punts had most of Wisconsin and many teammates endorsing his benching. Near the end of his tenure, Buckley received a piece of fan mail that contained nothing but a crumbed piece of toast. It took him awhile, but he eventually laughed at the joke.

No laughing matter: The play that defined Buckley's Packers career. It came in Game 3 of the 1993 season, with Green Bay leading the host Vikings 13-12 with less than 15 seconds remaining.

Vikings quarterback Jim McMahon faced a desperate third-and-10 from the

1993 draft
at a glance

The significant move was Wolf's pursuit of Alabama S George Teague. He traded two No. 2s, a fourth and an eighth to Dallas for its first and fourth pick, using the No. 1 to draft Teague. Both Teague and first-rounder LB Wayne Simmons have shown flashes of stardom, but haven't exhibited the consistent performance befitting their draft position, and Teague was traded to Atlanta prior to training camp in July 1996. T Earl Dotson was a solid No. 3 pick, QB Mark Brunell was a great find in the fifth round and CB Doug Evans was an excellent choice in the sixth round.

"Simmons has demonstrated he's capable of playing at an upper echelon," Wolf said. "Teague had a marvelous first year, then got sick and he hasn't been himself since. He's been a mere shell of himself. When you look at first D'Onofrio, then Teague, those are huge losses. But still, we picked up Evans, who we have high regard for, and Brunell, who would still be here without the new (free agency) system."

50-yard line. But Buckley, rather than running with rookie Eric Guliford on a fly pattern, inexplicably tried to help Butler cover Cris Carter on a 15-yard down-and-out. McMahon lobbed the ball to Guliford, who fell down at the 5. Fuad Reveiz kicked a 22-yard field goal on the next play, giving the disbelieving Vikings a 15-13 victory.

Said McMahon: "They just blew the coverage ... they should cover a guy going deep. Buckley thought, 'That's McMahon. He can't throw it that deep.' If I throw it any further, he scores."

Teammates' attempts to defend Buckley after that play were fruitless. Many confided they wanted him benched, and, in time, the lack of camaraderie began to impact the 23-year-old's psyche. An explosive runner who thrilled fans with a 58-yard touchdown in his first game as a Packer, Buckley began to struggle on punt returns as well. After seven fumbles and just a 6.9 yard return average midway through 1993, Buckley asked special teams coach Nolan Cromwell to release him from return duty. One of the Packers' primary reasons for drafting him – Holmgren called him an "offensive defensive player" – had been negated.

Though he lasted one more season – intercepting a team-high five passes in 1994 – he was unsuccessful in covering the NFC's leading receivers, especially taller players such as Herman Moore of Detroit, Cris Carter of Minnesota and Alvin Harper of Dallas, who burned him for a back-breaking 94-yard touchdown play in Buckley's final game as a Packer, a 35-9 playoff loss.

Buckley's confidence was gone and, after the 1994 playoffs, so was he – dumped to Miami in exchange for the humiliating "past considerations." The non-trade was a preferable alternative to waiving the former No. 1 pick, and Wolf believed Buckley might regain his confidence in Florida, site of his college accomplishments.

"He just didn't work out," Wolf said. "I don't have the answer, but my speculation is through all that bravado, he was not a self-secure individual. The game got too big for him. He couldn't make the plays like he wanted to, and he got down on himself."

1994 draft

at a glance

Wolf traded a third-round pick to move up four positions in the first round and select G Aaron Taylor, who has suffered season-ending knee injuries both years in Green Bay. Wolf then traded a second-round pick to the 49ers for four later-round picks. RB LeShon Johnson, chosen in the third round, never contributed but the subsequent three picks – DE Gabe Wilkins, WR Terry Mickens, RB Dorsey Levens – were significant role-players throughout 1995.

"We stuck all our eggs in one basket that year, for Aaron Taylor, and then he gets hurt," Wolf said. "LeShon Johnson didn't help us, but Dorsey Levens did pan out and developed into a pretty good player. Wilkins can be a starter. But thus far, that isn't exactly a powerful draft."

Most frustrating for Wolf: Buckley was not his top choice in the 1992 draft.

In the days before his first draft in Green Bay, Wolf confided that his favorite player was offensive tackle Bob Whitfield. But he knew the Packers had expended previous draft picks on linemen, and figured the franchise needed a boost – a marquee player who could provide an immediate impact. The draft was strong at cornerback – both Buckley and Wisconsin's Troy Vincent were highly rated on most teams' draft boards – and the Packers certainly needed help on defense, where Tony Bennett and then-rookie LeRoy Butler were their only talents of note.

Plus, adding a top-notch corner would allow Butler to move inside to strong safety, where his ball-hawking, big-play abilities could be maximized. Wolf viewed Butler as one of the Packers' greatest weapons, due in great part to the reaction of other NFL executives when the ex-Jet and Raiders executive moved over to the Packers.

1995 draft
at a glance

Top pick Craig Newsome is a fixture at left cornerback. Wolf compiled four third-round picks in deals with Jacksonville (QB Mark Brunell), Carolina (for moving down 10 picks in the first round in '95), and Seattle (as compensation for restricted free agent Corey Harris). All four third-round selections – DT Darius Holland, RB William Henderson, LB Brian Williams and WR Antonio Freeman – are expected to contribute in '96. Also, fifth-rounder Travis Jervey and seventh-rounder Adam Timmerman are potential contributors.

"It could be a good draft – but we'll see what happens," Wolf said. "It seems that for some reason, when you move down to where we are now (the later portion of the draft round, compared to the No. 5 position in 1992) you do a little bit better job."

"Most of the calls I got were for Butler," Wolf said. "In fact, I didn't get many trade-type calls that didn't include Butler. So right then, we knew we had something pretty special."

The Packers strongly considered the bigger, stronger Vincent, but Wolf and Holmgren both were captivated with Buckley's ability to "make things happen" when he handled the football. Buckley could help the team immediately as a punt returner, they reasoned, and could likely be counted on for a half-dozen interceptions at left corner as well.

Wolf now admits that Vincent would've been a better choice.

"The idea was adding some spark to our team but we made a mistake there," Wolf said. "Had I known what I know now, I never would've taken Buckley over Vincent. Not because of how Terrell played here, but because of the way you have to play here. It's so much different, playing in this weather instead of where he came from (Florida State). You need a bigger person, a stronger person to play corner in Green Bay."

**Wolf on linebacker
Wayne Simmons**
'He's capable of playing
at an upper echelon.'

Wolf shakes his head at the impact Vincent, Whitfield or several other players in that draft (DT Chester McGlockton, DB Dale Carter) might've made in Green Bay.

"Fortunately, we've been successful here … or we might've been right out the door, with some of the moves we've made," Wolf said.

Buckley, though, wasn't the biggest disappointment of the first Wolf-Holmgren draft. Hours after selecting Buckley, the Packers chose a linebacker who Wolf believed had Pro Bowl "written all over him." D'Onofrio, son of a New Jersey union leader, was another in a long line of outstanding Penn State linebackers. Early in his first exhibition season, he flashed the aggressiveness and agility that had Wolf "doing a backflip" when he was available with the 35th pick in the second round.

But D'Onofrio's career ended almost before it began. He suffered a devastating hamstring tear in just his second regular-season game and, despite more than a year of rehabilitation, never returned to active duty. It's worth noting that, before drafting D'Onofrio, the Packers desperately pursued a trade for a late first-round pick with the intention of taking Tennessee receiver Carl Pickens. Wolf wasn't successful – "we didn't have enough ammunition," he said later. Pickens has become a dominant player for the Bengals, who tabbed him at No. 31. Green Bay got D'Onofrio four picks later.

Still, the first Wolf-Holmgren draft is an unquestionable success, even with the disappointments of Buckley and D'Onofrio. The Packers found Robert Brooks in the third round, Edgar Bennett in the fourth and Mark

Chmura in the sixth.

An interesting element of that draft, and with the majority of players Green Bay has acquired during the past four seasons, is their winning background. When Wolf and Holmgren joined the Packers, only three of their starters – safety Mark Murphy, guard Ron Hallstrom and defensive end Robert Brown – had been in an NFL playoff game, and none of those players remained on the roster one year later. To generate a positive attitude in Green Bay, Wolf and Holmgren had to bring in players who were accustomed to the success Holmgren, Ray Rhodes and Sherm Lewis had enjoyed in San Francisco. It was with that intention that the first six players Wolf drafted in 1992 had won 79.7 percent of their college games the year before. In Tom Braatz's last draft in Green Bay, the five players chosen on the first day of the draft had a college winning percentage of just 40.7. Wolf has continued to select players from larger, successful schools. His first four picks in 1996, for example, came from USC, UCLA, Notre Dame and Nebraska.

1996 draft
at a glance

For the first time during the Wolf-Holmgren era, the Packers did not make a trade on draft day. T John Michels heads a beefed-up offensive line, with C Mike Flanagan (UCLA, third round) and G Marco Rivera (Penn State, sixth round) expected to contribute. WR Derrick Mayes (Notre Dame, second round) was expected by some to be a first-round pick; in time, he could be a terrific complement to Robert Brooks. RB Chris Darkins (Minnesota, fourth round) may be employed as a change-of-pace for Edgar Bennett, much like the Eagles use Charlie Garner to supplant Rickey Watters. "Edgar won't like that too much, but I think in the long run, I can show him why it will be a good thing for him," Holmgren said. "I'd like to be able to insert one of those young guys (Darkins or Travis Jervey) and get them in the game as a spark."

"They're accustomed to being successful, and they're accustomed to winning," Wolf said. "That's why they were selected."

Wolf is probably his own worst critic, willingly discussing what he could have and should have done throughout the player personnel sphere. In late 1993, for example, he evaluated himself and his scouting staff through comparisons against the best NFC teams, noting that the Packers likely wouldn't win the NFC Central until they had a 1,000-yard rusher to compare with Minnesota's Terry Allen, Detroit's Barry Sanders, Tampa's Reggie Cobb and the Bears' Neal Anderson. He was correct: The Packers' first division title in the Wolf-Holmgren era came in 1995, when Edgar Bennett became the team's first runner in 17 years to surpass the 1,000-yard mark.

An interesting assessment of the Packers' drafts can be gained through a comparison to the NFC's premier teams, Dallas and San Francisco.

The Packers have retained 19 players from their first four drafts. Three others – Ty Detmer, Mark Brunell and Buckley – are competing for starting jobs with other teams.

In 1992, the Packers drafted three current starters: Brooks, Bennett and Chmura. Dallas picked up DB Kevin Smith and S Darren Woodson. The 49ers didn't gain any starters.

In 1993, the Packers found Simmons, Teague, Dotson and Evans. The Cowboys picked up LB Darrin Smith, S Brock Marion and WR Kevin Williams. The 49ers drafted DT Dana Stubblefield.

In 1994, the Packers found Aaron Taylor and Dorsey Levens. Dallas picked up DE Shante Carver and T Larry Allen. The 49ers chose DT Bryant Young, RB William Floyd and LB Lee Woodall.

The tally: Packers 9, Cowboys 7, 49ers 4.

"You could find teams that have done better: Pittsburgh, for example," Wolf said. "But I think we've done OK – and that's a tribute to the players we've taken, and the job our coaching staff has done with them."

And the scouting staff that found a Pro Bowl tight end (Chmura) and a potential Pro Bowl cornerback (Evans) in the sixth round?

"They're doing OK, too." ❖

Day One

Mike Holmgren and general manager Ron Wolf meet the media Jan. 11, 1992, the day Holmgren was hired as the 11th head coach in the history of the Green Bay Packers.

Return to Glory

Keith Jackson
Jackson combines with Mark Chmura to form the best tight end combination in the NFL. Against the 49ers and Dallas in the '95 playoffs, he totaled six catches for a 30-yard average and two touchdowns.

Return to Glory

Sterling Sharpe

During Sharpe's seven-year career in Green Bay, only one player (Jerry Rice) caught more passes. The NFL leaders from 1988-94: Rice, 620; Sharpe, 595; Andre Reed, 518; Henry Ellard, 478.

Return to Glory

Sean Jones

The former Raiders and Oilers defensive end has 108 sacks in 186 games, including 19.5 in two seasons with the Packers. His best season: 1986, when he had 15.5 sacks for the Raiders.

Return to Glory

Antonio Freeman
The rookie wide receiver made a splash on special teams in the 1995 playoffs, recording a 76-yard touch-down on a punt return.

Return to Glory

Edgar Bennett
Not only did he become the first Packer in 17 years to gain more than 1,000 yards rushing, Bennett in 1995 set a team record for most receiving yards by a running back with 648.

70   **Return to Glory**

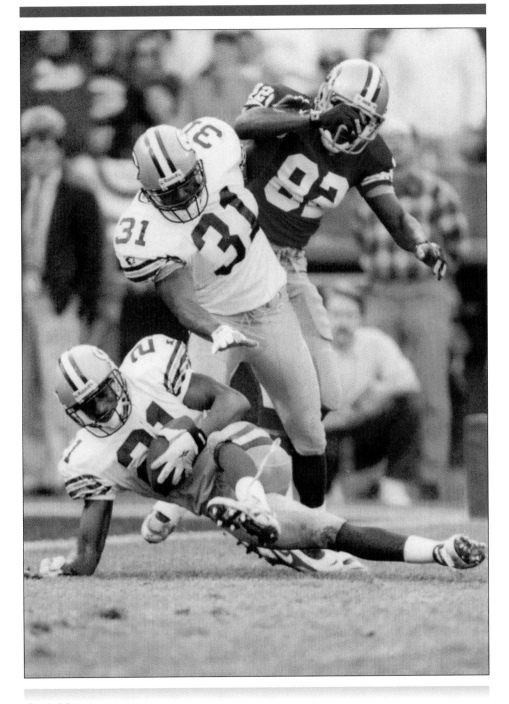

Craig Newsome
The rookie left cornerback provided everything Terrell Buckley didn't, including this interception and a fumble he recovered and returned for a touchdown in the stunning playoff victory over the 49ers.

Return to Glory

Ken Ruettgers

Green Bay's key lineman for a decade, his value was never more evident than in the 1995 opener, which he missed with a back injury. St. Louis pressured Favre throughout a 17-14 Packers loss.

Return to Glory

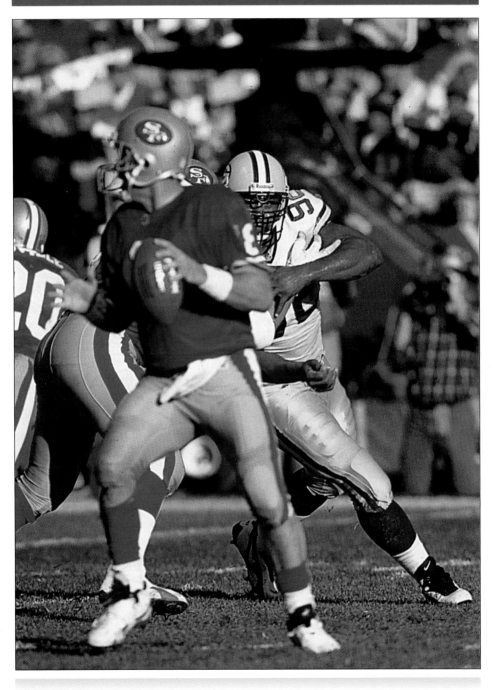

Reggie White
With the signing of Reggie White in April 1993, the Packers "turned the corner to becoming one of the upper echelon teams," GM Ron Wolf says.

Return to Glory 73

Holmgren's Offense

Mike Holmgren's reputation as an excellent offensive strategist has solid statistical backing. The NFL rankings of his offenses (49ers coordinator from 1989-91, Packers head coach 1992-95):

Year	Total Yards	Yards Rushing	Yards Passing	Points
1989	1	10	2	1
1990	2	18	2	8
1991	3	11	2	3
1992	15	21	9	17
1993	19	22	18	6
1994	9	19	9	4
1995	7	26	3	6

Robert Brooks

How good was Brooks in 1995? His 1,497 receiving yards were the most in Packers' history. Sterling Sharpe held the previous record with 1,461 in 1991; James Lofton had 1,361 in 1984.

Return to Glory

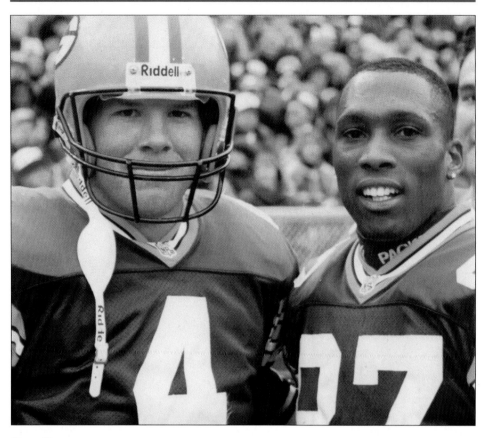

Brett Favre

How important is Brett Favre, pictured with primary receiving target Robert Brooks, to the Green Bay Packers? Consider these numbers from his four-year Packers career:

➤➤ When he throws more TD passes than interceptions (36 games), the Packers' winning percentage is 86.1.

➤➤ When he throws as many TDs as interceptions (11 games), the Packers' winning percentage is 36.4

➤➤ When he throws fewer TDs than interceptions (16 games), the Packers' winning percentage is 18.8

Dynamic Duo

Craig Hentrich, who averaged 41.7 yards per punt in '95, and kicker Chris Jacke (77.2 career field-goal percentage) lead a strong special teams unit, directed by assistant coach Nolan Cromwell.

Return to Glory

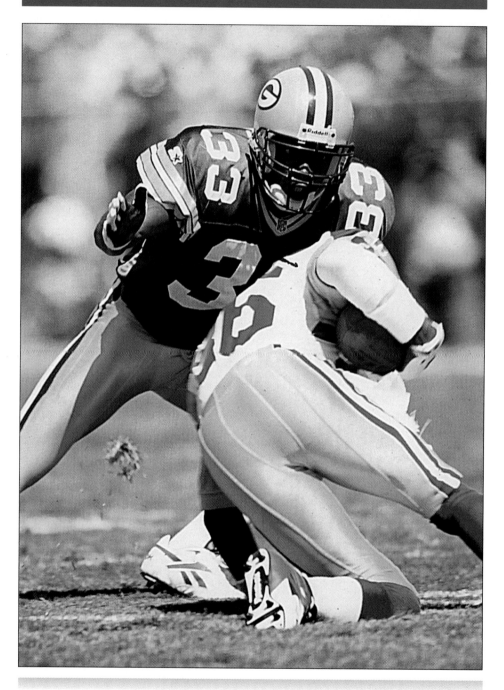

Doug Evans

The former sixth-round draft pick has developed into a Packers defensive leader. In 1995, he led the Packers with 27 passes defensed and contributed 90 tackles, third-best on the team.

Return to Glory

Reggie White
The NFL's career sack leader has 157 in 168 games. He had 12 sacks in an injury-hampered 1995. His best season: 1987, when he had 21 sacks in 12 games for Philadelphia.

Return to Glory 79

MVP

Brett Favre is pictured receiving his NFL Most Valuable Player trophy on this SkyBox football card.

Return to Glory

Sterling

Sharpe played a critical role in
the Packers' resurgence, but couldn't
stay to enjoy the benefits

The player who contributed most to the Green Bay Packers' appearance in the 1996 NFC Championship game had to watch it on TV.

Sterling Sharpe deserved better.

The man who put the Packers' adolescent offense on his shoulders for most of Mike Holmgren's first three seasons as Green Bay head coach now reports on the NFL for ESPN, his career curtailed by a neck injury. Though he set dozens of team and league receiving records, Sharpe's career expired without the ultimate prize: The Packers' record during his career was 51-61, and he participated in just two playoff games.

He left the Packers angry and defiant, certain their doctors were wrong, convinced he'd play again. A year later, as Green Bay prepared to play for the NFC championship, Sharpe was little more than an afterthought.

"I'm sure a lot of people look at our record, and at Robert Brooks and Mark Chmura, and say, 'No, they don't miss him,' general manager Ron Wolf said. "In some ways, it would be nice to say, yes, we don't miss him.

"But that's not the truth. Good players win football games, and he was a great player."

Sharpe's stay in Green Bay was marked by achievement on the field and difficulty off it. Never was that contradiction more evident than in the days before the 1994 season.

Sharpe was playing under a "lifetime" contract, negotiated with former operations chief Tom Braatz, that carried through the year 2000. Sharpe's unique contract contained escalator clauses that always kept his salary among the five highest for NFL receivers. But after Favre signed a five-year, $19 million deal prior to the 1994 season, though, Sharpe began to complain openly to teammates that he was underpaid. His $2 million salary in 1994 did lag behind at least three teammates: Reggie White

($4.25 million average per year), Favre ($3.8 million) and defensive end Sean Jones ($2.6 million).

Sharpe's annoyance became apparent during a preseason practice, when Favre was struggling to gain command of his throwing. After several misfires, Sharpe chided the quarterback in the huddle, according to teammates, at one point saying, "You'd think for $19 million, you could put it in my hands." Favre had to be restrained from an altercation, teammates said.

Sterling Sharpe retired as the Packers' all-time leading receiver with 595 catches.

Sharpe carried his dispute much further than practice, however. In the days before Green Bay's regular-season opener against Minnesota, he began hinting to teammates that he might skip the game if his contract wasn't sweetened. Favre's comments about that possibility left no secret of his antipathy regarding the receiver: "If he walks out, he walks out. We have other guys who can step up and play."

After a week of uncertainty that Holmgren called "a distraction, and a shame," the dispute went public on Saturday, Sept. 3, when Sharpe skipped the team's mandatory 9 a.m. meeting, its walk-through practice and the 1994 team picture. Hours later, the Packers issued a statement announcing that Sharpe had left the team and planned to sit out the season.

"Bob Harlan, Mike Holmgren and I met and decided that, if he didn't show up, we were going to put him on reserve and he wasn't going to play that year," Wolf recalled. "There are several ways to skin a cat, as they say, and he tried one. It was that simple."

The Packers' message to Sharpe, the rest of their players and the NFL: No player would hold their franchise hostage. At the same time, though,

Holmgren was not relishing the thought of a season without Sharpe. He met with Sharpe that afternoon and convinced him and his agent, William "Tank" Black, to meet again with team negotiator Mike Reinfeldt. Sharpe's representatives and Reinfeldt reached agreement on an adjustment of Sharpe's contract – basically, money originally payable in 1999 and 2000 was moved to 1994 and 1995 and Sharpe returned to the team's hotel.

"We didn't change the overall dollar amount, but we changed how he got his money," Wolf said. "Given everything that was involved, the change in the money wasn't really that big of a deal."

Wolf and other team officials credit Holmgren with resolving the dispute. Without the coach's mediation, Sharpe wouldn't have played in 1994, they said. "I have a feeling for Sterling, and I think he has a feeling for me and the ballclub," Holmgren said. "Anything I could contribute, I'm glad I could. I'm not sure how much I did, though."

Not surprisingly, Sharpe played a key role in the next day's 16-10 victory over Minnesota. He caught seven passes for 53 yards, including a 14-yard touchdown from Favre.

"No matter what else you want to say about him," Wolf said, "the guy always showed up and played."

A sampling of Sharpe's incredible contribution to the Packers:

• Nov. 1, 1992: Sharpe catches six passes for 84 yards, outshining Detroit's Barry Sanders in a 27-13 victory. Favre capitalizes on the blitz package the Lions prepared for him, completing 22 of 37 passes. "We knew what the Lions were fixin' to do," Favre said. "So then it was just a matter of throwing and catching and running, which is what Sterling does best."

• Dec, 20, 1992: Sharpe catches eight passes for 110 yards and two touchdowns in a 28-13 victory over the Rams, including a 7-yard score just before halftime. It is the Packers' sixth straight victory.

"We've got 20 seconds to go in the half, we've got no timeouts, we throw him the ball and he's hit two yards short," assistant Gil Haskell says. "And he still gets into the end zone. That's pretty much his whole season for us."

• Dec. 27, 1992: Sharpe sets an NFL record with 108 receptions, breaking Art Monk's 8-year-old record midway through the second quarter of a season-ending 27-7 loss to Minnesota. Sharpe also finishes No. 1 in the league in receiving yards (1,461) and touchdowns (13) on a team without another legitimate offensive weapon. "Sometimes, he amazes me," running back Darrell Thompson said. "It's almost like Michael Jordan."

• Nov. 14, 1993: Plagued by turf toe, which limited his practice time, as well as a bloody nose and blurred vision, Sharpe caught a 54-yard desperation pass from Favre with 52 seconds remaining to set up Chris Jacke's game-winning field goal in a 19-17 victory over New Orleans. "I didn't want to watch," team president Bob Harlan admitted. "But somehow, Sterling came down with it." He finished the season with 112 receptions, breaking his own record and becoming the first player to lead the league in receiving two straight years since the Chargers' Kellen Winslow did so in 1980-81.

• Jan. 8, 1994: Slipping behind the Lions defense with just 55 seconds remaining, Sharpe catches a 40-yard touchdown pass from Favre, his third of the game, to give the Packers a 28-24 NFC wild-card playoff victory.

"I think when Brett rolled left, the defense was reading his eyes and they drifted to their right," Sharpe said. "Brett looked over and made a great throw."

Said Favre: "I don't want to say a hope and a prayer, but that's really what it was. I knew where Sterling was going to be and he knew not to give up on me, because who knows where I'll throw it. Sometimes I don't know."

• Nov. 24, 1994: In a 42-31 loss to Dallas, he catches nine passes for 122 yards and four TDs against the NFL's No. 1 rated defense.

• Dec. 24, 1994: Sharpe catches nine passes for 132 yards and three TDs in a playoff-clinching, 34-19 victory over Tampa Bay, his final game. He finishes the regular season with a league-high 18 receiving TDs, and extends his team record to 103 consecutive games with at least one reception.

"God truly blessed me by sending me Mike Holmgren and sending me Brett Favre and being able to be in a system where I can go out and I don't have to worry as much about what the alternate route is," Sharpe said on Holmgren's TV show. "I can just go out and do my thing."

He finished his seven-year career with 595 catches. Only one NFL player had more during that span: the 49ers' Jerry Rice, with 620.

Of course, Sharpe's achievements with the Packers go well beyond the statistics. It was his rare talent that helped Favre develop into the NFL's best quarterback. Remember how often Favre looked to Sharpe during his first two dozen games as a starting quarterback? Remember how often Sharpe somehow freed himself from two or more defenders, made the catch, got the first down, kept the drive alive? The Packers certainly do.

"He was a heckuva competitor and a marvelous receiver, no matter what anyone writes about him," Wolf said.

The media wrote a lot about Sharpe during his seven years in Green Bay, especially considering the no-interview policy he put in place early in his rookie season. Sharpe, apparently upset by stories documenting the excessive passes he'd dropped, began declining all interview requests. With the exception of a few national TV chats and a brief Q&A after the playoff victory at Detroit, Sharpe stayed silent.

In refusing to talk to the media or sign autographs, he built a wall between himself and Packers fans. While lesser talents such as nose tackle John Jurkovic were generating mini-celebrity status and the accompanying endorsement deals, Sharpe simply did his job and went home to his fiance, Susan, and their infant daughter. His unwillingness to participate in fan or media functions bewildered his family and frustrated Packers executives, including Holmgren.

Favre on Sharpe:
'I knew where Sterling was going to be, and he knew not to give up on me.'

"I talked to him about the positive benefits of that, many times," the coach said. "I can't make him do it."

It's interesting to consider whether Sharpe's off-field problems with the Packers impacted his departure. The Packers waived Sharpe on Feb. 28, 1995, after failing to restructure his contract. The neck surgery he underwent three weeks earlier kept him from playing in 1995 and, according to Packers medical staffers, ever again. The Packers, unable to utilize Sharpe's $3.2 million contract on the field, hoped to sign a top-notch free agent to replace him – but needed money under the salary cap to do so. Green Bay offered to pay him $200,000 in 1995 as a means of extending his relationship with the franchise. When Sharpe's agent, Tank Black, suggested the Packers release him, Wolf obliged, and Sharpe's spectacular career in Green Bay came to an unceremonious end.

Would the Packers have treated another player differently? Would another player have responded differently? Was Sharpe's waiving a payback for his one-day holdout before the 1994 season? Perhaps answers can be found in Sharpe's previous dealings: Everything he meant to the Packers was predicated on his athletic ability. When that was gone, nothing remained.

Wolf, who still talks to Sharpe on the phone occasionally, suggests the ex-receiver understands the team's perspective.

"What we tried to do is give him some dignity in getting out of the game," Wolf said. "We wanted to keep him on our roster, even though we had a salary cap situation. It would've given him some time to go out the way he wanted to go out. He can see what we were trying to do. It's just too bad it didn't work out."

In retrospect, Sharpe probably did his teammates a favor with his unhappy exit. It's human nature to unite against a common enemy, and the 1995 Packers were intent on proving they could win without Sharpe. It's highly possible he, unwittingly, was the impetus for the remarkable unity Holmgren's team enjoyed last season. Certainly, the spotlight made available by Sharpe's departure – despite Holmgren's attempts at a balanced offense, Sharpe accounted for nearly 40 percent of Green Bay's receiving yardage during his time in the system – was more than enough for Brooks, Bennett, Chmura and Keith Jackson.

Sharpe, to his credit, has been a strong supporter of the resurgent franchise though his work on ESPN, at times suggesting the Packers' offense is more diverse, and, ultimately, better without him.

The Packers aren't as certain.

"Just think if we still had him," Wolf says. "With the emergence of Brooks and Chmura, just imagine how effective we'd be.

"You couldn't stop us." ◈

The coach

Mike Holmgren's ability to teach
has taken him from a California high school
to one of the best franchises in the NFL

It was a brisk, winter day in 1993 and Reggie White was headed to Green Bay as part of his highly anticipated free-agent tour.

White was not seriously considering signing with the Packers at the time. But he was nearby in Detroit and believed it could not hurt to fly to Green Bay and hear what Packers Coach Mike Holmgren had to say.

What Holmgren said changed White's life. Due in large part to that meeting, White shocked the NFL and signed a four-year, $17 million contract with the Packers.

Ask the All-Pro defensive end why he decided to sign with the Packers and he lists several reasons. At the top of the list, though, is Holmgren.

So what was it about Holmgren that impressed White so much and led him to come to Green Bay?

"I think he saw not only the effect I could have on the field, but in the locker room and the community," White said. "I think he was just as much interested in that as he was in me playing. That says a lot to me about him."

Many other members of the Packers have a similar anecdote about their head coach. This is a result of Holmgren's personal, hands-on approach to coaching. Holmgren believes in being more than just a coach to his team. He is also a teacher and a confidant if need be. He is all of that – and more – to his players.

"It's all about character," wide receiver Anthony Morgan said. "He'll come into the locker room and see how you are off the field. Just see how you're doing, how your family's doing. When you hear that from a head coach, you respect that. And I respect Coach Holmgren a lot."

Tight end Keith Jackson, who joined the Packers in 1995, knows a thing or two about playing for a successful head coach, having spent three years with Don Shula in Miami. Jackson said it did not take him long to realize there was something special about Holmgren and his approach to coaching his team.

"When I was in Miami, Reggie was telling me what a great coach Coach Holmgren was," Jackson said. "I think he'll be judged when it's over on his personality, and I think he's an outstanding person."

Holmgren's ability to relate with his players in a positive manner was one of the key reasons Wolf hired him in 1992. Wolf said Holmgren's biggest strength is also his most prominent characteristic as a person.

"He's a genuine human being," Wolf said. "That may sound very trite, but when Mike Holmgren tells you something you believe it. I think you can go to the bank with it. He has such great character that I think people want to do things for him and people will respond to him.

"In other words, when Mike Holmgren talks with you, you're getting the whole package. You're not getting pieces."

That approach is something Holmgren takes pride in. And even though he has learned a great deal during his first four seasons as a head coach, his fundamental approach has stayed very much intact.

"I think I've learned something every year," he said. "My approach to the team, I hope it's been consistent and will remain consistent. I think I have to be myself, otherwise the players see right through you right away."

So who is Mike Holmgren and how has he become one of the NFL's most successful head coaches?

In many ways, Holmgren appears to be the quintessential Californian – laid back, a dry wit and always at ease. To an extent, this is true.

Perhaps nobody knows him better than his wife Kathy, the mother of their four daughters. Kathy says her husband's stoicism, that cool, calm and collected veneer that fans see on the sidelines even in the face of catastrophe, comes from a need to keep an even keel for his team.

"I think he's just good at concealing his emotions," Kathy said. "He just works real hard at putting on a good face. He never wants to appear overly optimistic, and if he's feeling down, he works real hard not to feel down."

And the coach has a fiery side rarely seen by the general public. It comes across mostly in-house, where he prefers to deal with his players one-on-one if he senses a problem instead of lambasting them in the media.

It also seeps through at practice where mistakes are not tolerated, where a lack of effort or a breakdown fundamentally is met with a tirade that would make Woody Hayes or Mike Ditka blush.

It is not uncommon to see a thoroughly disgusted Holmgren cut short a practice and order his players off the field, screaming at them that if they have no desire to focus on their jobs that day, he has no desire to work with them on the field.

"He knows how to motivate us," cornerback Doug Evans said with a laugh.

Keith Jackson
'I think (Mike Holmgren) will be judged when it's over on his personality, and I think he's an outstanding person.'

Certainly, nothing Holmgren does is without purpose. His anger may be genuine, but it is also done to provoke a response. He uses it as another tool to get his message across.

This is all part of Holmgren's coaching style. One part easy-going leader. One part stern taskmaster.

At the heart, however, is Holmgren's belief in himself as a teacher. He is fond of saying that the players he deals with now may be older and their problems may be more sophisticated and adult-oriented, but the fundamental approach to teaching his players now is pretty much the same as it was during his days as a high school coach in San Francisco.

"I love teaching," Holmgren said. "I thought I'd be doing that until I retired. Maybe that's why I'm having so much fun now."

Holmgren has had his share of fun and, at the same time, he has carved out a niche for himself as one of the NFL's elite coaches. Along with Wolf and team president Bob Harlan, Holmgren is one of the architects of the Packers' amazing turnaround.

One of Holmgren's greatest attributes as a head coach is his ability to keep his fingers firmly on the pulse of his team.

If he believes his players are mentally drained, he gently prods them forward. If he senses it is time to crack the whip, he does so without provocation. The key is finding the proper balance between the two and still be true to himself. Many have tried to do just that.

Holmgren has succeeded.

"He knows what we're going through – the emotional ups and downs," wide receiver Robert Brooks said. "I think he knows how far to go to get the most out of us."

Holmgren's coaching skills were tested more than ever in 1995. Faced with the loss of All-Pro receiver Sterling Sharpe, Holmgren embarked

upon a season filled with uncertainty. Many wondered if Green Bay had the talent to make it to the postseason for a third straight year.

Holmgren, though, remained steadfast in his belief in his team. By believing so strongly in his players, the players' belief in themselves never wavered.

"If one person gets down, you got another person who'll come in and say 'Don't worry about it. Let's go,'" Morgan said. "You got guys here that really care about one another. If you carry that onto the football field, you're going to win games."

Holmgren has fostered that belief by creating an atmosphere where the players truly believe

Mike Holmgren can be a disciplinarian and a best friend, and his players appreciate both.

they can rely on each other. Morgan says Holmgren has molded the Packers into a family. Although Holmgren is the family's patriarch, he stresses to his players that it is their team – not just his.

That is one reason he created an executive committee of players who often serves as his link to the rest of the team. Holmgren meets constantly with White, quarterback Brett Favre, tackle Ken Ruettgers and safety LeRoy Butler not only to discuss the events of games past and present, but also to iron out any problems that may be surfacing as the season goes along.

"He listens to the players," Butler said. "It's not a dictatorship. He knows that once the players feel good, they'll play good for you.

"If you try to do it like, 'You do this, it's my team,' players really don't want to play for you."

The sentiment of team that Holmgren has fostered was never more

Return to Glory

evident than in 1995.

No longer did Holmgren have Sharpe to rely on so heavily for his offensive production. Pro Bowl linebacker Bryce Paup was also gone, leaving via the free agent route to Buffalo.

The challenge facing the Packers would be great.

Yet Holmgren believed, as all good teachers do, that adversity can bring people closer together. He drew upon that idea early on and preached it continually – from the spring mini-camps, through training camp and the preseason and throughout the season.

Winning at home
The top 5 coaching records for games played in Green Bay in Packers history.

Coach	Years	Record	Pct.
Mike Holmgren	1992-95	19-4-0	.826
Vince Lombardi	1959-67	28-7-1	.792
Curly Lambeau	1921-49	95-30-9	.743
Phil Bengtson	1968-70	6-6-0	.500
Bart Starr	1975-83	17-18-1	.486

To win in 1995, Holmgren stressed, the Packers had to do it as a team. It was a theme he drilled into his players daily. And it was one they embraced wholeheartedly.

In the end, that belief translated into an 11-5 season, Green Bay's first division title in 23 years and a trip to the NFC Championship game. And Holmgren enjoyed the ride.

"I've really enjoyed coaching this group," he said as the season neared its conclusion. "To see how they practice, see how they rib each other, how they support each other.

"Every one of our 58 players (including the practice squad) has made a significant contribution in some way to the success that we've had this year.

"I've had more fun coaching this team this year than any team I've been around because they're so unselfish. This is as close as I've come to a total team concept."

While chemistry is an overused word in athletics, a bond existed among the 1995 Packers that was undeniable. It was evident very early in the season and remained in place until the final loss at Dallas in January.

Much of the credit for the team's unity could certainly be traced to

Don't let the casual, friendly approach Mike Holmgren displays in public eye deceive you. When the coach talks, his players listen.

Holmgren, who has always strived to create an atmosphere in which team goals are never sacrificed at the expense of individual accolades. That feeling has been in place ever since he took over in 1992.

In 1995, it was stronger than ever.

Like his players, Holmgren knew he would be tested without Sharpe. With his offensive centerpiece no longer around, everyone wanted to see exactly what Holmgren could do with his team.

Quite simply, how good of a coach was he?

What Holmgren did was use Sharpe's absence as a rallying point. Instead of bemoaning the fact their great receiver was no longer there, Holmgren told his team to turn that negative into a positive.

Holmgren said that this season, more players would have to contribute to the team's overall success. More players would have to raise their level of play considerably if the team was going to be successful.

And in the process, more players could feel a sense that they were contributing and were key cogs in the Packers' machine.

"There's a dynamic with this team that through a tragedy may have given us a little spurt," Holmgren said at one point.

Indeed it did.

The results were impressive. Not just for the team, but for Holmgren as

Return to Glory

well. Holmgren's offense was one of the best in the league. Favre – Holmgren's prized pupil – became the league's Most Valuable Player and the Packers came within one quarter of a trip to the Super Bowl.

Holmgren's abilities as a head coach were put to the test and he passed with flying colors. He did it by constantly emphasizing the word "team."

"Every once in awhile, it clicks into a team that they're united in one goal," Holmgren said at one point during the season. "They want to be the guy who makes the play to win the game, but if someone else does, that's good too.

"We've all been on teams where that wasn't the case. But I haven't seen any of that. It's been kind of refreshing."

His players took to the approach and ran with it.

"When we play the game, we play football," special teams standout Marcus Wilson said late in the year. "We don't go out there for certain individual accolades. We're together and we want to do what it takes to take the next step.

"Guys may be upset about something, but in the end what's more important? The greater good."

Holmgren had every reason to be proud. The students had taken their teacher's words to heart.

Perhaps one of Holmgren's greatest achievements in 1995 was forging the Packers into essentially a group of role players.

Favre and White were the two stars. Everyone else was a specialist of sorts. That became very evident as Holmgren continually juggled his lineup each game to get the most out of each player.

For example:

●Morgan and Mark Ingram were co-starters at split end.

●Dorsey Levens and William Henderson shared time at fullback.

●Jackson and Mark Chmura rotated at tight end.

●John Jurkovic, Gilbert Brown, Darius Holland, Bob Kuberski, Gabe Wilkins and Matt LaBounty all figured into the picture on the defensive line.

In an era when the egos of professional athletes have to be handled as gingerly as a newborn, Holmgren was able to get them to merge their personal goals with those of the team. He kept his players focused on the task at hand and not on how much playing time each player was getting each week.

Holmgren continually emphasized the greater good – winning – and the players took it from there.

"I think there is a feeling when they step on the field, they're going to win – regardless of the opponent," Holmgren said.

It was a feeling that came from the top. That was exactly what Holmgren preached to his team from the outset of the season. And as the season unfolded, it became clear his words did not fall on deaf ears.

"There are no egos here," Morgan said. "We're like a family. We're all pulling for each other."

For Mike Holmgren, the 1995 season was his high-water mark as an NFL head coach. And as he looks ahead to the 1996 season, Holmgren could look to the past and view his accomplishments with pride. He has helped revitalize the Packers' organization and turned the team into a winner once again.

But as he examines what he has done in four years in Green Bay, it is easy for Holmgren to look even further back, to remember his days as a high school coach in San Francisco.

And as he recalls those earlier days, he cannot help but be amazed at how far he has come.

"I still, at times, can't believe I'm doing what I'm doing," Holmgren said before pointing to a wall in his office of pictures of his friends from home. "I have my high school coaches, all my buddies are right there from 1978 and we were all together until 1981.

"It's still unbelievable to me. I never set goals that way in my professional life. I thought I'd be teaching history, quite frankly, and passing out jockstraps to freshmen, which is fine."

Instead, he has become one of the NFL's top coaches. Even Holmgren admits his journey has been a bit off the beaten path.

"I don't think it's the typical (NFL) coach's story because most guys don't coach in high school for 12 years," he said. "But it's worked. I can't say, however, that I'm having any more fun than I did at Oak Grove (High School). It's just different.

"You have to fight the temptation to get caught up in the adulation of it all, the fans and all the material things that the job brings to you. I think it's kind of easy to get swept up into a kind of 'king syndrome.'

"My family, my daughters, they obviously don't let me do it at home. And I have a couple of guys on my staff that are good friends of mine and we have an agreement that if I start jumping off the edge, they grab me.

"I'm just trying to keep things in perspective, realizing that I'm pretty fortunate."

It's not easy for a man who has risen to the top of his profession to keep his feet on the ground, but Kathy Holmgren said the coach is basically the same person he was 15 years ago.

"Fundamentally he hasn't changed at all," she said. "There are people who don't know him well that were afraid he would change. He's just the same person.

Leading the Pack

The top 5 coaching records in Green Bay Packers history (includes playoff games):

Coach	Years	Record	Pct.
Vince Lombardi	1959-67	98-30-4	.758
Curly Lambeau	1921-49	212-106-21	.656
Mike Holmgren	1992-95	42-29-0	.592
Phil Bengtson	1968-70	20-21-1	.488
Dan Devine	1971-74	25-28-4	.474

"The difference is the level of responsibility. You could see it (as he was) going up the ladder. When he was just the quarterback coach (for the 49ers), what happened was dependent on what one or two players did. Even if the team lost, if the quarterback functioned OK, he didn't feel so bad. Then it goes on to the offensive coordinator.

"But now every single aspect of the game is influenced by his leadership and everything hurts. ... There are a lot of people's jobs dependent on him, and he takes that very personally and seriously."

As head coach of the Packers, Holmgren has a record of 42-29 in four seasons. Only two coaches in team history have won more games: Curly Lambeau and Vince Lombardi. Impressive company, to say the least.

With success comes expectations, which Holmgren does not shy away from. He enjoys the challenge each season brings, the chance to do what others believe cannot be done.

Ultimate success in the NFL is measured in wins and losses. And of course, there is the ultimate glory – a Super Bowl championship. But for Mike Holmgren, there is more to his job than that. Much more.

"I think it's the development of the team and the getting there I like the most," he said. "All the things that go into coaching. I think I'm a people person and I like dealing with the players and I love my staff and the organization is a great one. I just love coming to work every day. I'm very lucky.

"I even like talking to (the media). For some guys it's confrontational, but I don't see it that way because everyone's been pretty fair with me here.

"I just love what I do. The hard part, conversely is on (his wife) Kathy and the girls because they just see the wins and losses and hear the comments on occasion. I just tell them 'Let's just enjoy this time.'"

And as long as he remains the head coach of the Packers, Holmgren's fundamental approach will not waver. His message will remain the same – no win is too great, no defeat is too difficult to overcome.

Mike Holmgren
'I'm just trying to keep things in perspective, realizing that I'm pretty fortunate.'

"That's one of the great lessons of this game," defensive coordinator Fritz Shurmur says. "Whether they're having great success or terrible difficulty, never take it too seriously ... and you'll have a future in this game."

The Packers believe in that message – and the messenger.

"He knows what we have to do on the field and he does his best to interject that and give us as much input as possible," White said. "He makes you feel good about being in this organization."

That is the Mike Holmgren approach. And it has been working wonders for the Green Bay Packers. ◈

Champions

For the first time since 1972, the Packers
could say they were the best
team in the NFC Central Division

Yancey Thigpen dropped the ball.

And as it hit the turf in the corner of the end zone at Lambeau Field, a roar erupted from the sold-out crowd unlike any the players had heard there before.

LeRoy Butler

'When he dropped it,
I heard the loudest
yell I've heard since
I've been living.'

"When he dropped it, I heard the loudest yell I think I've heard since I've been living," safety LeRoy Butler said. "Our fans went wild."

With that drop, the Green Bay Packers had beaten the Pittsburgh Steelers 24-19 at Lambeau Field in Green Bay, finished their season with an 11-5 record and were off to the playoffs for the third straight season.

But most of all, Thigpen's stunning miscue meant the Packers were the NFC Central Division champions. For the first time since 1972, the Green Bay Packers could say they were better than any other team in their division.

"I came in with coach Holmgren and Ron Wolf and I saw what they were trying to build," linebacker George Koonce said. "Sometimes, with players coming and going, you might think, 'The Packers have taken a step backwards.'

"But they knew what they were doing. They put players on the field and we made things happen."

It wasn't supposed to be this way. A division title. Another trip to the playoffs. None of this was supposed to occur in 1995.

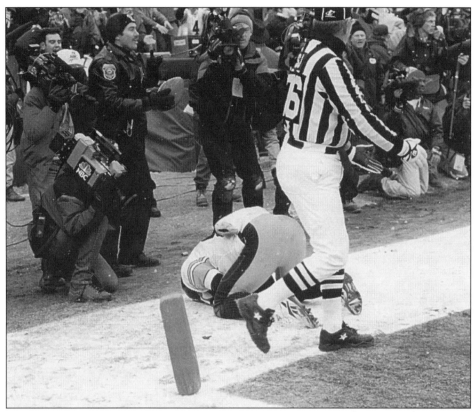

If Yancey Thigpen was holding the football, Green Bay wouldn't be holding its first Central Division title since 1972.

This was supposed to be the season when the Packers' rise to prominence under Ron Wolf and Mike Holmgren came to a crashing halt.

No Sterling Sharpe.

No Bryce Paup.

One of the greatest wide receivers in NFL history and a Pro Bowl linebacker were both gone. The Packers were coming off another loss to Dallas in the second round of the playoffs and the gap between the two teams seemed to be wider than ever.

No one believed the Packers would beat the overwhelming odds that were stacked against them. No one except the Packers.

The Packers spent the entire off-season, training camp and the exhibition season listening to the naysayers predict nothing but gloom and doom. No Sharpe. No Paup. No chance.

But while outsiders were busy focusing on who Green Bay did not have,

Return to Glory

the Packers believed they could reach new heights in 1995 because of who was still there.

Namely, Brett Favre.

"The real ace in the hole for us is our quarterback," Holmgren said before the season began. "We have a real fine quarterback."

Reggie White agreed.

"He's got to know that he's the man to carry us to a championship," White said. "The way he played the last eight games last year, I feel confident he can do it for us."

With Favre at the helm and a team full of young, hungry players surrounding him, Holmgren was confident the Packers could exceed the dismal expectations.

"I'm not a predicting guy, but I'd say we're going to do real well," Holmgren said, just prior to the season opener. "Everybody in that locker room wants to win and when push comes to shove, everybody's going to watch everybody's back on that field.

"I have no doubts about what we can do this year."

After the first game, however, many other people did.

The opener against the St. Louis Rams was supposed to be a showcase for Favre and a chance for the Packers to prove they could not only survive – but thrive – without Sharpe. Instead, they stumbled out of the gate against a team that had won only four games the previous season.

The Rams came into the season opener at Lambeau Field and promptly put a hurt on the Packers. With starting left tackle Ken Ruettgers out with a back injury, the Packers started Joe Sims – normally a right tackle – in Ruettgers' spot and the Rams took advantage.

Sensing a weakness on the Packers' offensive line, the Rams moved left end Sean Gilbert to the right side, where he could square off against Sims. Combined with Kevin Carter's work on Green Bay right tackle Earl Dotson, the Rams had Favre on the run all day long, sacking him four times.

Sims had so much difficulty that he was replaced at halftime by Gary Brown, who was making his first-ever regular-season appearance.

"I definitely felt like a rookie," said Sims, who admitted he was not adequately prepared to play left tackle after being acquired by the team the week before the season began in a trade with Philadelphia. "I'm normally a right tackle, you know?

"I figured they were going to do something, whether it was me or Gary

Brown over there. They got to me pretty good I guess."

Like the Rams' defense, the Packers' defense was also putting some heat on the opposing quarterback. Green Bay sacked Rams starter Chris Miller five times – including 2½ sacks in a vintage performance by White – and held St. Louis to only 187 total yards.

But, in a precursor to the rest of the season, the Packers were unable to force a single turnover. That was one of the most deciding factors in the 17-14 defeat.

"We just didn't get any turnovers for our offense in the red zone," Butler said. "I think that was the key today."

The loss was a total team effort. There were numerous penalties, dropped passes, one blocked punt and three interceptions.

"I'm angry, to be quite honest," Holmgren said the day after the game. "You're playing against really superb athletes on the other side all the time, unlike the preseason when there's a lot of substitution. There's very little margin for error.

"I'm not going to tolerate the mistakes we made in our execution, the sloppiness of play."

The season was only one game

Robert Brooks' 99-yard touchdown catch on Monday Night Football was a springboard to stardom.

old and already the Packers were forced to regroup.

A number of questions were tossed at the offense, which had struggled for the third straight time since losing Sharpe. With Sharpe in 1994, the Packers were fourth in the NFL in total points, averaging 23.9 per game, and Favre had thrown 33 touchdown passes.

Without Sharpe in the last three games, including two in the '94 playoffs, Green Bay had averaged just 13 points per game and Favre had only two touchdown passes.

To the Rams, at least, the key reason why the Packers were struggling was because they no longer had Sharpe around to utilize.

"Their offense has changed," Rams linebacker Shane Conlan said. "Obviously, (Sharpe) was a great, great player."

Again, outsiders were wondering if the Packers' rise to prominence had come to an end. But if anything, that made the team grow closer and its inner resolve become even stronger.

A little win at Chicago on Monday night the next week didn't hurt either.

The Packers went into Soldier Field hoping to shine in front of a national television audience, beat their biggest rivals and regain some momentum after their lackluster season debut.

With one play, they showed all of those things and gave a tantalizing preview of what was to come the rest of the season.

Leading 14-0 early in the second quarter, Green Bay faced a third-and-10 at its own 1-yard line. Instead of running a conservative play to give punter Craig Hentrich some extra room, Holmgren decided to go for the Bears' throat.

Thanks to Favre and Robert Brooks, the plan worked.

Favre dropped back to pass and looked toward Brooks, running down the right sidelines. Favre pump-faked and Chicago's star cornerback Donnell Woolford bit on the fake, allowing Brooks to breeze past him, catch Favre's perfect pass and race into the end zone for a 99-yard touchdown. The reception was the highlight of a breakthrough night for Brooks. He finished with eight receptions for 161 yards and two TDs and was named the NFC Offensive Player of the Week in the Packers' 27-24 victory.

It also was an indication the Packers would not be afraid to open things up in the passing game.

"You try to score every play and we have that ability," receivers coach Gil Haskell said. "If you make a mistake, we can go the distance."

After beating the Bears, the Packers won their next two games – 14-6 at home against the New York Giants and 24-14 at Jacksonville over the Jaguars – before taking off the bye week in preparation for what would be their annual date with destiny.

A trip to Dallas to face the Cowboys. It was the one game on the schedule the Packers had been targeting since losing 35-9 to Dallas in the '94 playoffs.

"When we came to the minicamps, a lot of guys were thinking about what we need to do to beat Dallas," Butler said. "We feel like, physically, we should beat anybody and Dallas just beat us physically (in the playoffs).

"That's not to say we're looking past anybody else. We're just confident we can beat anybody else. We just need to get to someone like Dallas."

At 3-1, the Packers had gotten themselves off to a good start despite their lackluster showing in the opener. Regardless of what happened at Dallas, Green Bay was a top contender for the NFC Central title.

But the Cowboys would provide the Packers with a stern test and their first opportunity to test themselves against a Super Bowl-caliber opponent.

"This is a good test," defensive lineman Gabe Wilkins said. "When we come out of this one, we'll know pretty much where we are."

The Packers did not come away with the answers they were seeking. Instead they were left to deal with another dismal trip to Dallas.

Dallas rolled up 448 yards of total offense and totally dominated the line of scrimmage in a 34-24 win. The Packers had come in with the NFL's top-ranked defense, but left a shell of their former selves and ranked third in the league.

"We had a good week of practice and I thought we were ready," White said. "Unfortunately, we weren't."

At one point, White began screaming at his defensive teammates on the sidelines, pleading with them to step up and assert themselves against the Cowboys.

It never happened.

Instead, the Cowboys maintained control and sent Green Bay packing. For the fifth time in the past three seasons, the Packers had ventured into Texas Stadium and been convincingly thwarted by the Cowboys. Dallas had shown its superiority and the Packers were left reeling.

Again.

"Maybe we're not as good as we thought we were," Butler said simply.

Once again, the Packers were forced to regroup. Once again, they did. Convincingly.

After losing to Dallas, the Packers faced two key division games at home against Detroit and Minnesota. This was an opportunity for Green Bay to make up for the disappointing loss at Dallas and assert itself as the dominant team in the NFC Central. And that is exactly what happened.

Favre passed for 342 yards and two touchdowns and Edgar Bennett – three days after signing a three-year contract extension worth a reported $3.9 million – rolled up 148 all-purpose yards in a 30-21 win over Detroit.

The next week, the Packers defense rose up for one of the first times in the season, forcing four turnovers and even scoring a touchdown on a fumble recovery by Sean Jones in the end zone in a 38-21 win over Minnesota.

Suddenly, the Packers were 5-2 and, with road dates at Detroit and Minnesota back-to-back, in a strong position to take complete control of the NFC Central.

But as they say about the best laid plans ...

The Packers went into Detroit and turned in one of their worst performances of the season. Four turnovers, including three interceptions by Favre, and two dropped passes in the end zone – one by tight end Keith Jackson in his Packer debut – spelled doom in a 24-16 loss to the Lions.

"They played like they thought they were better than they actually were," Holmgren said, reflecting on the loss at Detroit. "There is a danger with a young ballclub – and we're relatively young – that yeah, you start believing your press clippings.

"Once you start believing that, you run the risk of going through the numbers, thinking your great ability will carry you through. Quite frankly, anything we've earned around here has been because we've worked hard, not because we're the most talented.

"As soon as you start thinking you're pretty good, that's when you're going to get knocked off."

That is precisely what happened against the Lions. Now the Packers were hoping to remedy that the next week in their annual trip to what has become another one of their house of horrors – the Metrodome in Minneapolis.

If someone wanted to write a storyline for what possibly could go wrong for Green Bay that day, they could not have come up with a better script. First Favre was injured, severely spraining his ankle in the third quarter. Then backup quarterback Ty Detmer went out in the fourth quarter, suffering what would prove to be a season-ending thumb injury.

Then White limped off the field after a frightening collision with Jones while the two were trying to get to Vikings quarterback Warren Moon for a sack. As bad as all that was, the worst was yet to come.

With the game tied 24-24 late in the fourth quarter, third-string quarterback T.J. Rubley was driving Green Bay for a potential game-winning field goal. But on a third down and inches play, Rubley called an audible, changing a quarterback sneak to a rollout pass.

He rolled to his right and tried to hit Brooks in traffic. But the ball was tipped and intercepted by Minnesota linebacker and ex-Packer Jeff Brady. Moments later, Fuad Reveiz kicked a 39-yard field goal as time expired.

The Packers had lost 27-24 and were now 5-4.

"I made a poor choice and it cost us a victory," Rubley said. "I won't do it next time."

He never got the chance. Rubley never played another down for Green Bay and was waived five weeks later.

Next up was the Bears at Lambeau Field. Of more immediate concern to the Packers was the health of their two stars – Favre and White.

White suffered a sprained ligament in his right knee and injured his right thigh in the collision with Jones. Early reports had him being out 4-6 weeks, although White vowed to play the following Sunday against Chicago.

"I've done this before and I was able to play the next week," White said.

Favre, meanwhile, sprained his left ankle and was on crutches in the locker room the day after the loss to the Vikings. Like White, Favre intended to face the Bears.

1995 Game-by-Game

The regular-season results for the Green Bay Packers in 1995:

Opponent	W/L	Score	Rec.
St. Louis	L	14-17	0-1
at Chicago	W	27-24	1-1
NY Giants	W	14-6	2-1
at Jacksonville	W	24-14	3-1
at Dallas	L	24-34	3-2
Detroit	W	30-21	4-2
Minnesota	W	38-21	5-2
at Detroit	L	16-24	5-3
at Minnesota	L	24-27	5-4
Chicago	W	35-28	6-4
at Cleveland	W	31-20	7-4
Tampa Bay	W	35-13	8-4
Cincinnati	W	24-10	9-4
at Tampa Bay	L	10-13	9-5
at New Orleans	W	34-23	10-5
Pittsburgh	W	24-19	11-5

"I'll give it a go," he said.

The Packers were not so sure and, with Detmer through for the season, they signed veteran Bob Gagliano to compete with Rubley for the chance to start if Favre was unable to play. Matt LaBounty was expected to replace White if he could not go.

All week long there was uncertainty surrounding the Packers two stars. On the heels of a two-game losing streak against a pair of division teams,

Green Bay now trailed first-place Chicago (6-3) by one game.

The Packers desperately needed to beat Chicago to get back on the right track. Doing that without their two stars would be extremely difficult.

With practice closed to the media, Holmgren was doing his best to keep Favre and White's physical conditions a secret. He would say on Friday the two had practiced in limited fashion, but refused to speculate on their chances for playing Sunday against the Bears.

"I won't decide until Sunday," Holmgren said. "There's a chance neither one of them will play."

The Bears weren't buying that, however.

"We're not going to fall into any trap of thinking we're not going to get Green Bay at their best," Chicago coach Dave Wannstedt said.

That turned out to be a wise move. As it turned out, it did not do the Bears much good. Not only did White and Favre both play, once again both were magnificent.

White sat out the first 12 snaps in favor of LaBounty. He came in with just over 4 minutes left in the first quarter and played the majority of the game thereafter.

"He was going to go in there basically in the long-yardage situations," defensive coordinator Fritz Shurmur said. "As the game went on and he got (the knee) warmed up, it felt pretty good to him."

And bad for Chicago's James "Big Cat" Williams.

Much of White's work was directed at Williams, the Bears' 6-foot-7, 335-pound tackle. White tossed Williams aside repeatedly and finished with four tackles, one-half of a sack, one tipped pass and several pressures.

"I don't think he was anywhere near 100 percent," Shurmur said. "But there were some magnificent downs he played on one leg."

While White was terrorizing the Bears offense, Favre was busy carving up Chicago's defense. Despite the sprained ankle, Favre passed for 336 yards and a team record-tying five touchdowns in Green Bay's 35-28 win.

It was a performance that stunned the Bears and had the Packers raving.

"To get off the bed and play in a situation where 90 percent of the people wouldn't, I would say if it's not (Favre's best performance ever), I haven't seen the one that is," Wolf said.

White said Favre's effort was exactly what the Packers needed.

"If they'd have said, 'Reggie, you have to pick, you or Brett,' I'd have picked Brett (to play) because he's something special to this team and he showed it," White said.

The victory over the Bears seemed to energize the Packers. They promptly put together one of their most impressive stretches of the season, both offensively and defensively.

Green Bay piled up three straight victories – a 31-20 win at Cleveland followed by wins at home over Tampa Bay (35-13) and Cincinnati (24-10). The Packers were on a roll, and the contributions were coming from both sides of the ball.

Offensively, Favre was in complete control of one of the NFL's most potent offenses. The Packers' running game was one of the NFL's worst statistically, putting more pressure on Favre and the passing game to make things happen.

They did. And nowhere were they more potent than in the red zone.

Green Bay eventually finished first in the league in scoring inside the opponents' 20-yard line with 40 touchdowns on 60 possessions (66.7 percent). At one point in the season, the Packers converted on 17 straight attempts, including 16 touchdowns.

"We're pretty damn good down there," Favre said flatly.

Defending the Packers passing game had become something akin to a defense picking its poison. Of course, there was always Favre to worry about. Pressure Favre and maybe you have a chance.

But if Favre was not pressured, defenses suddenly found themselves with several problems.

Double-team Brooks and tight end Mark Chmura would emerge. Stop Chmura and Brooks and Anthony Morgan or Mark Ingram would run free. And there were always Edgar Bennett and Dorsey Levens lurking out of the backfield.

"We've got a lot of weapons, man," Brooks said, smiling.

Those weapons became nearly impossible for opponents to handle when the Packers ventured into the red zone. Holmgren spent a considerable amount of time in practice each week working specifically on red zone situations and the lengthy work paid off handsomely.

The Packers ran their red zone plays to perfection in practice and that resulted in near perfection during games.

"That's the ultimate goal," Holmgren said as the regular season neared its end. "We're not quite there yet, but we are closer than we've ever been.

"Just playing together. Look at our four-year guys – you got Favre, Chmura, Brooks, Morgan's a three-year guy, Levens. The longer you're together like that with that group of people that touch the ball, then you

George Koonce
'Sometimes, with players coming and going, you might think, 'The Packers have taken a step backwards.' But (Wolf and Holmgren) knew what they were doing.'

can do some pretty good things."

While the offense was on a roll, the Packers' defense was also faring much better.

In the win over Tampa Bay, the Packers held running back Errict Rhett to only 13 yards on 14 carries. The defense also had a key goal-line stand in the second quarter that held the Bucs to a field goal and provided impetus for the victory.

Then in beating the Bengals, Green Bay held the NFL's 10th-ranked passing attack to only 32 total yards in the second half.

One of the main contributors in the defensive resurgence was Jones.

After recording only 3½ sacks in the first 11 games, the critics said Jones was washed up and the Packers should consider dumping him and his $2.65 million contract when the 1996 season rolled around. Jones admitted he even wondered if his best days were behind him.

But after watching some film, Jones became convinced he was still playing effectively, even if the sacks were not there. He said his work against the run was better than it had ever been and that sacks were often a result of luck as much as anything else.

"I was coming off the ball, I was working my moves," Jones said. "I just didn't get (sacks)."

But then, the sacks began to come. He had 1½ sacks and a forced fumble in the home win over Tampa Bay and picked up another sack in the win over the Bengals.

Suddenly, Jones was no longer being asked if he was washed up. Instead, the questions were focused on his apparently new-found effectiveness as a

Return to Glory

pass rusher.

And Jones could not help but laugh at the sudden turn of events, how he went from being written off to being a valuable contributor in such a short period of time.

"I start off slow and (critics said) I've lost a step, that was kind of amusing to me," said Jones, who would finish the regular season with nine sacks. "I know when I'm not playing well and I'm painfully honest with myself. So there's nothing (the media) can say that I don't already know."

Now 9-4, the red-hot Packers strode into Tampa Bay for a Sunday night game on ESPN with an opportunity to clinch their third straight playoff berth. Just two weeks ago, Green Bay had thoroughly destroyed the hapless Bucs 35-13. A victory this Sunday appeared inevitable.

Unfortunately for the Packers, Tampa Bay decided to play the role of spoiler to the hilt.

Green Bay went into the game without

Sean Jones had his best season as a Packer in 1995, helping the Green Bay defense overcome injuries to Reggie White.

White, who had suffered a hamstring injury the previous week against the Bengals. Without one of their emotional leaders on the field with them, the Packers appeared flat and uninspired.

The Packers had everything to play for, but it was the Buccaneers who stepped forward with more energy on this night. Green Bay's struggles started early when Favre had a tipped ball picked off in the end zone on the team's opening drive of the game.

Despite struggling the entire night, the Packers still had a chance to win the game late. But Chris Jacke badly missed a 45-yard field goal with five seconds left in regulation.

"I just didn't hit it very well," Jacke said. "I think I was trying to kick it a little harder than necessary."

The game went into overtime and Tampa Bay won the toss. Green Bay's defense was unable to stop the Bucs on their opening drive and they moved downfield, setting up a 47-yard field goal by Michael Husted that won the game.

The Packers left Tampa Bay 13-10 losers and more than a little embarrassed by their performance on national television.

"It's disgusting when you look at the schedule and you see a team you're supposed to beat – let's not kid ourselves, an average team – and they beat you," Butler said. "What does that make you?"

It did not appear things could get any worse, but for a brief time they did. On Wednesday, the Packers announced that White's hamstring would require season-ending surgery. The Packers' most important defensive weapon and one of their most inspirational players would be lost for the season.

But in true White fashion, he quickly shocked everyone by bouncing back. He returned to practice on Thursday and claimed he could play that Saturday at New Orleans.

For the Packers, the Saints game meant redemption for their loss at Tampa Bay and another chance to clinch a playoff berth. For Favre, it meant an opportunity to shine in front of his friends and family.

With a national television audience, 3,000 members of his fan club and at least 60 friends and family members watching, Favre put on a clinic and staked his claim as the NFL's Most Valuable Player. He threw for 308 yards and four touchdowns as the Packers ran right through the Saints 34-23.

The win gave the Packers a 10-5 record, the first time under Holmgren they had won more than nine games. It also clinched a playoff berth for the third straight season.

For Favre, the game was sweet redemption after a dismal outing in Tampa Bay.

"He sure looked like the MVP to me," Saints safety J.J. McCleskey said. "He's the real deal."

And so, it appeared, were the Packers.

The final regular-season game would be at Lambeau Field against the Pittsburgh Steelers, who had become the AFC's hottest team.

Winners of eight straight games, the eventual AFC champions strode into Green Bay with an aggressive defense and a wide-open offense that often featured five wide receivers and a quarterback-running back-wide receiver simply known as "Slash" – rookie Kordell Stewart.

"You have to be aware of him all the time," Holmgren said. "It gives you one more thing to work on. It sure makes your opponent worry and lose sleep."

For the Packers, however, the Steelers represented simply another obstacle in their quest to attain another goal during this remarkable season. Green Bay had clinched its playoff berth, but the Packers wanted more.

They wanted the NFC Central Division title.

The last time a Green Bay team had won a division title was in 1972 under Dan Devine.

"Our word for the week is focus," Morgan said. "This is the time to put it all together."

That is precisely what the Packers did in front of an electric crowd at Lambeau Field. But it did not come without some anxious moments.

Favre again led the way, continuing his MVP run by completing 23 of 32 passes for 301 yards and two touchdowns. The Steelers put continual pressure on Favre – even knocking him out of the game twice – but Favre never wilted.

He passed for touchdowns to Brooks – who finished with 11 receptions for 137 yards – and Chmura. Bennett scored on a 9-yard run and Jacke booted a 47-yard field goal to keep Green Bay ahead the entire game.

Early in the third quarter, Favre was injured when he tried to dive into the end zone for a touchdown and was hit in the back by Pittsburgh linebacker Greg Lloyd. Although backup Jim McMahon began warming up on the sidelines, Favre did not leave the game and promptly threw a touchdown to Chmura on the next play.

"I wasn't going to let Jim steal my touchdown pass," Favre joked.

Favre did have to come out for two plays in the fourth quarter after being hit again, this time by linebacker Kevin Greene. But he would later return to put the finishing touches on the game.

"He's tough as nails – period," Brooks said. "What else can you say?"

Despite Favre's gritty disposition, the game remained in doubt until the closing seconds. The Steelers kept the heat on, and on their last possession of the game, trailing 24-19, they drove to the Green Bay 6-yard line.

There, on fourth down, quarterback Neil O'Donnell dropped back to

Brett Favre and one of his many deadly targets, receiver Anthony Morgan.

pass and looked for Thigpen, who had beaten cornerback Lenny McGill and was wide open in the end zone. O'Donnell lofted a perfect pass to Thigpen and it appeared the Packers were about to lose not only the game, but their first division title in 23 years.

"I couldn't bear to watch," Favre said. "I just waited to see if we cheered or started crying."

Then the unthinkable happened. Thigpen, a Pro Bowl receiver, let the ball drop through his hands.

"I came around the corner and I saw the pass go up and thought 'Oh no,'" Reggie White said. "But then I heard the crowd."

With a thunderous roar, the crowd reacted to the drop and to the fact that the 24-19 win gave Green Bay its long sought-after division title.

"Winning the division means we have reached another goal set by the team in training camp," Holmgren said. "It also is an indicator we are moving in the right direction."

When the game was over and after many of the players had departed the Packers' locker room, Butler stood in front of his locker, a throng of reporters hanging on his every word.

Butler's thoughts soon turned to the division title the Packers had just earned. He talked about how much it meant to him to win the title and how much it meant to the team in general.

Then, with a smile creeping over his face, Butler began to admire the

Quarterbacks coach Steve Mariucci congratulates Brett Favre after the Packers won the Central Division championship.

1995 NFC Central Division champions hat he was wearing. He removed the hat and held it up broadly for all to see.

Then, as he put it back on, he summed up an entire team's feelings in one sentence.

"To all the naysayers out there who said we couldn't do this," Butler said, his smile growing wider. "Take that." ◉

Stepping up

The emergence of Robert Brooks, Edgar Bennett,
Mark Chmura and Craig Newsome put the
Packers among the league's elite

A team is nothing more than the sum of its parts. That was especially true for the 1995 Green Bay Packers.

While Brett Favre and Reggie White carried the banner and garnered a great deal of the glory and attention for the Packers' scintillating season, there were many other players who played key roles in Green Bay's return to prominence. Wide receiver Robert Brooks, running back Edgar Bennett, tight end Mark Chmura and cornerback Craig Newsome are four of the players who stepped up and made significant contributions to a season the Packers and their loyal legion of fans will not soon forget.

ROBERT BROOKS

The season that put Robert Brooks on the NFL map almost never came to fruition.

With Sterling Sharpe released because of his career-ending injury, general manager Ron Wolf's top priority in the '95 off-season was to add a Pro Bowl-type receiver who could come in and assume Sharpe's role as the focus of the Packers' passing attack.

The man Wolf wanted was former Atlanta star Andre Rison.

"What we tried to do was replace a superstar with a superstar," Wolf said. "That was our sole purpose and our focus."

With that in mind, the Packers went after Rison with a vengeance. The former Atlanta Falcon eventually narrowed his choices to Green Bay and the Cleveland Browns.

The Packers reportedly offered Rison a five-year deal worth $13.5 million. The Browns countered with $17 million over five years.

Rison went to Cleveland and Wolf was left to look elsewhere for Sharpe's replacement. He did not have to look very far.

Robert Brooks, the Packers' third-round draft choice in 1992, would become the man and Wolf never once regretted the fact that Rison got away.

"We're not suffering at all," Wolf said with a sly grin late in the season.

While Rison was a flop in Cleveland, Brooks was a huge success in Green Bay. He led the Packers in receiving with 102 receptions, the third-most in team history. His 1,497 receiving yards were the most in Packer history and his 13 touchdowns equalled the third-best single-season total in team history.

Brooks may not have been Sterling Sharpe. He was simply Robert Brooks. And that was just fine with the Packers.

"He's just a heckuva football player," Brett Favre said at one point in the season. "I don't know how long it's going to take to convince people in this league that he's a legitimate go-to guy.

Robert Brooks was an unknown commodity entering the 1995 season. A 1,497-yard season changed that.

"I'll just keep throwing to him until somebody stands up and says, 'Hey, you're right, he is pretty darn good.'"

Actually, it did not take too long for the Packers' opponents to discover Brooks was the real deal. In fact, some of them had been convinced of it all along.

It was just a matter of Brooks getting the opportunity to prove himself on a grander scale. That occurred in 1995.

"I've been impressed," Vikings Coach Dennis Green said. "I always thought he had excellent hands and he's athletic.

"I think he sees an opportunity. You don't get a lot of chances to take

Return to Glory

advantage of it and that's what he's done."

Replacing Sharpe was nothing new for Brooks.

"At (college in) South Carolina, it was the same situation," Brooks said before the season began. "They'd lost Sterling Sharpe and who was going to take Sterling Sharpe's place? I jumped right in there and there was nothing said about it after the first season.

"I'm looking at it as the exact same situation (in Green Bay)."

And it was. Brooks had a fine season in 1994, catching 58 passes with four touchdowns as the starting split end opposite Sharpe. But in 1995, he truly exploded on the scene.

He had nine 100-yard receiving games, breaking Sharpe's previous team record of seven set in 1992. He finished eighth in the NFC in receptions and fifth in receiving yards. He caught at least one touchdown pass in 11 games and became the fifth receiver in team history to post a 1,000-yard receiving season. The others were Don Hutson, Billy Howton, James Lofton and Sharpe. Impressive company to say the least.

One of the keys to Green Bay's success through the air in 1995 was Favre's ability to spread the ball around to different receivers. But there was no question who was at the heart of the passing attack: Brooks.

"Everything about him was four or five stars (in 1995)," wide receivers coach Gil Haskell said. "God gave him the ability to run and catch the ball and he does not take that for granted. He works at that very hard.

"Our biggest thing was to get him in there and see what happens. We knew he was good. How good, we didn't know. Now what is happening is he is one of the top receivers in the National Conference and that is not a fluke."

But while the accolades were raining down upon him in 1995, Brooks shrugged all of them off. He was reluctant to talk about himself or separate his contributions from those of his teammates.

Brooks did not care to be singled out or talk endlessly about his stats or how he was shredding secondaries every week. For Brooks, his role was no bigger than anyone else's. He was simply another part of the Packers offensive machine.

"(The media) always asks me if there's pressure on me," he said, shaking his head. "There's no pressure on Robert Brooks because I'm not the Green Bay Packers. How can there be pressure on Robert Brooks? I don't make the entire team.

"There's pressure on the Packers, yeah, but there's no pressure on Robert

Brooks the individual. What I do, it affects the team, but it doesn't win or lose a particular game for us. I'm just going to pull my part of the chain."

Modesty aside, there is no ignoring Brooks' place of importance in the Packers' offense. He has become their go-to receiver and one of the most feared threats in the NFL.

If he wanted to, he could use his new-found position as a way of improving upon the three-year, $3.9 million contract he signed prior to the 1995 season. He also could point to other receivers such as Curtis Conway, Jeff Graham, Quinn Early, Shawn Jefferson, Willie Davis and Keenan McCardell, who all received more lucrative contracts than his during the 1996 offseason.

Catching on

The top five receiving seasons, ranked by touchdowns, in Green Bay Packers history.

Player	Year	Catch	Yard	TD
Sterling Sharpe	1994	94	1,119	18
Don Hutson*	1942	74	1,211	17
Robert Brooks	1995	102	1,497	13
Sterling Sharpe	1992	108	1,461	13
Bill Howton#	1952	53	1,231	13

*11 games, #12 games

If he wanted to, Brooks could go to the Packers' management and ask for some improvements on his deal or make some threats if they did not agree.

But that isn't Brooks' style.

"If the Packers would like to say, 'Hey Robert, you've done a great job for us' and they want to come in and reward me for it, hey, I'm not going to turn it down," he said with a smile. "But I'm under contract. I'm not going to sit here and create some hoopla over money.

"I'm here to play. I'm having fun, I'm playing where I want to play, I'm getting the ball and that's what I want. And we're winning. When you're doing those things, good things tend to happen to you."

Good things certainly happened to Brooks in 1995. Barring serious injury, there is no doubt that, due to his strong desire to improve, good things will continue to happen to him and the Packers in the future.

"I think I can do anything out there if I work hard and I pray," he said. "That's what I did last year.

"I'm not shooting for any numbers. I just want to help this team win more football games than they won last year and go further than we did."

EDGAR BENNETT

Edgar Bennett was walking back toward the Packers' locker room after a training camp practice prior to the 1995 season. The sun was bright in the sky and Bennett's thoughts were on the season ahead.

After three seasons as a fullback, the previous two as a starter, this would be Bennett's first as the starting halfback. He would bear the brunt of the running load. It was a role he welcomed eagerly and one he had been waiting to assume ever since he was drafted in the fourth round in 1992.

On this hot July day, Bennett was talking to a reporter about his goals, what he hoped to accomplish in his first season as the Packers featured running back.

As he walked closer to the entrance to the team's locker room, Bennett stopped and flashed a wide grin when asked what he hoped to do in 1995.

"It's going to be one of those things where I shock the world," he said, his grin growing broader. "That's the goal. God didn't bring me this far to leave me."

Bennett may not have exactly shocked the world in 1995, but he rushed for 1,067 yards to become Green Bay's first 1,000-yard runner since Terdell Middleton gained 1,116 in 1978. Many Packers fans wondered when – or even if – another Green Bay back would reach that landmark. But Bennett did. And in that respect, he fulfilled his training camp pledge.

"I think you can say the jinx is over," Bennett said after breaking the 1,000-yard barrier in the season's 15th game at New Orleans.

In typical Bennett fashion, the 1,000 yards did not come easily. For the second straight year, he had to battle through an injury-plagued season. After suffering with a badly-injured shoulder in 1994, he had to play through the pain of an injured ankle in 1995.

But just like in 1994, Bennett did not miss a game. He played hurt and always played hard – always there and always a big part of the offense.

It was the Bennett the Packers have come to respect and admire.

"He lined up every week even though he was hurt," offensive coordinator Sherm Lewis said. "He played every week and we admire him for that. We know he'll play hurt."

There is nothing flashy about Bennett. He does not have the eye-popping moves of a Barry Sanders, the power and strength of a Chris Warren or the cutback ability of an Emmitt Smith.

What Bennett has is relentless determination, a willingness to battle every second he is on the field. In other words, Edgar Bennett is a warrior.

"I feel like I might have gotten beaten up in certain games," Bennett said in mid-November. "But that's all a part of playing football. It's just one of those things where I have to get treatment and get ready for Sunday."

This is not to say Bennett is devoid of skills. On the contrary, he is arguably the NFL's top pass-catching running back. His 648 yards receiving in 1995 set a record for Green Bay running backs, and his combined 1,715 rushing and receiving yards also set a new mark.

Bennett is also a good short-yardage back with a knack for finding the end zone. In his first two seasons as a starter, he had been one of the most valued members of the Packers offense as their starting fullback. But he became frustrated watching so many others try and fail at half-back.

While Vince Workman, John Stephens, Darrell Thompson and Reggie Cobb came and went, Bennett wondered if his chance would come.

"I honestly felt that after starting two years at fullback I wouldn't get the opportunity to be the starting tailback," Bennett said. "But God works in mysterious

Edgar Bennett set a Packers record with 1,715 combined rushing and receiving yards in 1995.

ways. He made it so I did get the opportunity."

When the opportunity arose, Bennett went after it with gusto. He went to Arizona and worked with Frank Schroeder, a personal trainer and power-lifting champion. With Schroeder's help, Bennett dropped 12 pounds to 214 and dropped his 40 time from 4.51 to as low as 4.37.

"I wanted to do everything that was possible to make me better at that position," Bennett said. "At the same time I was working on speed, I had

Return to Glory

to work on strength also. So I feel I got a little stronger in some areas."

Unfortunately for Bennett, he could not shake the injury bug that haunted him the previous season. A badly-injured ankle that required off-season surgery hampered him for much of the 1995 season.

The Packers were forced to cut back on Bennett's practice time in order to keep him fresh for each game. While Bennett admits he wonders what it would be like to play an injury-free season, he insists he never wonders why he has been hit so hard by injuries.

"I don't question that because the man upstairs handles all that," he said.

Bennett has a few personal goals he is willing to share publicly. At the top of the list is a trip to the Super Bowl and a journey to the Pro Bowl.

Double duty

The top five combined receiving/rushing seasons in Green Bay Packers history.

Player	Year	Rush	Rec.	Yds.
Edgar Bennett	1995	1,067	648	1,715
Jim Taylor	1962	1,474	106	1,580
Jim Taylor	1964	1,169	354	1,523
Robert Brooks	1995	21	1,497	1,518
Jim Taylor	1961	1,307	175	1,482

But he also has something else in mind: Another 1,000-yard season.

"That is one of my goals, to do it back-to-back, just in case any of you guys (the media) think it was a fluke," Bennett said.

With that, his grin grew even broader.

MARK CHMURA

Mark Chmura is no dummy. He knows one way for a tight end to get his share of passes thrown to him is to become a quarterback's best friend.

So Chmura did just that.

Over the course of the past four years, Chmura and Favre formed a strong friendship in Green Bay. That friendship is at least partially responsible for Chmura's breakthrough season in 1995.

Not because Favre looks for his buddy at the exclusion of anyone else. But rather, it's a situation where the two know each other so well, Chmura can read Favre's mind on the field and vice versa.

"He knows what Brett is doing out there," said tight end Keith Jackson, who watched Chmura's progress up close last season. "You see about four or five busted plays where he gets the ball and I'll be like 'What do I do now?" during the same play. He's doing a great job with Brett."

Of course, to credit Chmura's breakthrough season in 1995 solely on his friendship with Favre would be a great disservice to Chmura. In reality, Chmura has earned everything he has attained.

A sixth-round draft pick in 1992, Chmura has faced an uphill climb from day one. As a rookie, he suffered through a painful back injury that put him on the injured reserve list for the entire season. The injury was so frustrating that not only did Chmura get down mentally, he even contemplated giving up the game he loved.

"I thought about quitting," Chmura said.

Holmgren thought it would be in Chmura's best interests to stay with it. After some prodding from his head coach, Chmura decided to stick it out.

He played sparingly as a backup to Jackie Harris and Ed West in 1993, catching only two passes. He then started the final four games of the 1994 season and finished with 14 receptions.

When the 1995 season rolled around, Jackson was expected to be the team's starting tight end. But Jackson spent the first six games as a no-show, giving Chmura his chance.

Chmura played so well that even when Jackson arrived, he could do little more than be a bit player until the playoffs, when he assumed a larger role. But while Jackson's regular-season contributions were rather scarce, Chmura was a major part of the offense. He caught 54 passes for 679 yards and seven touchdowns.

Ironically, one of Chmura's finest games came the Sunday after Jackson ended his lengthy holdout. With Jackson standing on the sidelines Oct. 23 against Minnesota, Chmura went out and strode firmly into the limelight.

He caught five passes for what was then a career-high 101 yards and one touchdown in the Packers' 38-21 win. Even though Jackson was there on the sidelines, Chmura said he did not feel any added pressure to perform.

"I don't have to go out and prove myself," he said after the game. "The Packers knew what I could do."

Jackson was one of those most impressed by his new teammate.

"He did an excellent job," Jackson said. "I told him we've got to find a way to get us both in the game."

In addition to his work as a tight end, Chmura also was the team's long snapper on punts. But it was his efforts as a receiver that caught most Packers fans' attention.

Chmura's work did not go unnoticed by others in the NFL. His peers voted him to the NFC Pro Bowl squad as a reserve.

"I'm very proud of him," Holmgren said. "He has worked and made himself into a Pro Bowl player.

"I think he deserves a lot of credit for that and I think (tight ends coach) Andy Reid deserves a lot of credit for helping him get there."

Mark Chmura went from backup tight end to Pro Bowler for the Packers in one season.

The Packers promptly rewarded Chmura by signing him to a three-year, $4.8 million contract. But that was only the beginning of what would be a hectic off-season for Chmura.

Almost immediately after playing in the Pro Bowl, Chmura was besieged by offers for personal appearances. He also was contacted by an East Coast talent agency that wanted to line him up for work as a model and actor.

On top of that, there were discussions about a future role as a broadcaster on the network level. All of a sudden, Chmura had become one of the Packers' most marketable players.

"I'll always be the same old guy, but you have to capitalize when you can," he said. "Ten years from now, people might not even care.

"I didn't get too involved in it this year, but next year I'm going to look into it. I told them that right now, because it kind of started late, that I wanted to concentrate on football.

"That's my bread and butter. That's what pays the bills. That's what I'm going to bust my butt to do."

Just three years after almost giving up the game, Mark Chmura had, through endless hours of hard work and a fierce determination, become one of the best tight ends in the NFL. Even he admitted it was often difficult to believe where his journey has taken him.

"I never imagined I'd make the Pro Bowl when I was a rookie," Chmura said, shaking his head at the memory. "I still know there are so many areas where I can improve and that's what I want to keep doing. I don't think I've reached my peak yet."

CRAIG NEWSOME

Craig Newsome was tired. Not a little run down, mind you, but tired. Dead tired.

It was the 12th week of the regular season and Newsome had been through a wringer. The rookie cornerback had played 14 games, including the preseason, and his body was feeling the effects of the constant pounding and energy he had to expend daily.

Newsome was tired and he needed a rest. Everyone around him could sense it. His teammates. His coaches. Everyone.

"As a rookie, everyone hits that lull," fellow cornerback Doug Evans said. "You want to do things, but physically you're not able.

"It usually comes about this time. It lasts about two or three weeks and then you just pick it right back up."

Through it all, however, Newsome battled. And battled. And battled. He proved to be one of the Packers' most tireless workers in 1995.

"He's as solid a guy as I've ever been around," defensive coordinator Fritz Shurmur said. "One thing about Craig Newsome that I know for a fact is he's going to compete every down. And he's got enough ability to go in there against anybody and compete and win his share of battles.

"I trust him with my life."

From the moment he was drafted, Newsome had great expectations heaped upon him. He was a No. 1 draft pick and a projected starter, manning one of the most difficult positions in the game. Those factors alone would have been pressure enough.

But Newsome had more. He had to prove to everyone he was not Terrell Buckley, a player scorned by Packers fans and the man Newsome was replacing as Green Bay's starting left cornerback. Newsome did just that.

"Craig's been a tough guy for us from day one," safety LeRoy Butler said. "Not just tough physically, but mentally too. That's the kind of attitude you need in a corner."

The Packers believed Buckley may have wilted under the strain of playing such a demanding position. They drafted Newsome in large part because they thought he had a stronger mental makeup and would not be as adversely affected by any difficulties he would encounter.

Return to Glory

"He's a good player and a tough person," Wolf said during the preseason. "That's what we need."

Newsome proved from the outset he was a much different cornerback than the beleaguered Buckley. Where Buckley often lacked an aggressive

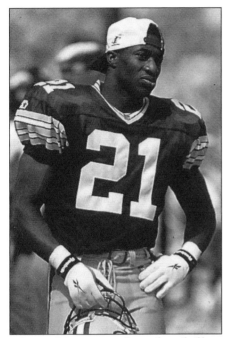

mentality, Newsome was relentless in his approach to his position. While Buckley's practice habits came into question, Newsome often had to be told by coaches not to overdo it in practice, to save himself for Sundays.

While Buckley was bombastic, Newsome was quiet and humble, soft-spoken and seemingly uncomfortable with the media attention he was drawing. Unlike Buckley, who usually was surrounded by reporters in the locker room before and after practice and after games, Newsome largely avoided the media. Only rarely could he be seen in the locker room when the media was present.

It was not that Newsome disliked reporters. He just preferred to spend his time on the task at hand.

Craig Newsome has the skills, both physical and mental, to battle the NFL's top receivers.

"I'm just going to focus on what I have to do," Newsome said prior to the season. "I'm not going to worry about the last person who was here or who's watching me. I'm just going to come out here and do my part."

As if all the attention Newsome received for replacing Buckley was not enough, he also had to deal with a steady diet of top-flight receivers each week. In the 1995 season, Newsome squared off against six of the league's eight Pro Bowl receivers.

- Michael Irvin
- Herman Moore
- Cris Carter
- Carl Pickens
- Yancey Thigpen
- Jerry Rice

Newsome faced them all. To say he paid some heavy dues in 1995 would be an understatement.

"Craig has taken his lumps this season," Holmgren admitted.

There were some touchdowns given up, a few missed tackles, some long gains by those premier receivers and others. Exactly the types of things you would expect veteran players to do to a rookie.

Newsome, though, never wavered. He learned from his mistakes and continued to stand his ground. His aggressive mentality was one of the bright spots on the Packers defense all season long.

"He's really come of age," Holmgren said after the playoff win at San Francisco. "He's gotten better and better every game."

One of Newsome's best games came in that playoff win over the 49ers. Facing the venerable Rice either alone or with double-coverage help, Newsome combatted Rice's unmatched physical skills with physical toughness of his own.

When Rice would bump, Newsome would bump back. When Rice would make a cut, Newsome would read it and stay one step ahead.

The future Hall of Famer resorted to all of his cunning, but never gained an advantage on the rookie. Although Rice caught 11 passes for 117 yards, his biggest gain – a 32-yard completion – came against Evans.

"Fritz said to be real, real tough with him," said Newsome, who picked off a pass, scored a touchdown on a fumble recovery and made six tackles in the game. "Play good, sound defense.

"I was just going out there and playing my game and I didn't care what Rice did or what he said."

That is precisely the approach Newsome used every week in 1995 and it served him well. It is also the attitude that will likely elevate him to new heights in 1996 and beyond.

In 1995, Craig Newsome did more than just replace Terrell Buckley. He made people start talking about him as well. While Newsome appreciates the accolades from fans and the media, he's much more concerned about his personal analysis.

"I can always take a look at the film and see the things I did wrong and then focus on that part in the next practice," he said. "Then after that, I just have to go out there and play." ◈

White Christmas

Reggie White's incredible recovery
from a season-ending hamstring injury
provided a huge lift to his teammates

Mike Holmgren stepped onto the podium in the Green Bay Packers media auditorium on Dec. 13, 1995, and before taking questions during his usual Wednesday afternoon press conference, he paused.

Then he delivered a bombshell.

Reggie White was done for the season. He would have surgery to repair a hamstring torn Dec. 3 against Cincinnati.

A hush fell over the room. For several seconds, no one uttered a word. Finally, one reporter spoke up and asked Holmgren if he was joking.

He wasn't.

For the second straight year, the Packers had lost one of their stars late in the season. In 1994, it was Sterling Sharpe. Now White was gone.

Holmgren did his best to maintain a positive attitude, just as he had done when Sharpe was lost the year before.

"When you lose a great player, it's going to affect the team," he said. "However, there's a possibility of losing a player every week. While I'd be less than honest to say that we don't depend on Reggie White – that'd be stupid if I said that – we have other good players and they have to step up."

White had been examined by team doctors after suffering the injury in the win over the Bengals. After sitting out the following week's game at Tampa Bay – snapping his consecutive games played streak at 166 – team doctors said White had no other choice, he had to have surgery.

"Doc said we can't wait too long because the scar tissue will build back in and we won't be able to get the muscle out of there," White said. "I pretty much made the decision and said 'OK Doc, let's do this.' "

With that, White's season was over.

The Packers' locker room was somber. The players put on a positive attitude, saying they just had to rally together even more as they made their playoff run.

"It's a really big loss, but we just have to push on," defensive tackle Gilbert Brown said. "We're not going to miss a beat. We can't miss a beat."

Underneath the bravado however, was the cold, stark reality.

Without Reggie White, the Packers had lost more than just their star defensive end. They had lost their inspirational leader and perhaps their best chance to make a run deep into the playoffs.

"We're all shocked," tight end Mark Chmura said. "I think that's the quietest (the locker) room has ever been."

The Packers' upcoming opponent – the Saints – were stunned.

"Reggie White is out for the season?" Coach Jim Mora asked reporters incredulously. "With a hamstring? Oh man, that's too bad."

That was an understatement.

New Orleans quarterback Jim Everett was just as surprised, although he admitted the thought of White not being able to chase him around was more than a little comforting. But even he found time to sympathize.

"Reggie White's one of the most dominant players on the defensive line and you have to know exactly where he's at," Everett said. "There's things that you do with Reggie White that you might never do with other football players."

As the news of White's impending surgery shook the Packers to the core, they began to make preparations for life without his considerable presence. Matt LaBounty would step in for White at left defensive end and right defensive end Sean Jones would need to offer more as a pass rusher.

"I think you scheme around it and you adjust what you do in your package depending on who's there," defensive coordinator Fritz Shurmur said.

Shurmur reflected on the 1989 season when, as the defensive coordinator of the Rams, he revamped an injury-depleted front line by using linebackers as down linemen. That formation, known as Shurmur's 2-5 "eagle" defense, finished fifth in the NFC in sacks with 42 and helped the Rams to two post-season victories.

But as Shurmur noted, "that group didn't have to replace Reggie White."

No one took the news harder than White. The hardest part was meeting with his teammates to tell them the news.

"It was pretty emotional for me because I didn't want to be out for the season and I knew the effect it could possibly have on the team," he said. "That was a hard situation because I couldn't get emotional with them and I probably would have if Keith (Jackson) and Sean (Jones) wouldn't have told me not to. That was good because the guys needed to believe that they could win without me."

But in the midst of the gloom and despair of that dark afternoon, something miraculous happened. White began to feel better. Much better.

"I was sitting at home playing with my kids, running around the house and it felt good," White said.

White called conditioning coach Kent Johnston and asked to meet him at the Don Hutson Center. White executed the same drills that left him in pain an evening earlier – said the hamstring no longer bothered him.

The two then made a bee line to Holmgren's house, where the head coach was just about to head to bed.

"I'm going outside to turn off the Christmas lights and there's a knock at the door," Holmgren said. "I thought it was Santa Claus."

It wasn't Santa Claus, but it was the next best thing.

"He starts saying 'I can play. I can play,' " Holmgren said.

White no longer believed his season was over. Neither did Holmgren, although he certainly had no explanation for the sudden turn of events.

"Don't ask me to explain it," he said. "It's rather remarkable."

The next day at practice, the players strolled onto the field inside the Don Hutson Center expecting the first day of life without Reggie White. Instead, there was White, working out as if nothing had happened.

"All of our chins hit the carpet when we saw him," Brett Favre said.

Even the normally bombastic LeRoy Butler was left speechless.

"I don't know what to say," he said, shaking his head in amazement.

The Packers had seen this before. White tore a ligament in his left elbow during the '94 season in a loss at Buffalo. Green Bay was set to play at Dallas four days later on Thanksgiving and White was not expected to play. In fact, the injury was severe enough to keep him out for 2-4 weeks.

White did not miss a game. He played in that Thanksgiving Day game and, essentially playing with one good arm, he wreaked havoc on the Cowboys, tossing tackle Larry Allen around like a rag doll.

Then earlier in the '95 season, White sprained a ligament in his knee after colliding with Sean Jones at Minnesota. Again, there was concern White would miss several games. Again, White continued to play.

The Packers, in fact, had gotten used to White being on the field no matter how severe the injury.

"Nothing Reggie does surprises me," Jones said.

"He's the type of guy who hates to miss games," Jackson said. "He hadn't missed a game in so long, not because he wasn't injured, but because he had the will not to miss a game."

Still, this was different. This injury was supposed to end White's season. Surely, he could not recover in time.

But he did. When the Packers set foot on the artificial turf of the New Orleans Superdome, White was there. He played sparingly that day, but considering his season was supposed to be over, his mere presence was nothing short of a miracle.

"I guess it's time to start reading my Bible," LaBounty said.

There are three grades of muscle tears, ranging from a minor strain, which requires only a few days to heal, to a complete tear (grade 3). White had at least a grade 2 tear, which generally would take at least four to six weeks to heal. White's pain tolerance, motivation, physical strength and the severity of the injury were crucial to his recovery.

Reggie White
'I look at (the recovery) as another opportunity to glorify God in any way that I can.'

No one doubts the existence of those factors. But White credited a much higher authority for his stunning recoveries – his strong faith in God. White is an ordained minister, and his fame as a sports superstar enables him to reach a great number of people. "I know God is not just healing Reggie White for Reggie White's purposes," White told the *Green Bay Press-Gazette*, adding that his recoveries show what is possible through faith. "I mean, he's showing some mercy through the healing. But when I have a lady come to me who says she was inspired by God healing my arm, that it made her evaluate her life and she's serving God more fervently, that builds my faith."

Media members – not to mention a few opposing players – questioned the incredible recovery, saying perhaps White was not as injured as he claimed to be. But White stood steadfast behind his belief that the answer could be directly traced to his powerful religious beliefs.

In fact, the hamstring injury further strengthened what was already a powerful Christian foundation for White.

"This has done wonders for my faith," he said. "I look at this as another opportunity to glorify God in any way that I can. It's exciting for me."

Despite facing the prospect of having his season come to an end, White said his outlook remained positive, even before his miraculous recovery.

"The Bible says in Romans 8:28, 'All good things work together for good for those who love God and for those who have been called according to his purpose,'" he said. "I knew something good would come out of it."

For the Packers, it meant having White's considerable presence around for their entire run to the NFC Championship game. And there was no way of placing a value on how important White was to this team.

During the regular season, he had a team-high 12 sacks and his production was arguably the highest it had been in several years.

"He was playing like a young kid," defensive line coach Larry Brooks said. "He had a good camp, he came in probably in the best shape he's been in since I've been here and he was on a level where he probably would've made a lot of people say, 'Wow.' "

Of course, White's impact on the Packers defense is unquestionable.

The Packers ranked 23rd in the NFL in defense in 1992, then signed White, the most sought-after player with the advent of unrestricted free agency in the NFL, to a four-year, $17 million contract on April 8, 1993. In 1993, White tied New Orleans' Renaldo Turnbull for the NFC lead in quarterback sacks with 13 and the Packers defense shot up to No. 2 in the league. Coincidence? Holmgren thinks not.

"He made us a better football team – no question about it," Holmgren said. "We went from 23 on defense to 2– with no noticeable dramatic personnel changes, except for one man."

The NFL's all-time leader in sacks with 157, White uses his considerable size (6-foot-5, 300 pounds), strength and speed (he has been timed at 4.6 seconds in the 40) to consistently stuff the run and get to the quarterback despite facing constant double- and sometimes triple-team blocking. By tying up multiple blockers, White frees teammates to make plays and his pressure on the quarterback means the Packers' pass defenders don't have to cover the receivers as long.

A defining moment in the White-Packers fan relationship came in the fifth game of the 1993 season. The Packers, despite White's contributions, had lost three straight games after a 36-6 season-opening win over the Rams. The first of those losses was a heartbreaking 20-17 decision to the

Eagles, with whom White had played from 1985-92 after beginning his pro career in the springs of 1984 and '85 with the Memphis Showboats of the now-defunct United States Football League. Against Philadelphia, White had an exceptional performance with eight tackles, one sack and two forced fumbles.

With a 1-3 record, the Packers braced for a Sunday night, nationally televised battle with Denver. The Broncos were 3-1 and led by their future Hall of Fame quarterback John Elway, known for his "howitzer" of an arm – as Monday Night Football commentator Frank Gifford once called it – his considerable scrambling ability and, most of all, his uncanny knack of leading Denver to come-from-behind wins in the fourth quarter.

Elway had all of his abilities on display as he rallied the Broncos from a 30-7 halftime

All-time QB sacks

The top five sack leaders since the NFL began counting in 1982.

Name	Years	Total
Reggie White	1985-95	157.0
Lawrence Taylor	1982-93	132.5
Rickey Jackson	1981-95	128.0
Richard Dent	1983-95	126.5
Bruce Smith	1985-95	126.5

deficit with 20 consecutive second-half points. Trailing 30-27 late in the fourth quarter, Elway brought Denver to the Green Bay 43-yard line. But White sacked the speedy quarterback on third- and fourth-down plays to preserve the win and, potentially, the Packers' playoff hopes.

As much as the Packers coaching staff appreciated White's play, the feeling was mutual.

"This is the first time in my career that my coaches realize that superstars need a pat on the back, too," White said. "My game has moved up and I let them know I appreciate it."

Toward the end of the 1995 season, the hamstring injury hampered White. But he was an active presence in the playoffs and again appeared to be the Reggie White of old.

"I think by the time the Dallas (playoff) game rolled around, you could see he was back and he had a good step," Brooks said. "We had him in the Pro Bowl and he played hard in the Pro Bowl."

Through it all, despite the knee and hamstring injuries, White was enjoying the '95 season. Even when the team was struggling, White remained upbeat, his faith in the team never diminished.

"This has been a very good year for me," White said as the team prepared for the playoffs. "Very peaceful. One of my prayers was that this would be my most peaceful year and it has been.

"Even in the midst of the losses, I could still see good things that we did. I think the thing that's making me feel more comfortable about this team is guys are taking losing more serious and more personal. In the past, it didn't seem like that was the case.

"So that gives me a lot of confidence that this team can win."

The emergence of quarterback Brett Favre helped take some of the attention away from White, a welcome development for the defensive end. Not only was he playing at a high level, but White also appeared to enjoy himself more in 1995 than at any other time during his tenure with Green Bay. He was more relaxed in the locker room than he had been in the past.

"On all the teams that I've lost with, I've always tried to figure out, 'What did I do wrong? What could I have done more to help this team win?' " he said. "It was all about putting all the pressure on me.

"If we lost, I would go home and it was like it was all my fault that we lost. This year, I came in with a different attitude. Fritz was saying, 'It takes 11 guys at a time to win and you can't put all the pressure on yourself.'

"So my attitude this year when I came in has been, 'OK, I know (opponents are) going to run away from me so I can't make plays. So let me just keep my concentration because sooner or later, I will make a play.' "

White credited his new-found focus to his family, teammates and coaching staff. But he also gave a great deal of credit to the team's legion of fans.

"I've never felt so accepted in all my life by a group of people in a whole state," he said. "I hate to say this, but I've found more favor here than I found back home (in Tennessee) with the people. So it's been great."

There is no question that White was embraced by the fans from the moment he signed his lucrative free-agent contract with the Packers in 1993. But White admitted the reaction in '95 was greater than ever before.

When his season was thought to be over, there was a genuine outpouring of affection toward White from the team's fans. It became even more apparent to White that they cared about him as something more than just a football player.

"It means a lot to me," White said. "I think these people appreciate not only what I do on the field but off the field (too) and I think they're willing to show their appreciation in many ways.

"They've helped me accomplish some of the things I wanted to accomplish in helping people. It's just a situation where it's been overwhelming to me and I've really been sitting back in awe of how the people have responded."

White was even more overwhelmed by the public's response to a personal tragedy he endured late in the season. In January, a church in Knoxville, Tenn., where he is an associate pastor was burned down, allegedly by a racial hate group.

Racial slurs were painted on the back door of the church, but federal investigators still were not ready to claim race was a motive in the fire. Their attitude toward the tragedy infuriated White.

"The only thing I'm upset about is maybe our police department is not taking this thing serious enough," he said. "All they're going to do is come back and say, 'Well, we're doing our best.'

"My stepfather got murdered four years ago and the Chattanooga Police Department says, 'Well, we're doing our best.' There's a murderer on the loose. So I'm getting tired of hearing, 'We're doing our best.' You've got to find out who did it."

White also said it was time for people to realize the severity of the racial problems that exist in this country.

"It's time for us to stop sweeping this attitude under the rug and saying 'We've made progress' because the progress hasn't been made," he said. "Until whites and blacks start working together and start fighting against this, we're going to continue to have these problems."

A sign of the unity White was hoping to find came in the state of Wisconsin. After news of the tragedy became public, White and his family were besieged by donations from people all over the state.

Businesses made lucrative donations. Pre-school children even gathered together and sent White their allowances. Six weeks after the fire, at a press conference in downtown Green Bay, White accepted a $143,261.42 check from donations to rebuild the church.

"You might see a grown man cry right here," White said. "I always believe that out of something bad comes something good. I think God had a plan in all of it. I think this is a step forward in defeating racism."

White said about 85 percent of the donations came from white people. "Their contributions said: 'We will not tolerate this,'" he said.

The roughly 3,000 donations sent to the Bank One fund ranged from

Return to Glory

$10,000 given anonymously by a Green Bay organization to 92 cents from a child who taped pennies to a sheet of paper in a "92" shape. While some contributions came from as far away as California, most came from Northeastern Wisconsin. Also, an anonymous private donor made a $25,000 pledge to the award for information leading to the arrest of the arsonist or arsonists responsible for the blaze that also damaged a wing that housed a nursery and radio station.

Reggie White led the Packers in sacks in 1995 with 12 despite almost constant double-teaming.

"The response here has been so great," he said. "It's been incredible."

White is entering just his fourth season with the Packers, but already is one of the most popular players in team history. White admits it means a great deal when people mention him with Starr, Hornung and Nitschke.

"That's what intrigued me when I came here," he said. "When you go out (in Lambeau Field) and you see the names up there and to be mentioned in those guys' league, that's a lot to say.

"It's like when they elected me to the (NFL's) 75th Anniversary Team. When I was told I was elected, it didn't mean nothing. But when I went to New York and sat with those guys, that's when it did mean something.

"I started thinking, 'Man, I can't believe this. God has blessed me this much to fulfill a dream of mine as a professional and to be among the elite of my profession.' In this situation too, I guess it probably won't do much inside of me until I quit."

Before he does, though, there is still some unfinished business.

His desire to win a Super Bowl has been well-documented. It is the one thing that drives him more than any other. White has his Pro Bowl trips. He has received enough personal honors. All he wants now is "the ring."

"He is obsessed with taking this team to the Super Bowl," Shurmur said. "He leads by example better than any player I've ever been around. Never misses a turn in practice."

Not only does White want to win a Super Bowl title for himself, he also wants to win it for Packers fans everywhere.

"That's what's driving me now," he said. "To see the affection that I'm gaining and the Lord has blessed me with this affection. He's given me favor here. To see that affection makes you not only want to win for yourself, but to win for them, too. To know that they had 25 years of losing and this stadium was still packed. They deserve (a championship) probably more than anybody."

And so White is determined to win one for them. It could be one way for him to show the fans just how proud he is to have become a member of the Packers' extended family.

"When I played for the Philadelphia Eagles, I took pride in playing for (then head coach) Buddy Ryan and the guys that I played with and the people in the city," he said. "But I didn't take pride in being a Philadelphia Eagle because the people up top (in management) didn't take pride in their players.

"But here, it's a different atmosphere. When you take pride in your team and you take pride in your organization, that's what makes you a champion. So yeah, I take a lot of pride in being a Green Bay Packer.

"I like people knowing I play for the Green Bay Packers."

All of which begs the question: When White is elected to the NFL's Hall of Fame, will he go in as Reggie White the Philadelphia Eagle or Reggie White the Green Bay Packer? Team president Bob Harlan had the answer in a *Milwaukee Journal-Sentinel* article.

"A year ago, (White) was on a television show and somebody asked him, 'Reggie, when you go into the Hall of Fame, will you go in as an Eagle or Packer?' He said, 'I can't answer that.'

"This spring in minicamp, I told him that when it comes time to go into Canton, I hope he goes in as a Packer. He said, 'I'm going to.'" ◈

The MVP

Brett Favre has developed
into the most productive
quarterback in the NFL

During the 1994 exhibition opener, the largest response the Packers received from the crowd at Camp Randall Stadium in Madison came after an incompletion.

Quarterback Brett Favre, fresh off a 24-interception season in 1993, was pressured in the pocket and his primary receiver was covered. But instead of forcing the ball into coverage, as he had done so often in '93, Favre heaved the ball out of bounds.

The crowd roared.

"I could've went 10-for-10 or 20-for-20 and that throwaway would've been the most exciting thing that happened," Favre said with a laugh.

At the time, Favre's decision was applauded as a sign of maturity. He was 24 years old and known as a gunslinger, both on and off the field. The Packers coaching staff, players and fans all knew the only thing separating Favre from greatness was maturity, that sometimes intangible quality that comes with years off the field and passes on it.

That incomplete pass in a meaningless game was a sign that Favre had taken another step on the road to being a top-flight quarterback.

In 1995, Favre not only was still on the road, he began to create some new paths for others to follow.

Instead of throwing the ball out of bounds when a difficult situation arose, Favre evolved into a confident quarterback who had the patience to go through his reads. Second, third, fourth, even fifth reads became the norm for Favre as he started carving up defenses with alarming ease.

And in 1995, no quarterback did it better. In fact, no offensive player was better than the Packers' leader.

He led the NFL in touchdown passes with 38 and passing yards with 4,413. His average yards per attempt of 6.7 was easily the highest in the league. Favre's quarterback rating of 99.5 was second only to Indianapolis' Jim Harbaugh and inched his career rating to 86.8, fourth in the history of the NFL behind future Hall-of-Famers Steve Young, Joe Montana and Dan Marino.

Clearly, in 1995, Brett Favre arrived.

"Even though I don't say many things, I believe I can win the MVP," Favre said at a Jan. 1, 1996, press conference announcing his runaway selection for the NFL's top individual award.

"I believe I can be the quarterback in the Super Bowl. Hall of Fame. Super Bowl MVP. I believe all of that," Favre said, a smile stretching across his face. "Keep it to yourself. Work hard. If it comes, it comes."

At 26, he became the second-youngest active quarterback to have won the MVP award. Dan Marino was 23 in 1984; John Elway and Boomer Esiason were 27 when they won in 1987 and 1988, respectively; Steve Young was 31 in '92, and Joe Montana was 33 when he won the award in 1989.

Favre said his focus, however, was on the Packers – not himself.

"Our players can say, 'Hey, if a Packer can win this award, then we're getting a little notoriety and people are starting to recognize us.' I can't say enough about what this award means for me and my team. You can't win something like this unless you win and be successful. That's a salute to all my teammates."

The MVP honor is especially notable because it came in a year when Jerry Rice and Emmitt Smith set NFL records, Rice for receiving yards (1,848) and Smith for touchdowns (25).

Favre received 69 of 88 votes from the media panel. Rice had 10, Smith 7, Jim Harbaugh 2. Favre was also named Offensive Player of the Year, a first-team All-Pro and a starter for the NFC in the Pro Bowl.

"Brett has really matured," teammate Reggie White said. "Other than Joe Montana and Phil Simms, Brett's the toughest quarterback I've ever seen.

"Brett realizes this is his team. I think it all boils down to recognizing that and (everybody else) playing a supporting role. He's come in with a great attitude every week.

"That's something you can build on. That's something you can put a lot of hope in."

No one was happier about Favre's emergence than head coach Mike Holmgren, whose patience was tested by his often-excitable quarterback during their first two-plus seasons together.

"He's a great player. He's had a great year," Holmgren said as the Packers were preparing for their playoff game with Dallas. "Now he's more relaxed. I don't have to do a lot of yelling and screaming. I just give him hand signals.

"We understand each other a little better. I wasn't wrong about everything I did with him, but it's much better now."

Much better than their first two-plus seasons together when Holmgren often vented his frustration at his young quarterback after witnessing another in a series of questionable decisions by Favre. Those

Brett Favre tied an all-time NFL record with 12 straight games with two or more TD passes, ending in Game 5 of the 1995 season.

moments left both Holmgren and Favre weary and the two were left wondering what the future would hold.

But then, after a dismal loss to Philadelphia in the third week of the '94 season, Holmgren brought Favre into his office for a meeting. His message was simple: "Don't worry about losing your job to (then-backup) Mark Brunell."

"I told him, 'Hey, you are the guy,'" Holmgren recalled. "I told him, 'Either we go to the top of the mountain together or we go to the dumpster together. From now on, what happens to me is tied in directly with you.'

"And really, from that point on, he has gotten nothing but better."

In 1995, there was no one better. Period.

With Sterling Sharpe gone, the spotlight fell directly on Favre. For the first time, Favre would be the central figure of his offense and his team in general. No longer would Sharpe be there to bail him out in times of trouble.

The challenge was there and Favre ran with it. Or more precisely, he threw. And threw and threw and threw.

Favre played at such a high level that opposing teams were left scratching their heads, trying to determine some way to keep him under wraps.

"He gets the ball off so quick," Saints Coach Jim Mora said. "They've got five receivers out much of the time and – bam! – it's in there to somebody.

"I don't think you can stop him. You just hope to slow him down a little bit."

Few have done that the past two seasons. In that span, Favre has completed 62.7 percent of his passes for 8,295 yards and 71 touchdowns. The most impressive stat is Favre's interceptions.

Make that his lack thereof. After throwing 24 in '93, he has tossed only 27 in 1994 and 1995 combined.

"After the second season, when Brett had the 25 interceptions or 24 or whatever – too many – Brett, to his credit, clearly understood what had to happen," Holmgren said. "And he worked very hard to make it happen.

"As a coach, you can tell if a player is not trying. He was trying, so I wasn't worried about that. It was just 'Show me.'

"And he did."

Favre still has that gunslinger mentality and is still willing to roll the dice and take a chance every once in a while. But now his gambles are more calculated.

Take, for example, a 13-yard missile to Mark Ingram in the end zone of the Dec. 3 victory over the Cincinnati Bengals. Ingram was double covered on the play by safeties Bracey Walker and Darryl Williams. Linebacker Andre Collins was also in Favre's line of fire.

Favre, though, was undeterred. He knew the throw had to be fine. And it was. It also had to have heat on it. It surely did. Most of all, it needed a quarterback brimming with confidence. Favre was just the one to make it.

"The one word that I think describes him best is he's been so resourceful," Pittsburgh coach Bill Cowher said. "I think you see a guy who's made,

Return to Glory

for the most part, all the right decisions."

Tampa Bay quarterback Trent Dilfer agreed.

"I don't think there's a question that Brett's the best," Dilfer said. "He's kind of unorthodox at times, but without a doubt he's highly intelligent, makes a lot of great decisions and makes a lot of great throws. He's a tough guy, he's a fierce guy and he's a fearless competitor and that's what I think quarterbacks should be.

Saints Coach Jim Mora on Favre:
'I don't think you can stop him. You just hope to slow him down a little bit.'

"He definitely makes that team run."

What is so ironic about the season Favre enjoyed in 1995 is that in his own mind, he didn't believe he could duplicate the success he enjoyed in '94 when he passed for 3,882 yards, 33 touchdowns and 14 interceptions.

"I can't play much better than I did last year," Favre said just prior to the start of the season. "I mean, that's pretty hard to do.

"I'm not going to concern myself with that. I'm just going to do the things that I do best and hopefully the other guys will follow."

As the Packers were preparing for their opening-round playoff game with Atlanta, Favre was reminded of that quote. And he couldn't help but chuckle at the fact that yes indeed, he had topped himself.

"I thought last year was a great year," he said. "I really thought it would be hard to top what I did, especially without Sterling, with a couple changes on our offensive line.

"We kind of started from scratch on offense. We had a new flanker, a new X (split end) receiver, a new tight end. That's tough."

Tough, but not impossible, as Favre proved conclusively.

"Everything we do on offense starts with Brett," tight end Mark Chmura said after Favre was named the NFL's MVP. "He makes it happen. He's really had a great year."

A great year by anyone's standards, but an even more impressive year considering he spent much of it hobbled by a badly injured ankle that would require off-season surgery.

Ironically, Favre's ankle injury may have made him a better quarterback. Limited with his mobility, Favre relied more on his mental approach, instead of letting his physical tools take over.

"He knows his legs and feet and all that running all over the place can't get him out of jams," Holmgren said. "Then how do you get out of jams? You get out of the jam by knowing where to go quickly and thinking."

Those were attributes Favre had possessed all along. It just took them some time to surface and become a dominant part of his on-the-field personality.

Favre showed hints of his vast potential during his first two seasons as Green Bay's starter. He led the Packers to back-to-back

Reggie White on Brett Favre: 'Brett realizes this is his team. I think it all boils down to recognizing that and (everybody else) playing a supporting role.'

9-7 records, a playoff berth and playoff victory in '93 and was selected to the NFC Pro Bowl squad twice, in 1992 and 1993.

But Favre knew there was still much more he could do. And as far as he is concerned, the turning point came after a Week 7 loss at Minnesota on Oct. 20, 1994.

Favre threw a costly interception that was returned for a touchdown and then was forced to leave the game in the first quarter with a badly bruised left hip. That was the first time he had ever been forced to leave a game because of an injury.

What was worse, the loss dropped the Packers to 3-4. The team, and Favre, were struggling.

"That was the lowest point of my career," Favre said.

What Favre did was fly home to Kiln, Miss. He sat down with his family and friends and tried to decipher exactly what was going wrong.

He knew he was a better quarterback than he was showing. In the end, he decided he was trying too hard to live up to the expectations caused by the five-year, $19 million contract he had signed prior to the season.

So what he did was immerse himself in the game. He spent countless hours at Lambeau Field, working out on his off days, watching film, studying defensive tendencies, doing everything in his power to become one of the NFL's elite quarterbacks.

"Basically, I was just burning myself out," he said with a laugh.

The plan worked. Favre regrouped and finished with a huge '94 season, passing for 3,882 yards and 33 touchdowns with only 14 interceptions. Despite those accomplishments, he was passed over by the Pro Bowl voters.

A similar lack of recognition occurred in 1995. While other young quarterbacks – such as Drew Bledsoe – were constantly touted by the media as the league's future stars, Favre was still ignored.

The lack of attention left Favre shaking his head. He did not begrudge others for the attention they received, he just could not understand why he was being slighted in the process.

Chmura said he and Favre often talked about the lack of recognition and Chmura said Favre would laugh it off. To Favre's teammates, though, it was no laughing matter.

In fact, very early in the season, wide receiver Robert Brooks issued a bit of a warning to those who were ignoring Favre and his accomplishments.

"They're going to eat their words," Brooks said. "They're going to see the numbers over and over and see that Brett Favre is the next great quarterback."

In 1995, through sheer force of will and eye-popping consistency, it eventually became impossible to ignore Favre any longer.

At first, many national media members tried to downplay his MVP credentials. But in the end, Favre would not be denied.

His numbers were too good. His production too impressive. Brett Favre was the NFL's MVP and made the Packers' offense nearly impossible to stop.

"That's a big advantage, having Brett," Brooks said. "It's Brett's team. We win and lose through Brett."

The statistics bear out Favre's importance. Favre has been forced out of only two games as a Packer because of an injury. Green Bay has lost both games and mistakes by the backup quarterbacks played significant roles in each defeat.

Need further proof? The Packers are 3-13 when Favre throws more interceptions than touchdowns in a game, 4-7 when he throws an equal number of each and 31-5 when he has more touchdown passes than picks.

Lofty territory

The top four regular seasons in terms of touchdown passes in the past 30 years:

Player	Year	Yards	TDs	INT
Dan Marino	1984	5,084	48	17
Dan Marino	1986	4,746	44	23
Brett Favre	1995	4,413	38	13
Steve Young	1994	3,969	35	10

"He's carried this team," fullback Dorsey Levens said. "No other individual does more for their team than Brett does for ours."

Favre's biggest improvement in '95 came with his ability to spread his passes around and keep a multitude of receivers involved in the passing game.

In the past, Sharpe was the key focus of the passing game and Holmgren did everything he could to get Sharpe open. Favre, meanwhile, relied heavily on his star receiver and turned to him repeatedly when all else failed.

But with Sharpe no longer around, Favre was forced to utilize more receivers. He began to develop the patience to go through his progressions and spread his passes around.

Even Sharpe was impressed.

"I think (their passing game) is better," Sharpe said in his role as an NFL analyst on ESPN. "In the past, they used to move me around a lot to get me the ball and I think a lot of guys lost their concentration.

"Now they're going to Robert Brooks, they're going to the tight end and the backs. (In '94), they talked about spreading the ball around. Now they're doing it."

Again, the statistics don't lie. The Packers are 10-3 over the past two years when at least eight receivers catch a pass. The most amazing aspect of that stat is that there are 13 games in the past two years in which eight receivers have even caught a pass.

"I think the best thing that's happened to this offense is Brett spreading the ball around," wide receivers coach Gil Haskell said. "If we continue to move the ball around, then we have a real offense."

Favre continued at that pace for the entire season. And even though he struggled somewhat in the final game at Dallas – throwing a costly fourth-quarter interception – nothing could diminish the year he put together and the impact he had on the Packers and the NFL in general.

Yet despite Favre's impressive achievements in 1994 and, especially in '95, there remain some critics who wonder if Favre is merely the product of an offensive scheme even Holmgren admits is "quarterback friendly." But to that, Favre has a simple retort.

"This is a very hard offense to run – for anyone," Favre said late in the '95 season. "A lot of teams are turning to this offense. I spent some time with (former Philadelphia quarterback) Randall (Cunningham) in the off-season and he said, 'We're putting in your offense,' and he said, 'It's going to be easy.'

"I said, 'It's not as easy as you think.' Well, he's watching Rodney Peete run it right now.

"I think a lot of times people take for granted how difficult this offense is because of the numbers that are put up. It hasn't been easy for me, I promise you that."

It only looks that way. And that is another tribute to Favre's progress.

"He has all the tools," Holmgren said. "He's big, strong, tough, great arm. He's got the package you look for physically."

Brett Favre the quarterback had arrived in 1995 and staked a claim as one of the best in the NFL. But for Brett Favre the man, another much more stern challenge was yet to come.

Favre's 1996 off-season took a somber turn in May when he announced he was entering the NFL's substance-abuse program. Favre entered the program due to an addiction to the painkiller Vicodin. He was also reportedly going to be evaluated for alcohol abuse.

The news came quickly and left Packer fans and NFL observers stunned. At first, there were a multitude of questions surrounding Favre and his dependency. Favre had little to say at his hastily-called press conference in May. But soon thereafter, details of his dependency began to come to light.

According to a story in *Sports Illustrated*, Favre was taking as many as 13 Vicodin pills at one time. Favre believed he was doing a good job of keeping his problem from his friends, family and teammates, but many of them – including Chmura and center Frank Winters – sensed something was wrong late in the '95 season.

Then on Feb. 27, Favre's dependency took a frightening turn for the worse. Favre was in the hospital that day to have minor surgery to remove bone chips from his ankle. What happened next was anything but minor.

Following the surgery, Favre suffered a 20-minute seizure in front of his fiance Deanna Tynes and their 7-year-old daughter Brittany. The *Sports Illustrated* story said that during the seizure, Favre's limbs thrashed and his body was shaking backward uncontrollably and he was gnashing his teeth.

At one point, Brittany turned to Tynes and asked in a terrified voice, "Is he going to die, Mom?"

After the seizure ended, Favre was told by Packers team doctor John Gray that another seizure could have serious consequences.

"I quit (Vicodin) cold turkey and I entered the NFL substance abuse program voluntarily," Favre told *Sports Illustrated*. "I don't want a pill now, because I want to make sure I'm totally clean.

"The one thing (the counselors have) taught me is that there will always be a spot in your brain that wants it."

The dependency on painkillers came as a result, Favre's father, Irvin, said, of the five operations his son has had in the last six years, dating back to the July 1990 car accident before his senior season at Southern Mississippi. Brett Favre suffered internal injuries in that accident and subsequently had 30 inches of his intestines removed one month later.

Since then, there have been several other injuries he endured on the field. A shoulder separation in 1992, a deep thigh bruise in '93, the hip injury in '94 and the ankle problem in '95. Yet Favre did not miss a game. His string of 61 regular-season starts is tops among NFL quarterbacks.

But in keeping that streak alive, Favre was paying a terrible price.

"During the last five years, Brett's had numerous injuries and operations," Irvin Favre told the Biloxi (Miss.) *Sun Herald*. "To help deal with

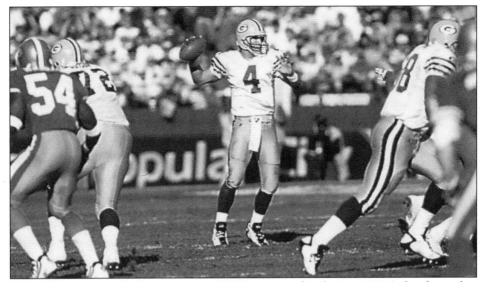

Brett Favre stood alone among NFL quarterbacks in 1995, leading the league in touchdowns and yards while winning the MVP award.

this, Brett needed prescription drugs … and Brett could not handle it."

Favre's admission came on the heels of other stories surrounding Dallas wide receiver Michael Irvin, Pittsburgh running back Bam Morris and former New York Giants linebacker Lawrence Taylor, who were all arrested on drug charges. But unlike those cases, Favre's situation did not appear to cast him in a negative light.

In fact, many Packer fans said they supported Favre and respected him for coming forward to admit his problem rather than denying it or attempting to hide it. One NFL observer, NBC analyst and former Giants quarterback Phil Simms, did not believe Favre's reputation would be harmed by his admission.

"I don't think it will be a problem for him in that regard," Simms said. "I think people look at how he handled it and I see a lot of positives.

"He's a young guy admitting he has a problem. I don't think people will look negatively at that."

The Packers, understandably, tried to focus on the big picture. Having Favre healthy and able to play at peak performance certainly is vital for the team's success in the years to come. But the Packers want more than just a healthy Brett Favre. They want to make certain Brett Favre is clean, healthy and ready to live a productive life long after his NFL days are over.

"We have to help him quite a bit," said Chmura, one of Favre's closest friends on the team. "There's going to be a change in our life and obviously a change in his."

Favre has sold his home in a popular Green Bay subdivision, which had become a frequent sight-seeing destination for Packers fans and at times the venue for players' postgame parties. His longtime girlfriend, Deanna Tynes, has purchased another home in one of Green Bay's more remote areas. Chmura and Winters, who were guilt-stricken at their unintentional, adjunct involvement in Favre's dependency, have pledged to drink soda instead of beer during their outings with the quarterback.

The Packers plan to be more vigilant in the drug/alcohol dependency area, though Wolf finds irony in that agenda.

"On May 10, we received our letter from the NFL saying that all of our records (regarding dispensation of prescription drugs) and everything else was up to date, and in perfect order for the 1995 season," Wolf recalls. "Two days later, our quarterback tells us he's entering a treatment center."

One source of concern for Packers executives: Where Favre got the pills. They discovered that, on occasion, Favre's teammates, aware of how battered their quarterback was, would slip him painkillers they'd requested, never thinking they were contributing to his addiction. He also received Vicodin from doctors outside the organization.

Ex-Packers lineman John Jurkovic says he personally supplied Favre with approximately 50 pain pills during their four seasons together.

"If my quarterback comes to me and says, 'Hey, tighten me up,' it's a no-brainer," Jurkovic said. "You give him the Vike."

Unknown to team doctors, Packers players regularly swapped medication. Those with access to pain pills, especially players who had undergone surgery, shared with teammates who wanted a boost before practice.

"All I know is, I've got this bottle of 30 Vikes, and if this were the season, these would be as good as gold," Jurkovic said.

Said Wolf: "The truth is, this is part of today's society. If anybody wants any type of drug, they can find a way to get it."

Jurkovic says he didn't know of Favre's addiction, but wasn't stunned by the news. Packers players had become accustomed to their quarterback's willingness to do anything to stay in a game.

"This is Brett's whole life. His thing is being a gritty performer and finding a way to play," Jurkovic said.

Jurkovic recalled a 1992 game against Philadelphia. Favre suffered a separated shoulder, received a pain-killing injection from team doctors at halftime and played the second half with minimal use of his shoulder. The Packers won 27-24.

"He comes to the sideline and sees (Don) Majkowski warming up and thinks, 'This is my shot. I might not get this back,'" Jurkovic said. "If the option is, 'Hey, tighten me up with a shot,' well, that's fine."

NFL players' reliance on painkillers is widespread. Simms, the former Giants quarterback, has estimated each NFL team would need a roster of 250 players to make it through a season if games were played with only healthy, non-medicated players. The league, wary of its liability, has become more vigilant in tracking prescription drug use. Jurkovic says players had easy access to painkillers when he entered the league in 1990, though it changed shortly thereafter.

"Now they're a lot harder to get. They no longer say, 'Hey, how ya feeling? Here's six of them for you.' After this (Favre's addiction), it's going to be damn near non-existent in that locker room, I'll tell you that."

Players often circumvent NFL controls by obtaining prescriptions from outside doctors. Jurkovic says he knows several veterans who "have their own medicine chest. They make sure they have enough of a supply so they don't have to rely on the team doctor."

Jurkovic believes 75 percent of NFL players take painkillers or anti-inflammatory drugs, mostly to survive midseason practices.

"Players can get through the games," Jurkovic said. "It's practicing when you're hurting that's tough. Playing isn't the problem."

Jurkovic wasn't surprised Favre continued taking the painkillers well after the season, noting that most NFL players need 1-2 months to recover from the demands of half a year of pro football.

"There's a medical need for painkillers," Jurkovic said. "When taken correctly, they could be a godsend for an individual. Like with any drug, if you don't follow the prescription, then the problems start. If you take 14 Advil, you're going to get sick.

"I'm not going to lie to you. I took a lot of them. I hurt after every game. There were times when I felt like absolute crap, and I took them. But I can also read the label."

Speaking by phone from his home on a Jacksonville, Fla., golf course, Jurkovic read from his Vicodin bottle: "1-2 pills every 4-6 hours, dependent upon need. Alcohol may intensify the effect."

Six pills remain in the 30-count bottle Jurkovic was issued by Packers physician Dr. Patrick McKenzie on Jan. 15, one day after the lineman suffered a severe knee injury in the NFC Championship game at Dallas.

Brett Favre answers a question as coach Mike Holmgren looks on during a press conference discussing Favre's return from a drug rehabilitation clinic.

Jurkovic has recovered from off-season surgery but will take the Vicodin to the Jaguars' training camp anyway.

"At Jacksonville, they've really tightened down," he said. "Training camp is going to be an absolute bear. I'm saving those six ... I might cut them in half, just to have enough to make it through."

If there is any comfort involving Favre's addiction, it is in his apparent motivation: He knew the Packers would struggle to win without him. Many in the Packers organization believe Favre subjugated his welfare and health to continue to present the strong, confident leader the team rallied around every Sunday. Unlike some high-profile sports addicts, Favre didn't expand his lifestyle based on newfound celebrity. His once-prominent social life was a non-factor late in the 1995 season, teammates have indicated. Favre spent most of his off-field time at home with Tynes and Brittany, who moved to Green Bay after spending the first three seasons of Favre's Packers career in Mississippi.

"The only reason I ever did this was because I had to. *Had to.* I had to play," Favre told *Sports Illustrated*. "Injuries have cost a lot of guys their jobs in this league, and there was no way an injury was ever going to cost me my job. Then it just got out of hand."

Holmgren said that, while the Packers are certainly concerned about Favre's ability to again play at an MVP level, they're much more concerned about Favre's life away from the football field: Brett Favre the man, the friend, the father.

Said Holmgren: "More important than the football part of this, really, is that he gets healthy." ◈

Finally, the 49ers

Mike Holmgren's return home – his first
since leaving San Francisco four years
earlier – couldn't have been better

The Packers opened the playoffs at home with a first-round date against Brett Favre's former team – the Atlanta Falcons. Poised and confident, the Packers were not about to stumble on their first step of what they hoped would be a run to the Super Bowl.

With Favre and Edgar Bennett leading the way, the Packers calmly dispatched Atlanta 37-20. Favre passed for 199 yards and three touchdowns and Bennett rushed for a team playoff-record 108 yards and a score to lead Green Bay into the second round of the NFC playoffs.

After the game, the Packers were brimming with confidence.

"With the Pittsburgh win and this win, we've sent a message to the league that we're a force to be reckoned with," special teams standout Marcus Wilson said.

The next game would put that feeling to the test.

The win over the Falcons placed the Packers in the second round of the playoffs for the third straight season. For the first time, however, their opponent was someone other than the Dallas Cowboys.

But the task was no less formidable. This time, the opponent was the defending Super Bowl champion San Francisco 49ers.

"I think that's a real challenge," defensive coordinator Fritz Shurmur said. "If you don't like to fight, you shouldn't be in this business. I think we like to fight."

The Packers were prepared to fight. Unfortunately, they would have to do so without one of their most gifted young warriors.

The one negative to come out of the Atlanta game was the season-ending knee injury suffered by starting left guard Aaron Taylor. It was the second major knee injury Taylor – a first-round draft pick in 1994 – had suffered in his brief career.

With Taylor out, the starting job fell into the hands of seventh-round draft pick Adam Timmerman, a scrappy competitor who had impressed the coaching staff all season with his determination and willingness to battle.

But he had never started an NFL game. Prior to the Atlanta game, he had not even seen any game action as a rookie. Now he was being asked to start against the defending Super Bowl champions and their two stand-out defensive tackles – Dana Stubblefield and Bryant Young.

"I'd better be ready," Timmerman said with a grin. "I don't have a choice."

That sentiment held true for the entire team.

The game had serious implications for the Packers. A victory on the road over the defending NFL champs would prove Wilson's point. The Packers would then have to be considered a team to be reckoned with.

Of course, they would also be just one more win away from the ultimate prize – a trip to the Super Bowl. With that in mind, it was left to Favre to send the 49ers a little message as the defending champs began to prepare for the Packers.

The San Francisco-Green Bay game was a coming out party for Packers linebacker Wayne Simmons, shown sacking Steve Young.

"If they were watching us today," Favre said after the win over Atlanta, "they know not to take us lightly."

The Packer players' confidence was higher than it had ever been before and they began preparing for the 49ers as if they were just another opponent. However, the game meant a great deal more to Holmgren.

For Holmgren, the game in San Francisco was more than just another game against a superb opponent. It was a chance to go home. A chance to return to the Bay Area and, for the first time, coach against the team that gave him his NFL start.

"It's special," he said earlier in the week as the Packers began their game preparations. "A lot of our family members are still out there, so it's special for a number of reasons."

There were moments when Holmgren stepped away from the game plan that week, from the endless hours of preparation, and tried to take it all in.

Going back to San Francisco. Playing the 49ers.

The team he grew up revering as a child. The team he later worked for as an assistant coach and the one where many of his coaching philosophies came to fruition.

The thoughts came crashing together as he pondered the playoff game between his Packers and the vaunted 49ers. They all merged together as he considered what the game truly meant.

What it meant to be going back home.

"It's going to be very emotional for me," he said. "I have to do my best to keep a lid on it."

Holmgren hoped for a pleasant response from those he left behind four years previous. But that did not prevent him from conjuring up a worst-case scenario.

"I don't want to go there and hear 'Holmgren sucks' from 60,000 people," he said with a grin.

There was not much chance of that.

Holmgren was a respected figure during his six seasons as a 49ers assistant. He began as quarterbacks coach under Bill Walsh and eventually became the offensive coordinator for new coach George Seifert in 1989.

Each year, there seemed to be a stable full of talent for Holmgren to work with. Joe Montana. Jerry Rice. Roger Craig. Steve Young.

To name a few.

But it was up to Holmgren to take that talent, mold it together and help the 49ers maintain the success that had become their trademark. He did so more than effectively.

During his tenure there, the 49ers had a winning percentage of .753 and won two Super Bowls.

"He played a huge part in my development," said Young, the NFL MVP in 1992 and '94. "When he coached me my senior year (at BYU), I was a little wild, running around a lot, not making reads.

"He settled me down and taught me how to play NFL-type quarterback. Then when I got to San Francisco, he taught me some more about being a dropback passer and what it takes to play at a high level in this league."

Holmgren's greatest work may have come in 1991. After losing Montana and Young to injuries, he took third-stringer Steve Bono and helped guide the 49ers' offense to the No. 3 ranking in the league.

That made Holmgren a hot prospect and, after the '91 season, six teams pursued him for head coaching positions. The Packers got him – "the prettiest girl at the dance, and he ended up with us," team president Bob Harlan said – and Green Bay hasn't had a losing season since.

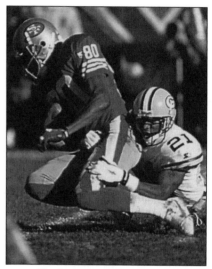

"He has helped take a program that had no life and really turned it around," Harlan said.

The week of the 49ers game Holmgren had ample time to ponder where he came from and what he has brought to the Packers organization.

"Like most teams, this team has had a lot of coaches over the years," he said. "When I was hired, I'm sure a lot of people in this building (at Lambeau Field) were saying 'We'll see if he's here in four years.'

Defenders like Craig Newsome held Jerry Rice in check with fine tackling.

"I've tried to get everyone in the building involved with winning. I told them 'Hey, I want you to be just as excited as I am on Sunday.' If I've brought anything, I think I've brought that."

The truth is, he brought a little something else to the party. He also brought the 49ers' exemplary West Coast passing offense. And that made the Packers-49ers playoff game even more fascinating.

For the first time, the NFL's two foremost practitioners of the West Coast offense were going to battle it out to determine which held the upper hand. The 49ers were still considered the master – the Packers the upstart young pupil.

But there was no denying they were gaining ground – fast.

The Packers had the 1995 MVP in Favre. The 49ers had the '94 model in Young.

Both had standout receivers to anchor their passing attacks. The 49ers

Return to Glory

had future Hall of Famer Jerry Rice, coming off his best season ever. The Packers had Robert Brooks, who had taken Sterling Sharpe's considerable shadow and trampled all over it during the regular season.

It was almost impossible not to look at the Packers and see them as an exact replica of the 49ers.

"In many ways, we're mirror images of each other," Young said just days before the game, "especially the base package."

Because of Holmgren's 49ers roots, many of the things he was doing with Favre, Brooks, Chmura and Bennett were the same things San Francisco was doing with Young, Rice, Brent Jones and Derek Loville. Despite that, as the '95 season had progressed, it became clear the Packers were not simply a junior version of the 49ers' present model.

"I think what Mike is doing is closer to what the 49ers ran when Joe Montana was there," Atlanta head coach June Jones said. "He uses more of their old formations. He's better balanced."

Holmgren agreed.

"It is different," he said. "You have different players, you're going to play to your players' strengths. I think what we run is probably closer to what I learned from Bill than maybe where they are now."

That is not to say Holmgren did not add his own personal little wrinkles to the scheme. He did. One of the biggest was the screen pass.

"We didn't run screens very often (in San Francisco)," said offensive coordinator Sherm Lewis, another ex-49ers assistant.

While Walsh and later Seifert did not feature the screen, Holmgren turned it into an art form. Each week, he featured a variety of screens in his game plan and, during the '94 and '95 seasons, no team in the NFL ran them better than the Packers.

"We always had one or two in the game plan (at San Francisco), but I don't think we called them as much," Lewis said. "Here, we may have four or five."

There were a few other changes as well. Holmgren often went to four wide receivers or two tight end looks, things the 49ers rarely did.

"It's little wrinkles," Young observed. "Their personnel might be better suited for two tight ends, so they go with that. We might figure three wide receivers in a little more.

"It's all about personnel."

Despite the often-subtle variations, the offenses of the Packers and 49ers bore a striking similarity. Both teams relied on the short-passing game for ball control and both teams were masters at it.

Two of the most high-powered offenses in the league were about to take center stage and battle it out for 60 minutes on Saturday afternoon. And that made the anticipation for the game even more intoxicating.

"Everybody in the world's going to be watching two good offenses going at it," wide receiver Anthony Morgan said.

With all of that buildup, who would've guessed the game would turn on one spectacular play made by the defense?

The Packers arrived in San Francisco calm, cool and collected as they made preparations for the game. Just a few hours before game time, Ingram was in the lobby of the team's hotel, waiting to check out when he spotted a reporter nearby.

Ingram saw the reporter and smiled.

"It's going to be a good day today," he said. "A real good day."

The 49ers pulled out all the stops for their first postseason game since their blowout win over San Diego in the previous Super Bowl. Skydivers soared into 3Com Park and fireworks filled the air during elaborate pregame festivities.

As it turned out, the real fireworks were yet to come. And they came courtesy of the Packers.

Most notably, linebacker Wayne Simmons.

Simmons had spent the better part of the season endlessly explaining to reporters that even though he was now manning Bryce Paup's left outside linebacker position, the two of them were not similar players. He was not Bryce Paup. Never had been. Didn't want to be.

Where Paup's forte was as a pass-rushing presence at linebacker, Simmons was asked to play the entire linebacker position. He covered tight ends and running backs in passing situations in addition to being asked to support the run from the outside. Only occasionally did Simmons rush the passer, although he was effective at it, finishing third on the team in sacks with four.

Paup had made his mark as a player with a penchant for making the big play. He spent the '95 season doing just that in Buffalo and he was honored as the NFL's Defensive Player of the Year.

The one thing the Packers coaching staff was waiting to see was whether Simmons could step up and be a big-play presence in a big-game setting. Simmons picked Jan. 6, 1996, at 3Com Park in San Francisco to prove that yes, he could.

Simmons made his presence felt on the 49ers' first play from scrimmage. Fullback Adam Walker took a swing pass from Young and was promptly drilled on a vicious hit by Simmons.

The ball popped out of Walker's hands and was scooped up by cornerback Craig Newsome, who raced 31 yards for a touchdown and a 7-0 Green Bay lead with 7:40 left in the opening quarter.

"That was a pretty intense play," said Simmons, who finished with 12 tackles, two passes defensed and one sack in addition to his forced fumble. "It set the tone for the rest of the day.

"We knew we had to be aggressive. We knew we had to lay the wood on 'em and hit 'em hard."

The Packers did all that. And much more.

Shurmur's scheme completely baffled the usually stoic 49ers. The venerable defensive coordinator had taken his share of heat during the regular season, but Shurmur was proving in the playoffs that he still had plenty of wizardry left.

After foiling Atlanta's run-and-shoot attack the week before, Shurmur tore the heart out of the 49ers on this day. He used a three-man front repeatedly and again used middle linebacker Fred Strickland as a pass rusher.

Other times, he dropped a lineman into coverage or rushed just three players and dropped eight players into the secondary. It was all designed to keep Young guessing.

It worked marvelously.

"I think the thing that helped us was they never got a rhythm going early because they're very good at what they do," Shurmur said.

The Packers consistently pressured Young, sacking him three times. They suffocated San Francisco's lackluster running game, holding the 49ers to just 87 yards on 18 carries, with Young gaining 77 of the yards on scrambles.

The Packers also defensed Rice as capably, if not better, than any team had done all season. They did so by playing man-to-man on Rice and utilizing zone coverage everywhere else on the field in an attempt to keep Rice from busting any big plays.

Even though Rice caught 11 passes for 117 yards, his specialty – yards after the catch – were reduced to almost nothing by Green Bay's aggressive, hard-hitting secondary.

"He was trying to get on the ground," safety LeRoy Butler said. "We got some good hits on him."

With the defense enjoying its finest hour of the season, that left the rest up to Favre and the Packers' offense. Unlike Walker, they did not drop the ball.

Favre had another brilliant day, completing 21 of 28 passes for 299 yards and two touchdowns. As had been his forte all season, Favre spread the wealth around, completing passes to seven different receivers.

Every time the 49ers would try to rise up defensively, Favre was there to cut them back down. He did it so effortlessly even Favre had to wonder what was going on.

This shouldn't be this easy, he thought to himself. Not against the Super Bowl champions.

But it was.

"At one point, I was just standing in the huddle checking out the cheerleaders," Favre joked afterwards.

It was that kind of day.

Favre's main target against the 49ers was a somewhat forgotten man on offense. A player the Packers acquired in the off-season with the hope that he could help them overcome the loss of Sterling Sharpe – former All-Pro tight end Keith Jackson.

After missing all of training camp, the entire pre-season and the first seven weeks of the regular season as a holdout, Jackson had been essentially a spot player during the regular season, catching 13 passes for 142 yards and one touchdown.

While Mark Chmura was garnering raves and a Pro Bowl berth, Jackson spent his time in the background, only occasionally being a featured player. And he never complained.

In fact, Jackson was truly enjoying his season with the Packers even though he was in a backup role.

"I told Mike and Ron Wolf that this is the most relaxing atmosphere I've ever been on with any team," Jackson said late in the season. "That's been great for me to come into a situation like this so late where a team could turn their back on me and actually accept me in.

"It's been a terrific situation. The unselfishness of this team, you just don't see that too many places around the NFL."

Jackson was a big part of that unselfishness. He realized Chmura had a better feel for the offense and deserved to be featured more at tight end. All the while, though, he quietly wondered when his time would come,

Legions of loyal Packers fans made the trek to San Francisco hoping for this moment – a chance to congratulate Reggie White in victory.

when he would receive the opportunity to step back into the limelight and show everyone there was still plenty of life left in Keith Jackson.

Jackson's time came against the 49ers. And he made the most of it.

He caught four passes for 101 yards and one touchdown. He torched the 49ers secondary with big plays, catching a 35-yard pass from Favre in the first quarter and another 35-yarder early in the second.

The Packers had waited for their biggest game of the season to use one of their most untapped big-play resources. And Jackson responded with his best game of the season.

"I was in the game plan more this week than any time this year," Jackson said after the game. "It was worth the wait. They seemed to be doubling Robert all day and that left a lot of guys open."

When it wasn't Jackson, it was Brooks on a slant or Chmura in the back of the end zone. The Packers' dominance over the 49ers was stunning. They had reduced the proud Super Bowl champions to rubble so swiftly, it was almost shocking to behold.

There was no question the 49ers were left staggering. While their defense was being carved up by Favre, their offense was going nowhere behind Young, who was misfiring much of the day.

Soon, the 49ers had lost all of their bluster and resorted to some late-game finger pointing and helmet tossing by veteran center Bart Oates.

"They definitely lost their composure," defensive end Sean Jones said. "I was surprised by that."

Oates even tried to carry on the 49ers' swagger after the game, proclaiming "Green Bay has solid coaching, (but) not the same talent as the 49ers or Dallas."

His words fell on deaf ears. With their 27-17 win, the Packers had proven that they had arrived as a legitimate NFL force. Nothing anyone could say could change what had transpired on the field. The Packers beat the 49ers in every facet of the game, and they beat them convincingly.

"I think this is vindication," Wolf said. "This is as nice as it gets."

And, of course, it was a sweet homecoming for

Mike Holmgren
'It was a very emotional week for me. To come back and play in front of family and friends is very special. It was like a dream come true.'

Holmgren. Even though Holmgren did his best to downplay the event during the week, his players could tell this game meant more to him than most.

"You could see it getting to him," Jackson said. "He was a little quieter this week than usual. He was intense this week."

And a winner in the Packers' biggest game since the second Super Bowl.

After the game, Holmgren stayed on the field for 10 minutes, basking in the glow of what his team had just accomplished. He waved and slapped high-fives with many of the Packer faithful who had made the trek out to San Francisco for the game.

"It was a very emotional week for me," he said after the game. "To come back and play in front of family and friends is very special.

"It was like a dream come true." ◉

Disappointed in Dallas

For the third straight season,
and sixth straight game, Green Bay
ran into a superior Cowboys team

After beating San Francisco on Saturday, the Packers had to wait and watch on Sunday to see who they would be playing the following weekend for the NFC championship.

Mike Holmgren
'We keep coming down here and getting lessons. I'm tired of lessons.'

A Philadelphia win at Dallas would mean the Eagles would travel to Lambeau Field, a factor the players naturally believed gave them a huge advantage. A Cowboys win meant Green Bay would make another trip to Texas Stadium to battle Dallas.

Outwardly, many of the players said they were hoping for an Eagles victory, saying Packers fans deserved another home game and how much they wanted to win the NFC title on their home field.

"Our fans deserve that game," Mark Ingram said. "They've been great all year and, if we can get that game there, that'll be great."

Privately, however, they knew that to truly make the season successful, they had to play the Cowboys again. Dallas remained the one thorn in the Packers' side and they had to eliminate it.

The Cowboys cooperated by thrashing the helpless Eagles. So for the sixth time in three seasons and for the third straight year in the playoffs, the Packers were headed to Dallas.

Once again, they were about to stare face-to-face with their biggest nemesis, the team that had a hold over them like no other. The Packers, though, were more than upbeat.

"I like our chances," Sean Jones said. "You just go out there and play football. You don't go in there in awe of what they've accomplished."

Ingram agreed.

"We're peaking at the right time and that's what it's all about," said Ingram, the only Packers player other than backup QB Jim McMahon with Super Bowl experience. "But we still have a large task ahead of us in Dallas and then going out to Phoenix (for the Super Bowl)."

Postseason records

The top five winning percentages in NFL postseason history:

Team	W	L	Pct.
Green Bay	17	8	.680
San Francisco	21	12	.636
Dallas	31	18	.633
Washington	21	14	.600
Pittsburgh	19	13	.594

Yes, for the first time, the Super Bowl had become a legitimate target. No longer was it something the Packers merely were hoping to accomplish.

Now they were standing right there on the threshold. A victory at Dallas would send them to a place they could barely imagine.

"Good things have happened to us lately and I think deservedly so," Brett Favre said early in the week prior to the game. "But we still have to get to the Super Bowl and we want to get there."

The question staring them in the face the entire week was how. How could the Packers reverse their miserable fortunes in Dallas. How could they defeat the powerful Cowboys, who also were peaking at exactly the right time despite a season filled with turmoil?

In Holmgren's opinion, the answer was simple: Prevent the Cowboys from making the plethora of big plays that had resulted in the Packers' downfall in the past.

In the previous five games, the Cowboys had 28 plays of 20 yards or more. They had five of those plays in their 34-24 win over Green Bay in October.

"Defensively, they've just gashed us," Holmgren said, summing up the problem succinctly.

Butler said the Packers had not helped themselves with some poor fundamental work.

"In October, I think we missed 12 tackles and they got 100-something yards after the catch," he said. "We have to tackle and make it a 6- or 7-

yarder and not a 70-yarder."

The Cowboys, meanwhile, were at a loss to explain their endless succession of big plays against the Packers defense.

"We've had some things called and we got the coverage that we were looking for," quarterback Troy Aikman said. "Other than that, I can't give you a reason for it."

Whatever the reason, the Packers knew it had to stop. The defensive players knew that if they could somehow find a way to keep Aikman, Emmitt Smith, Michael Irvin and company in check, Favre and the rest of the offense would give them ample opportunity to win.

The Cowboys appeared to recognize this as well.

"It's almost as if a monster is on the loose," Dallas safety Darren Woodson said. "Brett Favre is scary."

Irvin agreed.

"He's on a roll," Irvin said. "He's throwing balls while he's falling down and he's throwing them 50 or 60 yards. Usually, when you fall down you mess up your throwing. Not him.

"That's why he's the MVP. He's got confidence. Confidence is a dangerous thing."

After winning his battle over Young in the previous game, Favre had to brace himself for another test against one of the game's premier quarterbacks in Aikman. The two had faced each other before and each time Favre had come out on the short end of the stick.

In four matchups – Aikman missed the '94 Thanksgiving Day game with an injury – Favre had completed 55.7 percent of his passes for 1,011 yards, three touchdowns and four interceptions. Aikman had completed 76.9 percent of his passes for 1,272 yards, eight touchdowns and three interceptions.

Aikman held the edge in their personal matchups, but Favre was playing better then he ever had before. In the playoff wins over Atlanta and San Francisco, he had completed 45 of 63 passes (71.4 percent) for 498 yards, five touchdowns and no interceptions.

His quarterback rating in the regular season was 99.5, second-best in the NFL to the Colts' Jim Harbaugh. In the playoffs, it had risen to 121.0. Brett Favre was hot.

"He's playing well," McMahon said. "He listens to things that we tell him.

"In this offense, you're going to have people open. If you let the offense work for you, you're going to be successful."

No quarterback in the league had been as successful in 1995 as Favre. But in his next game, he would be facing the league's all-time postseason leader in completion percentage (69 percent) and average gain per attempt (8.72) and the NFL's No. 2 quarterback – behind Bart Starr – in quarterback rating (103.8).

It seemed likely whoever won the Favre-Aikman matchup would be moving on to the Super Bowl. Favre had no doubt who would come out on top.

"We expect to be in this game, we expect to beat Dallas," he said. "Now it's just a matter of doing it."

The Packers had plenty of confidence in the days leading up to the NFC Championship game. They were convinced this time it would be different. This time, it would be the Packers who had all the answers and the Cowboys who would be left searching.

Reggie White had an issue with the tactics of Dallas tackle Erik Williams.

This time, the Packers would knock that huge monkey off their backs. The Packers were convinced of it.

"We've got a lot of weapons that can get the job done," Anthony Morgan said. "That's what's been so successful for us.

"When we go into a game, everybody says, 'I'm going to be the guy who makes a play.' When you got a lot of guys thinking like that, you're going to make a lot of plays."

The team took its upbeat approach to Texas. The magnitude of the game was impossible to ignore, but the Packers maintained the loose approach that had worked wonders for them all season long.

How loose were they? Just to spice things up, Holmgren decided to lead the team and its motorcade to practice on Saturday. On a Harley-Davidson motorcycle.

No question about it, the Packers believed they were going to enjoy this trip to Texas Stadium.

The Cowboys, meanwhile, had their own agenda. For them, anything less than a trip to the Super Bowl would simply be unacceptable.

"Since we won the Super Bowl back in (January 1993), that's been a goal of this football team every year going in," Aikman said. "The whole goal of each year is to get in the Super Bowl and win the Super Bowl.

"When you come up short, it's extremely frustrating."

Dallas had come up short in 1994, getting defeated 38-28 by the 49ers in the NFC Championship game. The Cowboys entered the '95 season hoping to avenge that loss, but controversy was never far away.

If it wasn't the contract cornerback Deion Sanders received, it was Smith and head coach Barry Switzer having a run-in on the sidelines. Or Switzer's feud with Aikman or his questionable play-calling, including the infamous fourth-and-one call that cost the Cowboys an important late-season game at Philadelphia.

Yet the Cowboys were back in the NFC Championship game. Only this time, they were not facing the 49ers, the team they wanted to beat badly.

But even though the Cowboys had enjoyed so much success over Green Bay in recent seasons, they knew better than to take the upstart Packers lightly.

"We recognize Green Bay is playing outstanding and certainly had a big game last week against San Francisco," Aikman said just days before the championship game. "For us to win the ballgame, we're going to have to play the best game that we've played this year."

The stage had been set. It was just a matter of which team was going to step up and deliver first.

The Packers appeared to seize some momentum early in the game when backup linebacker Bernardo Harris blocked a John Jett punt after Dallas was stopped on its opening possession. It was the first block of any kind in Packers postseason history.

And it was a result of some studious film work on Harris' part.

"We'd seen that when (the center) puts his head down, he snaps the ball," Harris said. "I saw him put his head down and I shot the gap. I was shocked I got through there freely."

The Cowboys were also shocked. But only momentarily.

Although the Packers had a first down deep in Dallas territory, all Green Bay could muster was a 46-yard field goal by Chris Jacke. The Cowboys had taken the Packers' first shot and were still standing.

Now it was time for Dallas to come back with some hard body shots of its own.

Aikman and Irvin hooked up twice for touchdowns, first on a 6-yard toss and then on a 4-yarder, to give Dallas a 14-3 first-quarter lead. History, it appeared, was beginning to repeat itself.

Favre had looked shaky at the outset, misfiring badly on his first six attempts. The sixth was an attempted screen to fullback Dorsey Levens that was picked off by defensive tackle Leon Lett. Three plays later, Aikman and Irvin hooked up on their 4-yard score.

Favre hardly resembled an MVP quarterback on his first six passes. The seventh, however, was a thing of beauty.

On first down at the Dallas 27, Robert Brooks whipped past Cowboys cornerback Larry Brown on a post route and was wide open. Favre found him and Brooks raced 73 yards for a touchdown.

Suddenly it was 14-10. On just one play, the Packers were right back in the game.

"That play was big," quarterbacks coach Steve Mariucci said. "Until then, momentum was wearing a white jersey."

After that, Favre began to find his MVP magic. He moved Green Bay to a score on its next possession, a 24-yard hookup with Keith Jackson.

Trailing 24-20 in the third quarter, Favre brought the Packers back again. Another completion to a wide-open Jackson – this time a 54-yard strike down the middle – put the ball at the Dallas 2-yard line.

Three plays later, Brooks slipped into the end zone where Favre found him for a 1-yard touchdown and a 27-24 Green Bay lead. Even after Dallas regained the lead at 31-27, Favre had the Packers on the move again into Cowboys territory.

But then, perhaps the biggest play of the game went to the Cowboys. On second down at the Dallas 46, Favre rolled to his right and looked downfield for Chmura. But Chmura was covered on the play, forcing Favre to improvise.

Favre pumped once and then fired downfield toward Ingram. But Ingram was not expecting the pass, which was badly underthrown. Brown picked it off and returned it 25 yards to the Cowboys' 48.

"I saw Ingram looking at me," Favre said after the game. "I thought he was going to stop. Larry had his back turned when I threw the ball and then he turned and made the play."

"That was a big break for them," Mariucci said. "A big play."

The Cowboys sensed the game had turned and they promptly seized the opportunity to put the Packers away.

On first down, Aikman and Irvin teamed up for a 36-yard pass to the Green Bay 16. Irvin appeared to interfere with Evans on the play, but while Evans turned to complain to the official, Irvin snared the pass and darted to the 16.

"I guess the refs see things differently than us," Evans said. "I didn't even know that (Irvin) caught the ball."

On the next play, Smith scampered into the end zone for a 38-27 lead with 9:28 left to play.

Doug Evans and the Packers secondary have had trouble stopping the physical play of the Cowboys' Michael Irvin.

In a little over three minutes, the Cowboys had made three big plays – Brown's interception, the Irvin completion and Smith's touchdown. They had given the Packers a lesson in championship-caliber football.

And Holmgren wasn't too thrilled about it.

"We keep coming down here and getting lessons," he said. "I'm tired of lessons."

It had been the Cowboys' trio of superstars who stepped up when the team needed them most. Aikman passed for 255 yards with two touchdowns and no interceptions. Irvin caught seven passes for 100 yards and

For the title

The Green Bay Packers' history in championship games:

1936 NFL Championship
Packers 21, Boston Redskins 6
1938 NFL Championship
NY Giants 23, Packers 17
1939 NFL Championship
Packers 27, NY Giants 0
1944 NFL Championship
Packers 14, NY Giants 7
1960 NFL Championship
Philadelphia Eagles 17, Packers 13
1961 NFL Championship
Packers 37, NY Giants 0
1962 NFL Championship
Packers 16, NY Giants 7
1965 Western Conf. Championship
Packers 13, Baltimore Colts 10
1965 NFL Championship
Packers 23, Cleveland Browns 12
1966 NFL Championship
Packers 34, Cowboys 27
1966 Super Bowl I
Packers 35, KC Chiefs 10
1967 Western Conf. Championship
Packers 28, LA Rams 7
1967 NFL Championship
Packers 21, Cowboys 17
1967 Super Bowl II
Packers 33, Oakland Raiders 14
1995 NFC Championship
Cowboys 38, Packers 27

Championship game record: 12-3

two scores, while Smith rushed for 150 yards and three touchdowns.

"I think when it's crunch time, you see the real character," Dallas linebacker Darrin Smith said. "We had a whole lot of character out there."

In addition to that, the Cowboys also beat the Packers at their own game. Dallas held the ball a stunning 23 minutes to Green Bay's 7 in the first half and for the game, the Cowboys held a 38:56-21:04 time of possession edge. A big reason was Green Bay's inability to mount any sort of a running game.

In the previous five losses to Dallas, the Packers had averaged just 53.8 yards rushing per game and only 2.96 yards per carry. Their best individual effort was Bennett's 50 yards on 16 carries in an October, 1995 loss.

On this day, the Packers managed only 48 yards rushing on 12 carries. Bennett gained 46 yards on nine carries, but 18 of his yards came on one carry.

"I don't know what happened," Chmura said. "Even though we scored a lot of points, we didn't control the ball too well. Our defense was on the field a long time."

However, the Packers defensive players said the fact they were on the field so long was not a decisive factor.

"We just didn't get any turnovers," Butler said. "I don't think wearing down and getting tired had anything to do with that. We just didn't make any plays."

Dallas' defense did. And that proved deadly to the Packers.

Favre's interception had been a critical mistake the Cowboys utilized to take control of the game. On a day when Favre had hoped to prove that he not only could be an MVP quarterback, but also a Super Bowl quarterback, Favre fell victim to his own mistakes and Aikman's brilliance.

While Aikman was enjoying a stellar day, Favre was picked off three times despite passing for 307 yards and three touchdowns.

"Turnovers were very costly," he said. "You can't turn the ball over with this good of a team. You can't make it easy for a team this good.

"We had them right there until the end. I put us in a position to win, and then I took it away."

As if the defeat was not bad enough, the game was marred by two unfortunate occurrences involving the Packers.

John Jurkovic
'A guy cuts a man and injures his knee and that's all fun and games in the NFL.'

The first came when Brooks was pushed out of bounds and collided with Green Bay receivers coach Gil Haskell. Haskell's head slammed into the concrete-like surface of the artificial turf and the game stopped for several minutes while he was examined.

Haskell, perhaps Holmgren's closest friend in Green Bay, was taken to a Dallas hospital and remained there for several weeks while doctors diagnosed the severity of the injury. Haskell suffered a skull fracture and there was some question whether he would be able to return to his duties with the Packers.

Fortunately, he has since made a complete recovery and as the '96 season began, he was back coaching Green Bay's wide receivers.

The second incident involved nose tackle John Jurkovic, who had to leave the game after tearing a ligament in his knee when he was cut-blocked from behind by Dallas All-Pro offensive tackle Erik Williams. The play would prove to be Jurkovic's final one as a Packer. He departed in the 1996 off-season, signing a free-agent contract with the Jacksonville Jaguars.

Brett Favre
'This year was a great run. We had some great wins, some tough losses. This is just one of those tough losses.'

Williams' block on Jurkovic enraged the Packers.

"The NFL calls that kind of thing legal," Jurkovic said. "You touch a quarterback in the head and they fine you a million bucks. A guy cuts a man and injures his knee and that's all fun and games in the NFL."

Reggie White was also livid. At his postgame press conference, he lashed out at the league and, more specifically, at Williams.

"This league is doing nothing about illegal chops," an enraged White said. "We get punched in the face. I've got a scratch under my eye from getting punched in the face.

"And (the media) are just going to write about how we complain too much. I'm sick of it. I'm ticked off.

"I work my butt off to get here. I work too hard. I'm sick of this. I'm not happy because I got an official tell me I'm whining too much.

"(Williams is) going to go home tonight and sleep. I'm not. I'm going to be up all night."

White insisted the officials deprived the Packers of a chance at victory and called the pass interference penalty on Evans "ridiculous." And he clearly was not happy with what he perceived to be a bias toward the Cowboys in a game of this magnitude.

"Don't get me wrong, these guys have a great team," White said. "They deserve to be here. But when we come down here, they're going to get the calls."

Williams, meanwhile, defended his block on Jurkovic.

"It was a legal block," he said. "There are blocks like that every week. It was just unfortunate that he got injured on the play.

"I never intended for him to get hurt. I'm not like that. Reggie was pretty mad about the play, but hey, it's football."

The Packers thought otherwise and, after the block on Jurkovic, tempers began to flare. Wayne Simmons and George Koonce argued with Irvin, nose tackle Gilbert Brown got into a shoving match with Williams and White could be seen jawing with Dallas defensive end Charles Haley, who was on the sidelines in street clothes due to an injury.

It was one of the few times during the season the Packers had lost their composure, and Jones was not happy about the timing.

"You can't start that game where you're screaming at the officials because you didn't get a call," he said. "We missed like three (defensive) calls in that series because we were screaming back and forth and not looking to the sidelines.

"We got taken out of our game a little bit."

Questionable tactics aside, the truth remained the Cowboys won because they were the superior team. When push came to shove, they had the ability to rise up and make the big plays that decided the game.

The Packers were game challengers and they certainly pushed the Cowboys further than they had pushed them before. But in the end, the Cowboys had prevailed.

Again.

"I'm glad it struck midnight," a beaming Irvin said. "Cinderella can go home."

Before the Packers departed, however, they were left to think about what might have been and to ponder their stature in comparison to the Cowboys.

"I think the gap is close," Chmura said in a somber locker room after the game. "It'd be nice to get them up in Lambeau for once."

When the game had come to an end, the Cowboys trotted off the field with a chorus of "Super Bowl, Super Bowl, Super Bowl" ringing in their ears.

Those were the words the Packers so desperately wanted to hear. But on this day, they found no joy in them.

LeRoy Butler
'If we ever beat these guys, we will be in the Super Bowl.'

Instead, the words stung like salt on an open wound.

"This year was a great run," Favre said, summing up the season. "We had some great wins, some tough losses. This is just one of those tough losses."

But tougher than any of the others. For this one came just one game away from the Super Bowl.

"We had champagne to celebrate on the plane (if we had won)," Holmgren said. "We'll still drink a toast to this team."

The Packers had every reason to be proud, but it was difficult to do so in the aftermath of this defeat. They had come so close to their ultimate prize, but the Cowboys snatched it away from them before they could ever get a grip on it.

It had been a superb season and one that had produced many wonderful moments. But in the locker room after the loss to the Cowboys, it was difficult for any of the players to remember the good times.

All they could think about was they had made another trip to Dallas and come away with another loss to the Cowboys. In the end, it was left to Butler to sum up the situation for the rest of his teammates.

"If we ever beat these guys, we will be in the Super Bowl." ◈

The legends

Green Bay's stars of the 1960s
are thrilled with their team's
return to NFL prominence

They would gladly share the glory.

Stars of the Green Bay Packers "Glory Years," the teams that achieved an NFL record three consecutive titles and five championships in seven seasons during the 1960s, say there is plenty of room in the hearts of Packers fans for more heroes.

"There isn't a Packers player from our era that doesn't want us to win the Super Bowl again," said Bob Skoronski, a Green Bay tackle in 1956 and 1959-68. "There is great tradition in that town. It was there before we got there. With the small town competing against the big guys, it's a special place in football."

Super Bowl talk is prevalent around Green Bay with the Packers coming off their finest season since the 1967 team won the famous "Ice Bowl" over Dallas 21-17 and then crushed Oakland 33-14 in Super Bowl II. Green Bay's 11-5 regular season, pair of playoff wins and hard-fought 38-27 loss to the Cowboys have everybody, including the former players, expecting big things this year.

"We've been waiting 25 years for the Super Bowl," said Willie Wood, a Packers free safety from 1960-71 and one of only six free agents to make the Pro Football Hall of Fame. "There have been times I thought we were going to be competitive and then when we were not, it was very disappointing to me. I'd be very excited if we could do it. I think Green Bay, with all of the tradition that goes with the city and state, is certainly deserving of a Super Bowl."

Willie Davis, a Packers defensive end from 1960-69 and another member of the Pro Football Hall of Fame, said there is no concern that a new group of heroes will enable the past to be forgotten.

"In my mind, it adds luster because one of the biggest questions most of us have to react to is, 'When will the Packers come back?' " Davis said. "I think it's like in your family. You hope your son or daughter reaches your level of achievement as you move from the spotlight.

"I have that kind of reaction to the Packers of today. You would hope they would give you bragging rights."

Skoronski said it is time for the passing of the Packer torch. "The reason the players of the '60s are held in such high regard is because we haven't won since," Skoronski said. "To Packers fans, there is still only one middle linebacker, Ray Nitschke, because there hasn't been anyone as good since he retired."

"It's very nice that people show such great appreciation for what we did during the 10 years I was up there," Davis added. "It's also somewhat disappointing that, until the last couple of years, people had more respect for past Packers than for current Packers. Now there is appreciation for Packers of both eras."

Skoronski warned the Packers need to build on the disappointment of the NFC title game and realize they need to accomplish their goals soon.

Hall of Famers

Packers who are in the Pro Football Hall of Fame:

Player	Pos.	Year
Earl "Curly" Lambeau	*	1963
Robert "Cal" Hubbard	OT,DT	1963
Don Hutson	E	1963
Johnny "Blood" McNally	HB	1963
Clark Hinkle	FB	1964
Mike Michalske	OG,DL	1964
Arnie Herber	QB	1966
Vince Lombardi	Coach	1971
Tony Canadeo	HB	1974
Jim Taylor	FB	1976
Forrest Gregg	OT	1977
Bart Starr	QB	1977
Ray Nitschke	MLB	1978
Herb Adderley	DB	1980
Willie Davis	DE	1981
Jim Ringo	C	1981
Paul Hornung	HB	1986
Willie Wood	FS	1989
Henry Jordan	DT	1995

*Founder, player, coach, et. al.

"Once you get as close as they were last year, you realize you don't get too many opportunities and you fight a lot harder," said Skoronski, a retired businessman who lives in Middleton, Wis. "On defense, they're starting to age. Reggie (White) is getting older and he's a big force on the team. You have to have that sort of talent on defense to contend in championship games."

Bart Starr, Jerry Kramer, Ken Bowman and Fuzzy Thurston re-enact Starr's game-winning TD in the Ice Bowl during a "Packers Fantasy Camp" reunion at Lambeau Field.

Skoronski added that a successful return by Aaron Taylor, the offensive lineman coming off the second major knee injury of his two-year career, is essential to the Packers' title hopes.

"I don't care how good your quarterback, running backs and wide receivers are, you can't win a championship without a strong offensive line," said Skoronski, who played with Pro Football Hall of Fame offensive linemen Forrest Gregg and Jim Ringo.

"When you can open holes and protect the passer every play and every game, you don't have to depend on the weather and things like that."

The ex-Packers said they are not concerned about Green Bay quarterback Brett Favre, the 1995 NFL Most Valuable Player who entered a drug rehabilitation clinic in May for his addiction to the pain-killer Vicodin. Favre was ready for the start of training camp in July.

"I think that an athlete so many times is left with the challenge of doing what he has to do," said Davis, the Packers all-time leader in fumble recoveries with 21. "Today, as in the past, all athletes play with a certain amount of pain and I respect and appreciate that he came forward. Sometimes

Return to Glory   173

when you get something off your mind, your concentration can be better."

Added Skoronski: "He's a young, tough kid, he can overcome all that stuff. He's sitting on top of the world in football, has the most understanding fans in the world and a great coaching staff."

Davis, Skoronski and Wood were members of the 1960 Packers team that played in its first NFL championship game since 1944 and its first under legendary coach Vince Lombardi. Green Bay led 13-10 before a fourth-quarter touchdown gave Philadelphia a 17-13 win. It was the only blemish on Lombardi's 9-1 postseason mark.

The Packers of last season endured a similarly frustrating experience in the NFC Championship game on Jan. 14 in Dallas, blowing a 27-24 fourth-quarter lead in their sixth consecutive loss to the Cowboys in three seasons. As in 1960, Packers fans were especially hungry for a winner in 1995 since it had been 28 years since Green Bay came within one victory of the Super Bowl. The Packers stars of the '60s said the enthusiasm shown by fans in 1995, highlighted by the ritual of players jumping into the stands to celebrate touchdowns with fans brought back memories of what was happening in Green Bay as the team moved toward its first title under Lombardi in 1961.

"From the fans' point of view, excitement is based on winning," Davis said. "One of Lombardi's best quotes was, 'There's no laughter in losing.' Clearly, the best times we all had were when all of us, players and fans, shared those winning moments and championships. The winning last season brought things to an excitement level I hadn't seen since the '60s."

Skoronski said "Packer Backers" make the unique player-fan relationships possible.

"There's not any of us former players who don't envy those guys thinking to jump into the crowd with the fans," Skoronski said. "That's fantastic. Where else would you do that? Green Bay fans know who the players are, what they do and they're well-informed on the game."

Skoronski added that today, as in the Packers' heyday, the team's following is not confined to Wisconsin.

"I travel quite a bit and it is absolutely shocking how many people are infatuated with Green Bay and how they do," Skoronski said. "They want to see the small-town team get back there."

Davis agreed that the Packers are the true "America's Team."

"Because of its size and community support, Green Bay will always be a team that fans across the country will appreciate," Davis said. "The

Packers are considered underdogs in a sense."

Davis, who was elected to the Packers Board of Directors in 1994, said the current Green Bay players appreciate the team's tradition.

"Almost every Packer of the old days has some identification for the current Packers," Davis said. "The current organization and the players have shown a little more appreciation for us. I find the current players saying, 'These are the guys who did it then, let's go do it now and be a part of this rich tradition.' I don't think every team shares that sense of past and present."

Willie Davis, shown with Ray Nitschke and Bart Starr during the team's annual alumni celebration, says Green Bay's players and administrators have a strong appreciation for the Packers' past.

The ex-Packers, however, noted one key difference between the Green Bay teams of the Glory Years and the current one.

"This team has a good defense," Skoronski said. "We had a great defense. This team depends on the offense a lot to win games and doesn't seem to win low-scoring games."

Said Wood: "We won ballgames we had to win, by hook or by crook. If the offense was not playing good, the defense did well and vice versa."

Among the greatest moments enjoyed by the Packers of the '60s were the pulsating victories over Dallas in the 1966 and 1967 NFL title games. Tom Brown's end-zone interception saved the 34-27 win in '66 and Bart Starr's quarterback sneak gave Green Bay a 21-17 victory in the famous "Ice Bowl" of 1967. The Packers followed the triumphs over the Cowboys with victories in Super Bowls I and II.

Ironically, it is the Cowboys of the '90s that not only stand in the way of the Packers' hopes for a return to glory but also are challenging the standard of excellence Green Bay set three decades earlier. Dallas is the reigning Super Bowl champion and has three NFL titles in the past four seasons.

Not surprisingly, when the talk turns to the Cowboys, the age 60-ish ex-Packers talk like they're ready to suit up.

"I'm just sick that we couldn't beat Dallas last year," Skoronski said.

Wood, who led the NFL in punt returns with a 16.1-yard average in 1961 and topped the league with nine interceptions in 1962, knew how to play in big games. With the Packers leading just 14-10 in the third quarter of Super Bowl I, it was Wood's interception of a Len Dawson pass and 50-yard return to the Kansas City 5-yard line that triggered the Packers to a 35-10 win.

"There are ballgames you must win, certain teams you have to beat," Wood said. "The Packers played championship ball in the playoffs against San Francisco, but then dropped off against Dallas the next week. We have to find a way to beat the Cowboys."

Skoronski predicted a different outcome should the old adversaries meet in the playoffs again.

"When all the guys talk about Bob Harlan, Ron Wolf and Mike Holmgren on down, we feel the organization is in very good hands," Skoronski said. "The Packers are not afraid to go out and do whatever it takes to win, whether it's getting another player or improving the facilities.

"We have served our time and want to go to the Super Bowl. Our stars are at their peak. It is their time." ◈

Something Super?

1995 was great, but Ron Wolf,
Mike Holmgren & Co. believe the Packers'
future will be even better

There is a feeling in the Green Bay Packers organization that this team is on the verge of something special. It is a confidence bolstered by the success of 1995 and the feeling that the best for this team is yet to come.

In the span of four seasons, Ron Wolf and Mike Holmgren have directed the Packers from the depths of the NFL to a deserving place among the elite. In Wolf's opinion, the Packers are the second-best team in the NFC and perhaps the NFL.

"We're getting a little better week after week, year after year," Wolf said. "I think we're at the point right now where we're up among the better teams.

"I think when we went to San Francisco, we demonstrated walking away from there that we had the capability of playing with anybody, anytime. We still have certain areas that we have to improve in, but I think the maturation process of our football team enables us to move up a little bit."

And then Wolf sent a message to the rest of the NFL.

"You're going to have to contend with the Green Bay Packers," he said simply.

The Packers have made great strides the last four seasons. Four straight winning seasons. Four playoff victories. One division title.

But one task remains. One chore that must be finished before the Packers can accomplish all the lofty goals they have set for themselves.

Beating Dallas.

The Cowboys remain the yardstick by which the Packers will be measured until Green Bay somehow finds a way to defeat the reigning champions. And the Packers know it.

"That's the team," cornerback Doug Evans said. "They're the obstacle we have to overcome."

And it has been quite an obstacle.

Although the Packers were much more competitive in the NFC Championship game against the Cowboys than in previous defeats, the fact remains that they have squared off against Dallas six times in the last three seasons and lost all six games.

In those six defeats, the Packers have allowed 422 yards and 35 points per game. While many are searching for an answer to the Cowboys' stunning dominance over Green Bay, Wolf said the answer is very simple.

"You listen to all the constant talk about Dallas, and it's all about the 11 or 12 Pro Bowl players that they have," Wolf said. "That's what we have to do. That's how you catch Dallas, you have to have 11 or 12 Pro Bowl players.

"We've gotten a little closer to them. How far, I'm not too sure. The only place that can really be answered is on the field of play."

The Packer players, however, believe they have closed the gap significantly on the Cowboys and are now in a position to make a legitimate run at the Super Bowl. They are confident they can become the team to overtake Dallas as the NFL's best.

"I think we can be that team," Evans said. "We're taking the same steps (Dallas and San Francisco) took.

Ron Wolf
'That's how you have to catch Dallas. You have to have 11 or 12 Pro Bowl players. We've gotten a little closer to them. How far, I'm not too sure.'

"Dallas didn't start out a championship team, they had to build. I think we're on that same path. We're getting better and better each season."

The Packers' optimism stems from the fact they are coming off the team's most successful season since 1967. It was a return to prominence that was long overdue for a franchise steeped in championships and success.

Green Bay went 11-5, won its division, posted a convincing win at San Francisco and had a strong showing against the Cowboys in the NFC Championship game.

The Packers have one of the league's most explosive passing attacks, led by reigning league MVP Brett Favre. They also possess one of the league's most feared defensive players in Reggie White.

The fact Green Bay's two best players play two of the most pivotal positions on the field makes this a dangerous team.

What's more, the Cowboys suffered through a trying off-season. They lost four defensive starters through free agency and star receiver Michael Irvin became embroiled in a highly publicized drug scandal.

Put it all together, and it leads the Packers to believe their time may have arrived to step up and become the team to beat in the NFL. But they know it will not come easily. They know everyone will want a piece of them in 1996.

"We're not going to surprise anybody, and that's when they put you up there with the elite teams," safety LeRoy Butler said. "And that's where we're going to be."

The Packers prepared for the '96 season in relatively low-key fashion. Seeking to shore up their middle linebacker position, they made a strong bid for free-agent linebacker Cornelius Bennett, but were rebuffed.

Wolf later signed former ex-Bear Ron Cox and ex-Lion Mike Johnson to compete with talented Bernardo Harris for the starting middle linebacker position created by the free-agent departure of Fred Strickland.

For the record

Team records set by the Green Bay Packers in 1995:

Most TD Passes, Season
Brett Favre 38, Team 39
Most 300-Yard Passing Games, Season
Brett Favre, 7
Most 100-Yard Receiving Games, Season
Robert Brooks, 9
Most Yards Receiving, Season
Robert Brooks, 1,497
Most Rushing Attempts, Season
Edgar Bennett, 316
Longest Pass Completion
99 yards, Favre to Brooks
Most Consecutive Games With TD
Team, 58

The Packers' most significant free-agent signing was the addition of former Tampa Bay defensive tackle Santana Dotson. Dotson's presence is expected to significantly improve the defense's interior pass rush – a weak spot in '95 – and give some needed, youthful pass-rushing help to Reggie White and Sean Jones.

"You can never have enough defensive linemen," Wolf said. "What Santana brings is a unique skill as an inside pass rusher. That's probably the most difficult position to fill in the National Football League.

"He's demonstrated in his years in Tampa, particularly against the Packers, that he more than has enough skill to be an effective force as an inside rusher. We knew we had an opportunity to get him and where we had him rated, we did not let that rest."

Dotson is excited about the prospect of joining a team that may be on the verge of greatness.

"I definitely feel that I was on the (free-agent) market as the top pass-rushing linemen out there," he said. "When you have the pass rushers of the capability that Reggie and Sean Jones have, it just enables me to get better penetration and upfield rush.

"It's much more difficult for a team to game plan for me when I'm paired with Reggie or with Sean."

Dotson is not the only presence on the defensive interior the Packers are counting on to help them significantly bolster their defense. Defensive tackle Gilbert Brown, who has battled injuries the past two seasons, is healthy and the coaching staff believes he may be on the verge of stardom.

"Gil is way ahead of where he's ever been conditioning-wise and he's coming into the season relatively injury free," defensive coordinator Fritz Shurmur said. "As a result, I think you'll see him have a big season.

"If he can stay free of injuries ... he's had two years in a row where he hasn't done that. If we can get 16 games out of him, that will go a long way in determining how we do, against the run especially."

Another key defensively is keeping White fresh for the entire season. White appears to have recovered from his hamstring injury, but the Packers would like to rotate their defensive linemen this season with the hope that White can be rested during each game and maintain a higher level of effectiveness.

"We would love to have a system where we can keep as fresh as we can," defensive line coach Larry Brooks said. "Most of that depends on how the young guys mature. You know you've got a constant in the veteran guys, but to take a guy out and lose something or drop off dramatically, that doesn't make sense.

"If we put the young guys in and the level of play is not a dramatic change, then we're getting to where we want. In Fritz's concept, we'd love to have those kinds of options and use the whole roster."

Green Bay's defense must create more turnovers. The Packers forced only 16 turnovers in 1995, the fewest in a season in NFL history since the advent of the 16-game schedule in 1978.

Forcing more turnovers is something Shurmur has stressed repeatedly during training camp. That, combined with improving the work against the run and with the pass rush, have been Shurmur's primary points of emphasis during training camp.

"I'm not one to set those superfluous goals that don't mean anything," he said. "What we need to do is control the front, control the line of scrimmage on the run and be more effective rushing the passer."

The offense, meanwhile, has returned pretty much intact. Of course, the '95 unit was extremely productive.

Green Bay had the NFL's seventh-rated offense in 1995, including the league's third-best passing attack. Only San Francisco, Detroit, Dallas and Pittsburgh scored more points than the Packers' 404, and Green Bay had to travel longer than any team in the league on most possessions because of that

The Packers are hoping for more in-the-stands celebrations from Robert Brooks.

aforementioned lack of opportunism on defense.

At the heart of the offense, of course, is Favre. The main on-the-field question that surrounds him entering the 1996 season will be:

What can the NFL's MVP do for an encore?

"That's a good question," first-year quarterbacks coach Marty Mornhinweg said with a smile. "He had a wonderful season.

"His decision-making is up there with the best right now. If he can put four or five or just multiple seasons like he had last year back-to-back-to-back, now you're in the league of quarterbacks who don't get forgotten for awhile."

On the surface, it may seem next to impossible for Favre to improve upon his superb 1995 season. Yet the Packers believe Favre can get even better.

Mark Chmura
'We're not making it a point to be unselfish, that's just the kind of guys we are.'

"I think he can improve," offensive coordinator Sherm Lewis said. "There's areas as far as decision making, pre-snap reads of defenses. I think he can get better at that. He's made great strides and he was a lot better at that last year than he was before.

"I think with maturity and experience, he's going to get better. A lot of times he has to read fronts and make decisions on running plays, whether to stick with them or get out of them. He did an excellent job last season, but there's room for improvement.

"There's nobody in the league you say can't get any better. You stop getting better and then you go downhill."

One thing the Packers hope to continue is Favre's amazing streak of durability. Since becoming the starter four games into the '92 season, Favre has started 68 straight games, including the playoffs. That is the longest streak in the NFL among quarterbacks. And in this day and age when teams lose quarterbacks weekly, it is nothing short of remarkable.

"We know we could be one hit away from our second-string quarterback, there's no question about that," Lewis said. "He is durable. He's a big, strong man and hopefully, we can keep him in there."

If he is not, the Packers' season could be a big disappointment, but the fact remains Favre's presence in the lineup each week is pivotal to the Packers' quest for the Super Bowl.

"I don't think they can get there without him," NBC's NFL analyst and former Super Bowl MVP Phil Simms said. "You're talking about one of the best players in the league. There's no way you can replace a Brett Favre."

While the Packers look to fine-tune Favre and keep him healthy, they are hoping for more dramatic improvements in the running game.

Despite the fact Bennett rushed for 1,067 yards, the Packers still finished with their lowest rushing numbers in Holmgren's tenure. Green Bay finished 26th in the league in rushing, averaging 89.3 yards per game. Bennett averaged only 3.4 yards per attempt.

Holmgren, though, believes the Packers can make some significant improvements in the running game with the group already on hand.

"Another year of putting Edgar at halfback, that in itself, we should get better doing certain things," he said. "We, as coaches, have to come up with an improvement in our schemes, also.

"I would like a little more balance (offensively) and I would like our yards per carry to improve."

The Packers believe the running game can improve if Bennett can stay healthy, something that has not happened the past two seasons. The coaching staff would also like to improve the ground game by adding some speed.

That speed could come in the form of rookie draft pick Chris Darkins or second-year back Travis Jervey, who has been timed at 4.31 seconds in the 40-yard dash.

Ideally, the Packers would like to use Jervey as a complementary back for Bennett, much the same way Philadelphia uses Ricky Watters and Charlie Garner as a backfield tandem.

"He has all the speed and all the moves," running backs coach Harry Sydney said. "He could be that X factor. I think he's ready to step into a role where he's ready to push Edgar.

"That hole is only open for so long and if you have a 4.3 guy, boom, he's in the secondary with the threat of going all the way. Opposed to a 4.5 guy who's in there, (the defense) can react to him."

Getting more out of the running game would also take some pressure off Favre. As superb as Favre was in 1995, the Packers essentially fared as he fared.

When he was on – which was often – the Packers won. When he struggled, even in the slightest of fashions, the team struggled.

That is what happened in the championship loss to the Cowboys.

But the Packers are confident the seeds for success were planted in 1995. They believe they have a young nucleus of players who have continued to improve each year as they grow more comfortable with the offensive and defensive systems.

Players such as Favre, Brooks, Chmura, Bennett, Evans and

Newsome – their continued improvement will be the determining factor in how far the Packers go in 1996.

The Packers have placed their faith in the players already on board. That is why they did not plunge head-first into free agency and that is what allowed them to build for the future in the draft.

Brett Favre enters the 1996 season with the strongest supporting cast of his five-year Packers career.

"I like the group we have here," Holmgren said. "We can get a great team out of this group right here."

Wolf took things one step further.

"There are certain players here that have to become accountable," he said. "For instance, last year Robert Brooks became accountable. Edgar Bennett became accountable. Wayne Simmons became accountable.

"We need some more young players to step up and get us to that level."

Another key factor in 1996 is maintaining the team chemistry that was so abundant in 1995. As the season went along, there was an undeniable feeling among the team that their sense of closeness was a tangible feeling that was aiding them each week on the field.

Maintaining chemistry can be difficult in this era of free agency. Players come and go with alarming regularity.

But Chmura said the key is to keep the core players around as long as possible and then bring in players who will adapt to the team-first concept.

"I think it's something new guys really pick up on their own," he said.

"We're not making it a point to be unselfish; that's just the kind of guys we are.

"I think once they come in and see that, they either have to conform or they won't be here."

Holmgren, for one, said he will continue to stress team unity as a rallying point in 1996.

"The big challenge right now until the end of (the '96) season is to maintain the same type of attitude we had last year," he said. "Skill level and all that will come because the coaches will coach that.

"I thought we had tremendous team attitude last year and that has to be maintained."

One way of doing that is to keep the core players happy and under contract. As far as Green Bay's core players are concerned, the front office has done a good job of keeping as many of them around as possible.

On tap for 1996

Green Bay Packers records and landmarks that are within reach during the 1996 season:

➤With 118 points, Chris Jacke would surpass Don Hutson (823 points) as the team's all-time leader. He could also pass Paul Hornung (760) this season.

➤Brett Favre needs four 300-yard passing efforts to break the career record of 15 set by Don Majkowski.

➤Robert Brooks needs to open with two 100-yard receiving games to set a team mark with five straight.

➤The Packers can make the playoffs four years in a row for the first time.

➤The season finale against Minnesota at Lambeau Field will be the Packers' 1,000th game. Their record entering the season is 514-434-36.

There have been some free-agent losses – Tony Bennett, Jackie Harris and Bryce Paup come to mind. But Wolf has worked hard to make certain that several key figures have been signed to long-term contracts.

Favre and Butler were locked up two years ago. Brooks, Bennett and linebacker George Koonce were taken care of last year. Chmura and Morgan were re-signed to multi-year deals this past off-season. Keith Jackson rejoined the fold just before training camp.

"That's very important," Brooks said. "We kind of established something (last season) that no other team here had and that's the kind of a team unity where we're all for one common goal.

"I think it's good to keep all those players who were here last year and that feeling together."

The next task for the Packers is to reach the Super Bowl. They know it and are not shying away from the challenge of making a run at it this season.

"Our objective (for the '96 season) is nothing less than the Super Bowl," offensive coordinator Sherm Lewis said. "We expect to get to the next level. We want them (to think about that), that we've got to get to the next level, and that's the Super Bowl."

It is a message the players have taken to heart.

"We're going to try to go all the way," offensive tackle Earl Dotson said. "I know if we don't, I'll be disappointed.

"We can't have the letdown we had last year. Hopefully, it's our year. If everything works out right, we're going to be there."

The Packers have made great strides since Wolf and Holmgren took over in 1992. The one step that remains, however, is the Super Bowl.

If they are able to take that giant step, the return to glory will truly be complete. ◈

Brett is back!

The quarterback returns from a treatment center
with a new wife, a fresh outlook and a promise:
'I'm going to win a Super Bowl.'

It was the message the Packers desperately wanted to convey – and the message Packers fans desperately wanted to hear: Brett Favre is back!

"I'm going to beat this thing," he said. "I'm going to win a Super Bowl."

A confident, positive Favre discussed his treatment for painkiller dependency July 17 at the best-attended press conference in team history. Nearly 100 media representatives, including reporters from ESPN, CNN and 12 other TV outlets, packed the team's media room for a 45-minute session with coach Mike Holmgren and the league's Most Valuable Player.

"All I can tell people is, if they don't believe me, bet against me," Favre told the largely partisan gathering. "Because eventually, they'll lose."

Favre opened the event by presenting four charities with checks totaling more than $75,000 and also told of his marriage, three days earlier, to long-time girlfriend Deanna Tynes. (Strength coach Kent Johnston and his wife, Pam, were attendants. Favre's and Tynes' mothers and the couple's daughter, Brittany, were the others in attendance). The event's celebratory nature was in dramatic contrast to his last public appearance two months earlier, when he gave a brief statement regarding his dependency to perhaps 20 reporters and left the makeshift podium with tears in his eyes.

In between the briefings: 46 days of treatment at Menninger Clinic in Topeka, Kan., an NFL-sanctioned drug and alcohol rehabilitation center.

"It was tough. It was kind of like being in college again, except you couldn't leave the campus," said Favre. "It was a good time to concentrate on what I had to do, and that was get well and get in good shape for this season. I'm in the best shape ever ... but it was a long six weeks."

The 26-year-old said he left the clinic with an improved grasp of addictions, no outstanding dependencies, and a renewed commitment to family.

On addiction: "When I was growing up, I thought an alcoholic was a bum on the street. That's totally the opposite. It doesn't make you a bad person to be addicted to anything. That, you can't control."

On his dependency: Favre said doctors told him he no longer has a dependency on Vicodin or any pain medication. Favre said his dependency had no relationship to alcohol. "I just don't want this to ever happen again. Whatever it takes for me to control this, that's what I'll do."

On wife Deanna: "She's a great woman. We have a beautiful daughter. She's been my better half. She's stood by me through all of this."

Favre said it was difficult to publicly confront the problem, but said he realizes he's fortunate it didn't continue any further.

"(Addiction) leads to rock bottom, death, losing your family, losing your job, everything you've worked hard for," he said. "Thankfully, I didn't lose those things. I was able to catch it, and be smart enough to take care of it."

Favre said he and teammates Frank Winters and Mark Chmura will substitute soda for their post-game beer; he will substitute non-narcotic, non-addictive medication if he is injured; and he will continue to visit with a therapist, though it is not required by his treatment agreement.

"I think we should all see a therapist every once in awhile," Favre said, drawing a laugh from the crowd. The trademark humor that has endeared Favre to teammates and fans was evident throughout the event. Included:

● On the clinic's pledge he'd be treated as a regular person, not the NFL MVP: "I go in there for lunch, and 10 people are asking for autographs."

● On marrying just before training camp, without time for a honeymoon: "We've been honeymooning for 12 years now."

● On opposing fans: "I kind of expect pill bottles, whiskey bottles and beer cans to be thrown at me. That's what makes (pro football) great – to beat those teams in a hostile environment."

Favre said the addiction and his treatment have helped him grow up.

"Heck, I have to remind myself, I'm 26 years old," he said. "A lot of great things have happened to me ... I've had a tough time dealing with them. My ways of dealing with things are not always the right way.

"Everyone has gone through that stage when they realize some of the things they used to do are not as fun as they used to be."

Favre said his treatment will make him better at home, better with his friends – and ultimately better on the football field.

"I won't allow myself to be defeated by this," Favre said. "My main focus is winning the Super Bowl. That's what I'm going to work on every day."

For Packers fans, there can't be any better news. ◈

Timeline

Tracing the return

Key dates over the past five years
as the Green Bay Packers
returned to prominence in the NFL

1991

Nov. 11 – Packers president Bob Harlan fires Tom Braatz, the team's chief of football operations for five years.

Nov. 27 – Harlan hires Ron Wolf and gives him full reign of the football side of the Packers organization with the titles of executive vice president and general manager.

Dec. 22 – The morning after a season-ending 27-7 win at Minnesota, Wolf fires coach Lindy Infante, who finishes his career at Green Bay with a 24-40 record.

1992

Jan. 11 – Wolf names San Francisco 49ers offensive coordinator Mike Holmgren the Packers' new head coach, the 11th in their history. "I don't know the timetable, but we'll turn it around," Holmgren said.

Jan. 12 – Two of Holmgren's coaching cohorts in San Francisco are offered jobs as his top two assistants. Ray Rhodes accepts the job as defensive coordinator, while Sherm Lewis takes over the offense. It marks the first time in the NFL that a team has two black assistant coaches.

April 26 – The first draft in the Wolf-Holmgren era includes first-rounder Terrell Buckley and second-rounder Mark D'Onofrio, both busts. Fortunes improve later in the draft with Robert Brooks, Edgar Bennett, and Mark Chmura.

Sept. 6 – Holmgren loses his first game, 23-20 to rookie coach Dennis Green and the Vikings on a field goal by Fuad Reveiz in overtime. Buckley is a holdout and doesn't sign his four-year, $6.8 million deal until Sept. 10.

Sept. 20 – Buckley returns a punt for a TD in his first pro game and Brett Favre replaces the injured Don Majkowski and throws the winning

TD pass, helping Holmgren win his first game, 24-23 over the Bengals.

Sept. 27 – Favre starts his first pro game and leads the Packers past the Steelers 17-3. He has started every game since.

Nov. 22 – Edgar Bennett rushes for 107 yards in his first pro start, a 17-3 win at Chicago.

Dec. 27 – Controlling their own destiny to make the playoffs, the Packers are whipped 27-7 at Minnesota to finish the season at 9-7.

1993

April 6 – The Packers shock the sports world by announcing that free agent defensive end Reggie White has signed a four-year, $17 million contract to play in the NFL's smallest city. The Packers also sign guard Harry Galbreath and nose tackle Bill Maas, making them one of the most active teams in the first year of NFL free agency.

Aug. 16 – Inside linebacker Johnny Holland is cleared to practice after having neck fusion surgery in the off-season. Holland would go on to lead the team in tackles with 134 before retiring after the season.

Sept. 5 – The Packers win their first season opener since 1990, a 36-6 whipping of the Rams in Milwaukee.

Sept. 12 – Inside linebacker Brian Noble's career comes to a close when he injures his knee in the fourth quarter against Philadelphia. In the final game of his career, he makes 13 tackles and recovers a fumble.

Oct. 10 – With a 1-3 record, Green Bay gains a key win and the franchise's 500th, 30-27 over Denver on Sunday night. The Packers bolt to a 30-7 halftime lead and Jackie Harris sets a team tight end record of 128 yards receiving, then the Packers hold on 30-27 as Reggie White saves the game with back-to-back sacks of John Elway.

Oct. 19 – Defensive end Sean Patterson injures his knee in practice and has surgery a week later, ending his promising career.

Oct. 24 – Sterling Sharpe ties a record set by Don Hutson with four TD receptions in a 37-14 win over Tampa Bay.

Oct. 27 – Linebacker Tony Bennett ends the contract holdout that cost him the first six games of the season. He is activated four days later and has a sack as the Packers beat the Bears 17-3 to improve to 4-3.

Dec. 26 – Green Bay whips the Raiders 28-0 at a frozen Lambeau Field as Darrell Thompson runs for 101 yards with a 60-yard TD gallop, qualifying the Packers for the playoffs for the first time in a non-strike season since 1972. The Packers also improve to 9-6, assuring their first back-to-back winning seasons since 1966-67.

1994

Jan. 2 – Sterling Sharpe catches his 109th pass of the season, a 7-yard slant pass from Brett Favre, to break his own record for receptions in a season (108 the previous year). He would finish with 112.

Jan. 8 – The Packers defeat Detroit 28-24 in the NFC wild card play-offs for their first post-season victory since 1968.

Jan. 16 – Dallas knocks visiting Green Bay out of the playoffs, 27-17.

March 26 – Former Packer linebacker Tony Bennett signs a four-year contract worth $11 million with the Indianapolis Colts.

March 31 – The Packers extend the contract of Ron Wolf as executive vice president/general manager for three additional years, through 1999.

May 20 – Linebacker Johnny Holland, a nine-year veteran and one of the Packers' team leaders and best defensive players, retires because of a herniated disk in his back.

June 10 – Safety LeRoy Butler signs a three-year contract extension, becoming the second-highest paid safety in the NFL.

June 22 – The Packers decline to match the four-year, $7.6 million offer sheet tight end Jackie Harris signed with Tampa Bay.

July 14 – Brett Favre signs a five-year, $19 million contract.

July 18 – The Don Hutson Center, the Packers' new $4.2 million indoor practice facility, is dedicated.

Aug. 25 – The Packers extend the contract of head coach Mike Holmgren for three additional years, through 1999.

Sept. 3 – Wide receiver Sterling Sharpe threatens to sit out the season opener against Minnesota due to a contract dispute. The dispute is resolved and Sharpe returns to the team without missing the game.

Oct. 12 – Team president Bob Harlan announces that, beginning with the 1995 season, the Packers will leave Milwaukee and play their entire home schedule at Lambeau Field in Green Bay.

Dec. 18 – The Packers end their 62-year stay in Milwaukee with a 21-17 win over Atlanta at County Stadium. Sharpe suffers a neck injury that would later be determined to be career threatening.

Dec. 24 – The Packers defeat Tampa Bay 34-19 to qualify for the play-offs for the second year in a row. Sharpe suffers his second straight neck injury. The game would be his last as a Packer. He scored four touchdowns.

Dec. 31 – The Packers hold Barry Sanders to minus-1 yard on 13 carries as Green Bay beats Detroit 16-12 in the first round of the playoffs.

1995

Jan. 8 – For the second straight year, the Packers lose at Dallas in the second round of the playoffs. This time, the Cowboys prevail 35-9.

Feb. 28 – Sharpe is released "with reluctance" after the team is told by doctors his neck injury will not allow him to play again.

March 10 – Linebacker Bryce Paup signs a three-year contract worth $7.6 million with the Buffalo Bills.

March 29 – The Packers trade a second-round draft pick in the '95 draft to the Miami Dolphins for All-Pro tight end Keith Jackson.

April 3 – Beleaguered cornerback Terrell Buckley is traded to the Dolphins for "past considerations."

May 8 – Running back Edgar Bennett signs a one-year tender offer of $714,000. Later in the season, he would sign a three-year contract extension worth a reported $3.9 million.

June 1 – Robert Brooks signs a three-year contract worth $3.9 million.

Dec. 13 – The Packers say defensive end Reggie White will miss the rest of the season due to a hamstring injury. One day later, White's hamstring is no longer causing him pain and he returns to practice.

Dec. 16 – With White playing sparingly, the Packers defeat the New Orleans Saints and clinch their third straight trip to the playoffs.

Dec. 24 – Pittsburgh wide receiver Yancey Thigpen drops the potential game-winning touchdown, enabling Green Bay to beat the Steelers 24-19 and clinch its first division title in 23 years.

Dec. 31 – Packers defeat Atlanta 37-20 in the first round of the playoffs, advancing to the second round for the third straight season.

1996

Jan. 1 – Quarterback Brett Favre is named the NFL's MVP. Favre is the first Packer so honored since Bart Starr won the award in 1966.

Jan. 6 – Packers win at San Francisco 27-17 to advance to the NFC Championship game for the first time in 28 years.

Jan. 14 – Packers come within 15 minutes of the Super Bowl, but lose 38-27 to Dallas in the NFC Championship game.

Feb. 16 – Mark Chmura signs a three-year, $4.8 million contract.

May 15 – Quarterback Brett Favre enters the NFL's substance abuse program because of an addiction to painkillers.

Game-by-Game

Scores and a highlight from every game
in the first four years of the
Ron Wolf-Mike Holmgren regime

1992

Vikings 23, Packers 20 (OT, Sept. 6)
Fuad Reveiz beats Green Bay, connecting on a 26-yard field goal in
overtime to help Minnesota win at Lambeau Field.

Buccaneers 31, Packers 3 (Sept. 13)
The Packers fall to 0-2 as Vinny Testaverde passes for 363 yards.

Packers 24, Bengals 23 (Sept. 20)
Terrell Buckley, playing his first game, returns a punt for a TD and
Brett Favre tosses a 35-yard TD pass to Kitrick Taylor late in the game.

Packers 17, Steelers 3 (Sept. 27)
Favre, starting his first NFL game, passes for two touchdowns – one a
76-yard bomb to Sharpe – as Green Bay stops Pittsburgh at home.

Falcons 24, Packers 10 (Oct. 4)
Andre Rison catches a pair of touchdown passes from Chris Miller.

Browns 17, Packers 6 (Oct. 18)
Green Bay's offense goes nowhere, managing only two field goals.

Bears 30, Packers 10 (Oct. 25)
Jim Harbaugh passes for 194 yards and helps Chicago gain 356 yards of
total offense in crushing the Packers at Lambeau Field.

Packers 27, Lions 13 (Nov. 1)
Vince Workman rushes for 101 yards and Favre throws for two TDs.

Giants 27, Packers 7 (Nov. 8)
Sharpe catches 11 passes for 160 yards, but the Giants score two
touchdowns in the fourth quarter to put the game away at the
Meadowlands.

Packers 27, Eagles 24 (Nov. 15)
Favre suffers an injured shoulder after being hit by Reggie White, but

stays in the game and passes for 275 yards and two touchdowns.

Packers 17, Bears 3 (Nov. 22)

Favre connects with Sharpe on a 49-yard TD and runs for another.

Packers 19, Buccaneers 14 (Nov. 29)

Jacke boots four field goals; Favre and Harris combine on a 19-yard TD.

Packers 38, Lions 10 (Dec. 6)

Favre completes 15 of 19 passes for 214 yards and three touchdowns.

Packers 16, Oilers 14 (Dec. 13)

Green Bay's defense forces four Houston turnovers and Jacke kicks three field goals to enable the Packers to win at the Astrodome.

Packers 28, Rams 13 (Dec. 20)

Favre and Sharpe connect for two TD passes and Buckley returns an interception 33 yards for a score.

Vikings 27, Packers 7 (Dec. 27)

Needing a win to clinch a playoff berth, the Packers get blasted in their season finale as Sean Salisbury passes for 292 yards and two TDs.

1993

Packers 36, Rams 6 (Sept. 5)

Edgar Bennett rushes for two touchdowns and Sterling Sharpe catches a pair of touchdown passes and accumulates 120 receiving yards.

Eagles 20, Packers 17 (Sept. 12)

Reggie White plays his first game against his former team, but comes up on the losing end as Randall Cunningham directs a late rally.

Vikings 15, Packers 13 (Sept. 26)

Terrell Buckley leaves his receiver alone in the secondary late in the game and Fuad Reveiz kicks his fifth field goal to win it for the Vikings.

Cowboys 36, Packers 14 (Oct. 3)

Troy Aikman passes for 317 yards and one touchdown as Dallas jumps out to a 29-14 lead after three quarters and coasts to the win at home.

Packers 30, Broncos 27 (Oct. 10)

Reggie White thrills the Lambeau Field crowd, coming up with back-to-back sacks late in the game to stop John Elway and preserve the win.

Packers 37, Buccaneers 14 (Oct. 24)

Sharpe catches four touchdown passes from Favre and Darrell Thompson rushes for 105 yards as Green Bay stomps Tampa Bay.

Packers 17, Bears 3 (Oct. 31)

Sharpe catches one touchdown pass and Thompson rushes for one as

Green Bay wins a defensive battle over the Bears at Lambeau Field.

Chiefs 23, Packers 16 (Monday Night, Nov. 8)

The Packers turn the ball over six times in losing at Kansas City.

Packers 19, Saints 17 (Nov. 14)

Favre and Sharpe hook up for a key reception late in the game, setting up a 36-yard field goal by Chris Jacke.

Packers 26, Lions 17 (Nov. 21)

Trailing 17-16 entering the fourth quarter, the Packers get a field goal by Jacke and a 2-yard TD run by Bennett to win in Milwaukee.

Packers 13, Buccaneers 10 (Nov. 28)

Green Bay struggles most of the game, but pulls out the win late in the fourth quarter when Favre and Sharpe hook up for a 2-yard TD pass.

Bears 30, Packers 17 (Dec. 5)

The Bears turn two Favre turnovers into TDs as Green Bay turns the ball over five times and loses despite outgaining Chicago 466-210.

Packers 20, Chargers 13 (Dec. 12)

Jacke boots two field goals, including a 51-yarder, as the Packers play an efficient brand of football in dispatching San Diego.

Vikings 21, Packers 17 (Dec. 19)

Jim McMahon tosses three touchdown passes – two to Cris Carter – and unknown back Scottie Graham rushes for 139 yards.

Packers 28, Raiders 0 (Dec. 25)

With the wind-chill at minus-22 degrees, the Packers blank the Raiders to clinch a playoff berth for the first time since 1982.

Lions 30, Packers 20 (Jan. 2)

Eric Lynch, subbing for an injured Barry Sanders, runs through Green Bay's defense for 115 yards and two touchdowns at the Silverdome.

PLAYOFFS

Packers 28, Lions 24 (Jan. 8)

George Teague returns an INT 101 yards and Sharpe catches a 40-yard TD in the closing seconds as Green Bay wins first playoff game since '83.

Cowboys 27, Packers 17 (Jan. 16)

Dallas takes advantage of some costly Green Bay turnovers and Troy Aikman passes for 302 yards and three touchdowns.

1994

Packers 16, Vikings 10 (Sept. 4)

One day after threatening to skip the season opener over a contract dispute, Sterling Sharpe catches seven passes, including a touchdown.

Dolphins 24, Packers 14 (Sept. 11)

Dan Marino passes for two touchdowns as Miami builds a 24-0 lead through three quarters and coasts to the win at Milwaukee.

Eagles 13, Packers 7 (Sept. 18)

The Packers force a Randall Cunningham fumble in the closing minutes, but fail to score deep in Eagles territory in losing on the road.

Packers 30, Buccaneers 3

Favre passes for 306 yards and three touchdowns to three different receivers – Bennett, Sharpe and tight end Ed West.

Patriots 17, Packers 16 (Oct. 2)

The Packers botch an extra-point attempt and a kickoff late in the game as New England rallies behind quarterback Drew Bledsoe.

Packers 24, Rams 17 (Oct. 9)

Robert Brooks returns a punt 85 yards for a touchdown as Green Bay overcomes a 17-3 halftime deficit to win at home.

Vikings 13, Packers 10 OT (Oct. 20)

Favre is injured early in the game and backup Mark Brunell commits a costly turnover late as the Packers lose again in Minnesota.

Packers 33, Bears 6 (Monday night, Oct. 31)

Bennett rushes for 105 yards in the wind, rain and slush at Soldier Field and Favre scores on a 36-yard scamper as Green Bay rolls.

Packers 38, Lions 30 (Nov. 6)

Favre passes for three TDs in the first three quarters and Green Bay holds off a spirited Detroit rally, led by Wisconsin native Dave Krieg.

Packers 17, Jets 10 (Nov. 13)

Favre passes for two TDs and Green Bay's defense steps up in the closing seconds to thwart Boomer Esiason and the Jets to win at home.

Bills 29, Packers 20 (Nov. 20)

Jim Kelly tears up Green Bay's defense for 365 yards and two TDs.

Cowboys 42, Packers 31 (Nov. 24)

Third-string quarterback Jason Garrett has the game of his life, passing for 311 yards and two touchdowns as the Packers lose at Dallas.

Lions 34, Packers 31 (Dec. 4)

Barry Sanders gallops for 188 yards and Herman Moore terrorizes Terrell Buckley as Detroit wins a slugfest in the Silverdome.

Packers 40, Bears 3 (Dec. 11)

Bennett rushes for 106 yards and Favre passes for three touchdowns.

Packers 21, Falcons 17 (Dec. 18)

The Packers keep their playoff hopes alive in the final game ever in Milwaukee as Favre scores the game-winning TD on a 9-yard run.

Packers 34, Buccaneers 19 (Dec. 24)

In his final game as a Packer, Sharpe catches nine passes for 132 yards and three touchdowns before leaving with a neck injury.

PLAYOFFS

Packers 16, Lions 12 (Dec. 31)

The Packers hold Barry Sanders to a stunning minus-1 yard rushing on 13 carries to remain perfect (8-0) in playoff games at Lambeau Field.

Cowboys 35, Packers 9 (Jan. 8)

Troy Aikman and Alvin Harper light up Buckley for a 94-yard touchdown pass as Dallas steamrolls Green Bay at Texas Stadium.

1995

Rams 17, Packers 14 (Sept. 3)

Green Bay's offense struggles, turning the ball over three times, allowing four sacks and committing nine penalties in losing the season opener.

Packers 27, Bears 24 (Monday Night, Sept. 11)

Brett Favre and Robert Brooks hook up for an NFL record-tying 99-yard TD pass to highlight Green Bay's thrilling win at Soldier Field.

Packers 14, Giants 6 (Sept. 17)

Favre throws touchdown passes of 11 yards to Mark Ingram and 19 yards to Brooks to stake Green Bay to a 14-3 halftime lead.

Packers 24, Jaguars 14 (Sept. 24)

Favre ties an NFL record held by Johnny Unitas and Don Meredith for consecutive games (12) with at least two touchdown passes.

Cowboys 34, Packers 24 (Oct. 8)

Troy Aikman, doubtful because of a sore right calf, starts and completes 24 of 31 passes for 316 yards and two touchdowns to lift Dallas to its fifth straight win over Green Bay.

Packers 30, Lions 21 (Oct. 15)

Three days after signing a contract extension, running back Edgar Bennett finishes with 148 all-purpose yards and one touchdown.

Packers 38, Vikings 21 (Oct. 22)

The Packers force four turnovers, scoring on one when Sean Jones recovers a fumble in the end zone, and tight end Mark Chmura catches five passes for 101 yards and a touchdown as Green Bay wins at home.

Lions 24, Packers 16 (Oct. 29)

The Packers turn the ball over four times and Detroit's Herman Moore (three TDs) and Barry Sanders (167 yards rushing) have big days.

Vikings 27, Packers 24 (Nov. 5)

Favre and backup Ty Detmer both leave the game with injuries and third-stringer T.J. Rubley throws a costly interception, enabling Minnesota to win at home on a Fuad Reveiz field goal as time expired.

Packers 35, Bears 28 (Nov. 12)

Favre and defensive end Reggie White both overcome serious injuries to play and Favre throws five touchdown passes.

Packers 31, Browns 20 (Nov. 19)

The Packers take a one-game lead in the NFC Central, whipping the Browns as Favre throws three touchdown passes in the first half.

Packers 35, Bucs 13 (Nov. 26)

Bennett totals 145 all-purpose yards and Green Bay's defense holds Tampa Bay running back Errict Rhett to 13 yards on 14 carries.

Packers 24, Bengals 10 (Dec. 3)

Chmura catches a career-high seven passes for 109 yards and a TD.

Bucs 13, Packers 10 OT (Dec. 10)

With injured Reggie White on the sidelines, Green Bay falls after Chris Jacke missed a 45-yard field goal with 5 seconds left in regulation.

Packers 34, Saints 23 (Dec. 16)

Favre passes for 308 yards and four TDs as Green Bay clinches its third straight playoff berth.

Packers 24, Steelers 19 (Dec. 24)

Green Bay claims its first division title in 23 years when Pittsburgh receiver Yancey Thigpen drops a touchdown pass in the final seconds.

PLAYOFFS
Packers 37, Falcons 20 (Dec. 31)

Rookie Antonio Freeman returns a punt 76 yards for a touchdown to help Green Bay take a 27-10 halftime lead and roll over Atlanta.

Packers 27, 49ers 17 (Jan. 6)

Rookie cornerback Craig Newsome returns a fumble 31 yards for a touchdown on San Francisco's first play from scrimmage and Favre completes 21 of 28 passes for 299 yards and two touchdowns.

Cowboys 38, Packers 27 (Jan. 14)

Green Bay takes a 27-24 lead into the fourth quarter, but the Cowboys pull away on two Emmitt Smith touchdown runs.

Return to Glory

Writing history

Co-author had a feeling that
the 1995 Green Bay Packers
were a special team

It is a common response and one I hear whenever I tell someone what I do for a living.

"You cover the Packers? That must be such a great job."

My response is usually to tell them the truth. "It has its days."

In 1995, there were many more than I could have ever expected.

I recall the first day of training camp when the team embarked upon the season with the first of its grueling two-a-day practices. I remember thinking that this was a team full of question marks.

Of course, I was hardly the only media member who thought that. Without Sterling Sharpe – and to a lesser extent, at least in my opinion, Bryce Paup – many wondered what would become of the Packers in 1995.

But as training camp progressed, I began to have a feeling that something was different about this team. I certainly did not envision the season that transpired, but I honestly believed the Packers would not be left for dead, as so many others predicted.

As the season progressed, I found myself truly enjoying it. Not that I hadn't enjoyed my job in the past, but I had to admit there was something different in 1995. And most of these feelings had to do with the team.

I am not about to kid you. Covering a professional sports team is hardly a bed of roses. Many athletes look at the media as the enemy, people who simply want to start controversy whenever and wherever they can find it.

I have had a few such disagreements with players in the past and during the '95 season. But even those moments could not detract from the fact that there was something different, something special about this team. And I was interested to see what would ultimately transpire.

From top to bottom, this team was filled with interesting personalities.

Let's start at the top. I have always found General Manager Ron Wolf to be up-front, honest to a fault and a straight shooter, qualities that completely endear him to someone in my profession.

Coach Mike Holmgren is a bit more evasive , but I have had the opportunity to sit down one-on-one with Holmgren and found him to be engaging, witty and a man thoroughly in love with his job.

As far as the players were concerned, in 1995, they were a very tight group. Without Sharpe around, the decibel level in the locker room was turned down a notch or two, but it was still lively.

On most days, it would not be difficult to spot LeRoy Butler or John Jurkovic holding court. Like any reporter, there were players I enjoyed talking to more than others. Butler, Anthony Morgan, Ty Detmer, Edgar Bennett, Mark Chmura and Keith Jackson were among those I found interesting both on and off the field.

Of course, it certainly is more enjoyable to cover a team that is winning. And in '95, the Packers certainly were winning.

As the team continued its quest for the Super Bowl, the intense devotion that surrounded the team was stronger than ever. And considering how devoted Packer fans are to their team, that is really saying something.

The players were convinced there was something special about their team. Now the fans were convinced as well.

I remember sitting in the press box in Texas Stadium when the Packers played the Cowboys in the NFC Championship game. I remember when the game entered the fourth quarter, a thought crept into my mind. One that had never been there in all my years covering this team.

"The Packers may be going to the Super Bowl."

They were that close. Everything they had insisted upon all season long was very close to actually coming true. It did not occur, of course.

But the Packers' loss to the Cowboys could not diminish what they had accomplished. They beat all the odds and put together one of the most enjoyable seasons in team history. In 1995, the Packers came of age. It was a season the Packers and their loyal legion of fans will not soon forget.

Nor will I. ❧

Tom Kessenich
Oshkosh Wis.
July 15, 1996

Bios

Four years, 140 players

A player-by-player list of
those who have played a game in the
Ron Wolf-Mike Holmgren era

LESTER ARCHAMBEAU
POS: DE, **HT:** 6-5, **WT:** 275, **COLLEGE:** Stanford, **ACQ:** 7th round, 1990
Archambeau played three seasons with Green Bay, accumulating 20 tackles in each of the final two years before leaving for Atlanta in 1993. He registered 4½ sacks in 1991 and one in '92.

MIKE ARTHUR
POS: C, **HT:** 6-3, **WT:** 280, **COLLEGE:** Texas A&M, **ACQ:** Trade, 1995
Acquired in a trade with New England to back up Frank Winters, Arthur never played a down on offense, appearing in 11 games on special teams.

SEBASTIAN BARRIE
POS: DE, **HT:** 6-2½, **WT:** 280, **COLLEGE:** Liberty, **ACQ:** FA, 1992
Barrie played in three games during 1992, his only season with Green Bay. He was activated from the practice squad for games 8-10, but was placed on the injured reserve after a knee injury. Tallied three tackles (two solo), including a four-yard tackle-for-loss against Chicago.

MIKE BARTRUM
POS: TE, **HT:** 6-4½, **WT:** 243, **COLLEGE:** Marshall, **ACQ:** FA, 1995
Won the job as a reserve tight end and appeared in the team's first four games, along with being the long snapper on punts, but suffered a broken arm against Jacksonville in Week 5 and didn't play in another game. Didn't catch a pass in the 1995 season.

SANJAY BEACH

POS: WR, **HT:** 6-1, **WT:** 194, **COLLEGE:** Colorado State, **ACQ:** Plan B, 1992

Beach started 11 of 16 games in 1992 with the Packers. The ex-49er finished fifth on the squad with 17 receptions for 122 yards and one touchdown – a four-yard pass from Don Majkowski. It was Beach's first career scoring reception and his only TD with Green Bay. Beach was with Green Bay for three games in 1993 before being waived.

EDGAR BENNETT

POS: RB, **HT:** 6-0, **WT:** 216, **COLLEGE:** Florida State, **ACQ:** 4th round, 1992

With 1,067 yards rushing in '95, Bennett became Green Bay's first 1,000-yard runner since Terdell Middleton in 1978. Starting all 16 games in 1995, Bennett smashed Jim

Taylor's team record of 1,580 total yards from scrimmage in a season, accumulating 1,715. Bennett's 316 rushing attempts in 1995 broke Middleton's 1978 mark of 284. The ex-Seminole finished second on the club with 61 receptions for a career-best 648 yards and four touchdowns. Going into the 1996 season, Bennett is ninth on the Packers' all-time rushing list with 2,454 career yards. His 211 career catches place him 10th on Green Bay's all-time list. Bennett is the only running back in team history to have three 50-reception seasons. He's tied with Don Hutson, Bill Howton and Paul Coffman for third place all-time for the most 50-catch seasons. He hasn't fumbled in 684 rushing attempts, his last coming as a rookie in 1992 at Soldier Field.

TONY BENNETT

POS: LB, **HT:** 6-2, **WT:** 243, **COLLEGE:** Mississippi, **ACQ:** 1st round, 1990

The 1993 season was Bennett's last in Green Bay. After missing the first part of the season because of a contract holdout, Bennett played in 10 games, starting seven. He finished with 36 tackles that season to tie George Teague for ninth on the team. He was third on the team – behind Reggie White and Bryce Paup – with 6½ sacks. He racked up 13½ sacks in 1992 to pace Green Bay, good enough to tie him for sixth in the NFC. His personal best of 3½ sacks came in 1992 against the New York Giants. Bennett also returned a fumble recovery 18 yards for a touchdown in 1992. In 1991, he totaled 13 sacks to finish third

in the NFC. In his rookie season, Bennett amassed three sacks, the most by a Packer rookie linebacker since Tim Harris in 1986. Bennett started 39 of 56 games as a Packer. Bennett signed a free agent deal with Indianapolis following his stormy 1993 season.

LEWIS BILLUPS

POS: CB, **HT:** 5-11, **WT:** 185, **COLLEGE:** North Alabama, **ACQ:** Plan B, 1992

Billups started at left cornerback the first four games of the 1992 season and subbed at defensive back in the fifth game before being waived. Billups had 13 total tackles, along with one fumble recovery and two passes defensed.

DIRK BORGOGNONE

POS: K, **HT:** 6-2, **WT:** 221, **COLLEGE:** Pacific, **ACQ:** FA, 1995

Borgognone was signed as a deep kickoff specialist, appearing in games against the Giants and Jaguars before the Packers thought the better of using a roster spot for a backup kicker. After Borgognone was released, punter Craig Hentrich took over kickoff duties.

JEFF BRADY

POS: LB, **HT:** 6-1, **WT:** 238, **COLLEGE:** Kentucky, **ACQ:** Plan B, 1992

The current Minnesota Viking played eight games as a Packer in 1992, his only season in Green Bay. Spent seven games during the middle of the season on the IR with a knee injury. Recorded seven tackles and one pass defensed, as he played mostly on special teams and in the "nickel package." He finished fourth on the Packers with nine special teams tackles in 1992. Has played with six teams, including Pittsburgh as a rookie (1991).

MATT BROCK

POS: DE, **HT:** 6-5½, **WT:** 280, **COLLEGE:** Oregon, **ACQ:** 3rd round, 1989

Playing six years (1989-94) in Green Bay, Brock's best season came in 1990, when he totaled 59 tackles and four sacks. He also blocked an extra point in 1990. Brock paced all Packer defensive linemen in total tackles for three consecutive seasons (1990-92). His best game probably came in 1992 against Pittsburgh, when he registered two sacks and forced a fumble. In his final season – 1994 – Brock backed up Steve McMichael at defensive tackle. He spent the first 11 games of the '94 season on the inactive list, before recording two tackles in the final five games. He left Green Bay to sign a free agent contract with the New York Jets after the 1994 season.

ROBERT BROOKS

POS: WR, **HT:** 6-0, **WT:** 180, **COLLEGE:** South Carolina, **ACQ:** 3rd round, 1992

Brooks' breakout season came in 1995 when he established career highs for receptions

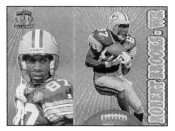

(102), receiving yards (1,497) and touchdown catches (13). He smashed Sterling Sharpe's team records in two categories – most yards receiving and most games with 100 or more yards pass receiving in a season (9). The Brett Favre to Brooks 99-yard scoring strike against the Bears in 1995 on Monday Night Football posted a new team record, and it was only the eighth time in league history the feat has been accomplished. His 13 TDs tied him for fourth in the conference and equalled the third-best season total in club history. Brooks scored at least one touchdown pass in nine games in 1995. He also became the fifth receiver in Packers history to post a 1,000-yard season. Brooks led the NFL in kickoff returns in 1993, as he averaged 26.6 yards on 23 attempts. The speedy receiver has chalked up two kickoff returns for touchdowns (95 yards in 1993 and 96 in 1994). He also ran a punt back 85 yards for a TD in 1994. Brooks became well-known nationally for jumping into the stands after touchdowns in 1995, at home as well as on the road.

GARY BROWN

POS: T, **HT:** 6-4, **WT:** 315, **COLLEGE:** Georgia Tech, **ACQ:** Waivers, 1994

Brown was claimed off waivers from Pittsburgh in 1994, spending all but two games on the Packers' inactive list and playing special teams in the other two. In 1995, he was inserted at left tackle at halftime of the season opener when Ken Ruettgers was hurt and Joe Sims was ineffective. Also played second half of a game a few weeks later at right tackle when Earl Dotson was injured.

GILBERT BROWN

POS: DT, **HT:** 6-2, **WT:** 325, **COLLEGE:** Kansas, **ACQ:** Waivers, 1993

Picked up off waivers from Minnesota, the former third-round draft pick played in only two games as a rookie but was impressive in tying up blocks and collapsing the pocket. Was Steve McMichael's replacement on passing downs in 1994, registering three sacks in the first 13 games when a knee injury ended his season. Also finished fourth among linemen with 30 tackles that season. Came back in 1995 and would have claimed a starting spot, but hurt an elbow and missed three weeks before regaining his starting spot in Week 9. Played in 13 games and finished with 23 tackles.

ROBERT BROWN

POS: DE, **HT:** 6-2, **WT:** 268, **COLLEGE:** Virginia Tech, **ACQ:** 4th round, 1982

Brown played 11 consistent, hard-working seasons for the Packers, plugging the middle for more than a decade. Started the final 108 games of his career and played in every non-strike game, 165 in all. He accumulated 25½ sacks in his career, although he was more noted as a run-stopper. Started all 16 games of his final season, compiling 37 tackles, one sack and a fumble recovery. Had four fumble recoveries in both 1985 and 1987. Had a career-high five sacks in 1984. The Packers released him after the 1992 season and he didn't catch on elsewhere.

MARK BRUNELL

POS: QB, **HT:** 6-1, **WT:** 208, **COLLEGE:** Washington, **ACQ:** 5th round, 1993

Wearing the green and gold for two seasons (1993-94), Brunell received his first taste of NFL action when he replaced Brett Favre in the second quarter after Favre suffered a badly bruised hip in a 1994 game at Minnesota. He scored his first NFL touchdown on a five-yard quarterback draw late in the second quarter. In the game, he completed 11 of 24 passes for 79 yards. He also saw action against the Bears in December 1994 when he completed one of three passes for 16 yards. He spent the entire 1993 season as the No. 3 quarterback. In 1994, he was named the second-string QB over Ty Detmer for 11 of the 16 games.

Prior to the 1995 season, Brunell was traded to Jacksonville for a 4th-round draft choice.

TERRELL BUCKLEY

POS: CB, **HT:** 5-9, **WT:** 174, **COLLEGE:** Florida State, **ACQ:** 1st round, 1992

Buckley never equaled the hype he brought with him from Florida State. Though he didn't earn his four-year, $6.8 million contract, he did pay off to a certain extent in 1994 when he led the Packers in interceptions with a career-high of five, which tied him for fith in the NFC. The INT total equaled his total of his first two NFL seasons combined, a far cry from his goal of 20-plus he set early in his career. Buckley did lead the team in passes defensed in 1992 and 1994. He had a career-best 59 tackles in 1994, along with three forced fumbles. In his three seasons with the Packers (1992-94), he picked off 10 regular season passes to go with two in the playoffs. Speaking of the postseason, Buckley's interception in the end zone in Detroit was a huge key to the Packers 28-24 victory. The following week in Dallas, "T Buck" picked off Troy Aikman. In his NFL debut, Buckley returned a punt 58 yards for a touchdown to help lead the Pack to a 24-23 victory over Cincinnati, Coach Mike Holmgren's first win. Averaged 10 yards per punt return as a rookie, but fumbled seven times and was taken off the job. Traded to Miami prior to 1995 season. Started four games and had one INT for the Dolphins.

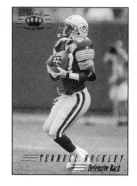

LEROY BUTLER

POS: S, **HT:** 6-0, **WT:** 200, **COLLEGE:** Florida State, **ACQ:** 2nd round, 1990

In 1995, Butler led the Packer defense with 102 total tackles. He was the first defensive back to lead the team in tackles since Mark Murphy in 1990 with 128. Butler's five interceptions in 1995 led the team. His career-best interception mark came in 1993 with six. His key play in 1995 came in the division-clinching victory over Pittsburgh on Christmas Eve day when he stopped Kordell Stewart for a one-yard loss on a third-and-goal play at the Packers five-yard-line with 16 seconds left in the game. Of course, this set up the fourth-down pass that fell incomplete through Yancey Thigpen's hands. Butler has started 76 of 92 regular season games for the Packers. Another career highlight came in 1993 against the Los Angeles Raiders in Lambeau Field when Reggie White scooped up a fumble and lateraled it to Butler who raced 25 yards for a touchdown. To celebrate the touchdown, Butler jumped into the stands, thus beginning the Packer tradition of celebrating with the fans. Through the 1995 season, Butler has amassed 432 total tackles.

JAMES CAMPEN

POS: C, **HT:** 6-2½, **WT:** 280, **COLLEGE:** Tulane, **ACQ:** Plan B, 1989

Spending five years in Green Bay (1989-93), Campen started 47 of 50 games, including 46 straight from 1990-93 before suffering a career-ending hamstring injury at Dallas in October of 1993. He was selected to the USA Today's All-Pro team in 1990. In 1989, Campen served as a third tight end in goal-line and short-yardage situations. In additon, he filled in as a backup defensive tackle against the Los Angeles Rams when injuries depleted that unit. He logged one solo tackle with a stop of Greg Bell, who ironically was traded to the Packers in the mid-1990s but failed his physical.

Return to Glory

CARL CARTER

POS: CB, **HT:** 5-11, **WT:** 190, **COLLEGE:** Texas Tech, **ACQ:** FA, 1992

Carter's only season in a green and gold uniform was 1992. Carter started one of seven games during the season. He subbed in five others and was inactive for one game. Carter recorded seven tackles from scrimmage and four special teams stops. His one start came at Houston when he played at right inside cornerback for the suspended LeRoy Butler. In the game he had six tackles and a forced fumble.

CHUCK CECIL

POS: S, **HT:** 6-0, **WT:** 190, **COLLEGE:** Arizona, **ACQ:** 4th round, 1988

Cecil spent five years (1988-92) in Green Bay and became known as a fierce hitter throughout the NFL. Had 13 INTs as a Packer, including four in 1992 to match his career high as a rookie. Best season might have been 1991, when he played injury-free for the first time, finishing fourth in tackles with 110 and setting a career-high with 13 passes defensed. Heavy hitting landed him on the All-Madden Team that year. Was second on team in tackles in 1992 with 102 and made the Pro Bowl, then signed a free agent contract with the Phoenix Cardinals in 1993.

MARK CHMURA

POS: TE, **HT:** 6-5, **WT:** 242, **COLLEGE:** Boston College, **ACQ:** 6th round, 1992

Chmura had the kind of season in 1995 that Ron Wolf and Mike Holmgren had waited for since they drafted him in 1992. He was voted to the Pro Bowl as a backup, after he posted a career-high 54 receptions for 679 yards and seven touchdowns. His catch total was two shy of Paul Coffman's single-season mark for most tight end receptions. Before last season, Chmura's career best was 14 catches in 1994. He caught his career-high seven passes against Cincinnati in 1995. Another highlight from 1995 came when he tallied the first 100-yard receiving game by a Packer tight end since 1993 (Jackie Harris). In 1994, he will be remembered for his two clutch catches of 25 and eight yards on the Packers' game-winning drive in a last-minute 21-17 win over Atlanta that kept the Packers alive for a playoff spot. Chmura also serves as the long snapper on punts.

SHANNON CLAVELLE

POS: DE, **HT:** 6-2, **WT:** 287, **COLLEGE:** Colorado, **ACQ:** FA, 1995

Clavelle was signed to the practice squad in Week 3 and brought up to the big club in Week 9 when Gabe Wilkins was injured, but was inactive the rest of the season except for Week 11 against Chicago when Reggie White was nursing an injury. Only appeared on special teams in that game.

VINNIE CLARK

POS: CB, **HT:** 6-0, **WT:** 204, **COLLEGE:** Ohio State, **ACQ:** 1st round, 1991
Clark never panned out as the 19th pick in the draft, intercepting two passes in each of his two seasons with Green Bay before being traded to Atlanta. Clark, who had 65 tackles in his two seasons, is a strong physical specimen who has played with three teams since the Packers and had five interceptions in 1994.

MARK CLAYTON

POS: WR, **HT:** 5-9, **WT:** 185, **COLLEGE:** Louisville, **ACQ:** FA, 1993
Clayton was brought in to be the starter opposite Sterling Sharpe in 1993. He caught 32 passes for 331 yards and three TDs to finish fourth on the team. His best game as a Packer came against the Bears in December when he caught a season-high six passes for 44 yards and one TD. He made a reception in 14 of 16 games in 1993, missing against the Eagles and the Raiders. A highlight of his 1993 season was a 28-yard reception during the Packers game-winning drive vs. Tampa Bay which put the ball at the Bucs' 17-yard-line. Clayton was not offered a contract for the 1994 season.

REGGIE COBB

POS: RB, **HT:** 6-0, **WT:** 215, **COLLEGE:** Tennessee, **ACQ:** UFA, 1994
Another attempt to find a quality running back that fell short. Cobb, who had one 1,000-yard season for Tampa Bay in four years, had a decent season for the Packers, finishing second on the team with 579 yards on 153 carries (3.8 average) and also catching 35 passes. Started 13 games. His long-gainer of the season was only 30 yards and he scored just four TDs, three rushing. He went to Jacksonville in the '95 expansion draft.

KEO COLEMAN

POS: LB, **HT:** 6-1, **WT:** 255, **COLLEGE:** Mississippi State, **ACQ:** FA, 1993
The Wisconsin Player of the Year while at Milwaukee Tech in 1987, he played in 12 games – two as a starter – with the Packers before suffering a broken ankle in the 1993 season finale. He ranked fifth on the team that year with nine special teams tackles. Coleman started the first game of his NFL career vs. Detroit on Nov. 21 at Milwaukee in

front of his hometown fans. He started the next game vs. Tampa Bay; it was the last start of his career. His highlight came when he recovered a Curtis Conway fumble on a third quarter kickoff at Chicago, which led to a Brett Favre touchdown pass to Mark Clayton.

BRETT COLLINS

POS: LB, **HT:** 6-1, **WT:** 234, **COLLEGE:** Washington, **ACQ:** 12th round, 1992

Collins played in 11 games as a rookie, making eight tackles, five on special teams. He survived four games into his second season before the Packers released him. Helped the Huskies share the national championship in 1991 with Miami.

SHAWN COLLINS

POS: WR, **HT:** 6-2, **WT:** 207, **COLLEGE:** Northern Ariz., **ACQ:** FA, 1993

Collins was with the Packers for seven games in 1993. He did not catch a pass.

KEITH CRAWFORD

POS: CB, **HT:** 6-2, **WT:** 198, **COLLEGE:** Howard Payne, **ACQ:** FA, 1994

Crawford was picked up by the Packers as a wide receiver in 1994, released, then signed again. Converted to a defensive back in 1995, playing in 13 games. Finished second on club with 13 special teams tackles. Missed three games with a sprained knee. Had a team-leading and career-high nine tackles against New Orleans, when he replaced Lenny McGill as the team's nickel back, and appeared in the secondary in three other games.

DON DAVEY

POS: DL, **HT:** 6-4, **WT:** 270, **COLLEGE:** Wisconsin, **ACQ:** D3, 1991

A local favorite from Manitowoc, Davey was the Badgers' MVP in 1990 and the first-ever four-time Academic All-American at Wisconsin. Played in all 16 games as a rookie, then was released for six weeks in the 1992 season before being re-signed. Forced a Herschel Walker fumble to set up the winning field goal in a Packer victory over Philadelphia on Nov. 15, 1992. Three weeks later, he forced a Barry Sanders fumble in a win over Detroit. Used as Reggie White's backup for nine games of 1993, registering two sacks. Played in all 16 games in 1994, starting two and finishing with 11 tackles and 1½ sacks. Got extensive playing time late in season when Gilbert Brown got hurt, and was impressive enough to be signed as an unrestricted free agent by expansion Jacksonville .

BURNELL DENT

POS: LB, **HT:** 6-1½, **WT:** 238, **COLLEGE:** Tulane, **ACQ:** 6th round, 1986

Played all seven seasons of his career with Green Bay, starting 11 games while making 166 tackles. Was waived in September of 1992, then picked back up four days later, and played the rest of the season. Wasn't offered a contract for 1993.

TY DETMER

POS: QB, **HT:** 6-0, **WT:** 194, **COLLEGE:** Brigham Young, **ACQ:** 9th round, 1992

The Heisman Trophy winner in 1990 is undersized by NFL quarterback standards, which is why he lasted until the ninth round in the 1992 draft. Proved himself an excellent backup in preseason and his brief regular-season appearances in 1993 and 1995. Signed with the Eagles as an unrestricted free agent,hoping for a starting role. Completed 3 of 5 passes in 1993 and went 8-for-16 with a TD and INT in his one game in 1995, when he replaced the injured Brett Favre and threw a TD pass to tie the game before tearing a ligament in his thumb in a loss to Minnesota.

MARK D'ONOFRIO

POS: LB, **HT:** 6-2, **WT:** 235, **COLLEGE:** Penn State, **ACQ:** 2nd round, 1992

A one-time star at Penn State, D'Onofrio never had much of a chance in the NFL. He made nine tackles in his first five pro quarters, then injured his hamstring so severely, he spent the rest of 1992 and all of 1993 on the physically unable to perform list. Long-time trainer Domenic Gentile called it the worst hamstring injury he'd ever seen.

MATTHEW DORSETT

POS: CB, **HT:** 5-11, **WT:** 187, **COLLEGE:** Southern, **ACQ:** FA, 1995

Played in 10 games as a rookie in 1995, mainly on special teams, and was inactive the other six games. Finished the season with 10 special teams tackles.

EARL DOTSON

POS: T, **HT:** 6-3½, **WT:** 310, **COLLEGE:** Texas A&I, **ACQ:** 3rd round, 1993

Dotson started all 16 games at right tackle in 1995. He made the highlight reels with his crunching block on Detroit's Robert Porcher on a Robert Brooks reverse in 1995. His first

NFL start came when he opened at right tackle vs. the St. Louis Rams in the 1995 opener. Played in 13 games as a rookie and four in 1994, all off the bench.

FOREY DUCKETT

POS: CB, **HT:** 6-3, **WT:** 196, **COLLEGE:** Nevada-Reno, **ACQ:** Waivers, 1994

Duckett was picked up for six weeks in 1994 when the Packers had injury problems in the secondary. He appeared in only three games, making one special teams tackle.

JAMIE DUKES

POS: C, **HT:** 6-1½, **WT:** 295, **COLLEGE:** Florida State, **ACQ:** Trade, 1994

Dukes added much-needed depth for the Packers, who wound up inserting the nine-year veteran into the starting lineup when Guy McIntyre had a blood clot, causing a chain reaction on the offensive line that led to Dukes starting at center for six games. He didn't play in the team's final eight games of 1994 and wasn't back in 1995.

DOUG EVANS

POS: CB, **HT:** 6-0, **WT:** 188, **COLLEGE:** La. Tech, **ACQ:** 6th round, 1993

Evans has started the last 31 of 32 regular season games at cornerback for the Packers. In 1995, he finished third on the team with 90 total tackles and led the team with a career-high 27 passes defensed, which was 12 more than his pevious career-best in 1994 and set a club record, surpassing LeRoy Butler's previous mark of 25 in 1993. In three years, Evans has three regular season interceptions. The best game of his career was in 1995 when he paced the team with nine tackles, two INTs and seven passes defensed against Minnesota.

BRETT FAVRE

POS: QB, **HT:** 6-2, **WT:** 220, **COLLEGE:** Southern Miss, **ACQ:** Trade, 1992

The NFL MVP in 1995 after throwing for 4,413 yards, second in Packer history to Lynn Dickey's 4,458, and 38 TDs, an NFC record and behind only Dan Marino's 48-and 44-TD seasons. Has been the Packers starter since replacing an injured Don Majkowski in the third week of 1992. Led the team to a 9-7 record that year and has started every game since. Stolen by Ron Wolf from Atlanta for a first-round draft choice in February of 1992.

Appeared in two games as a rookie for the Falcons, going 0-for-5 with two interceptions. Completed 64.1 percent of his passes in 1992 for 3,227 yards, 18 TDs and 13 INTs. Was erratic in 1994, completing 60.9 percent for 3,303 yards and 19 TDs but 24 INTs. Was the third QB taken in the 1991 draft, in the second round behind first-rounders Dan McGwire (2 career TD passes) and Todd Marinovich. Is the fourth-rated passer in NFL history (1,500 attempts minimum) at 86.8 behind Steve Young, Joe Montana and Dan Marino. Made the Pro Bowl in 1992, 1993 and 1995.

ANTONIO FREEMAN

POS: WR, **HT:** 6-0, **WT:** 187, **COLLEGE:** Virginia Tech, **ACQ:** 3rd round, 1995

Freeman was a pleasant surprise as a rookie in 1995, showing great escapability and starring as a return man. Finished fifth in the NFC with a kickoff return average of 23.2 and was 10th in punt returns at 7.9. Set a club record for punt returns as a rookie with 37. Used as the fourth receiver, finished with eight catches for 106 yards and one touchdown.

HARRY GALBREATH

POS: G, **HT:** 6-1, **WT:** 285, **COLLEGE:** Tennessee, **ACQ:** FA, 1993

A steady performer for the Packers, Galbreath started all 16 games at right guard in 1995 to increase his consecutive game streak to 48 with Green Bay. Galbreath was one of the reasons the Packers allowed an average of only 1.2 sacks per game over the final nine games of the 1994 season. His contract was not renewed after the 1995 season.

DAVID GRANT

POS: DE, **HT:** 6-4, **WT:** 275, **COLLEGE:** West Virginia, **ACQ:** FA, 1993

Grant was inactive the first two games of 1993, but did see action as a reserve the next seven games. He made three tackles vs. Chicago in October 1993.

CECIL GRAY

POS: T, **HT:** 6-4, **WT:** 292, **COLLEGE:** North Carolina, **ACQ:** FA, 1992

Drafted by Philadelphia in 1990 as a defensive lineman, Gray was converted to offense but was waived in 1992. Packers picked him up and he played special teams in two games.

RON HALLSTROM

POS: G, **HT:** 6-6, **WT:** 315, **COLLEGE:** Iowa, **ACQ:** 1st round, 1982

This dependable lineman played in every game after the strike of 1982 until the Packers released him before the 1993 season. Played every position on the offensive line during his career, but mainly at right guard. Was a backup to Karl Swanke in his second season, 1983. Took over for Syd Kitson as starter at right guard in fourth game of 1984. Had a contract holdout in 1990 and lost starting job for a few weeks. Played in 163 games for Packers; started 124. He played most of the 1993 season with Philadelphia, then retired.

RUFFIN HAMILTON

POS: LB, **HT:** 6-1, **WT:** 242, **COLLEGE:** Tulane, **ACQ:** Sixth round, 1994

Hamilton spent two stints on the active roster in 1994, coming off the practice squad to play in four games. He assisted on one special teams tackle and wasn't back with the team in 1995.

BERNARDO HARRIS

POS: LB, **HT:** 6-2, **WT:** 243, **COLLEGE:** North Carolina, **ACQ:** FA, 1995

A second-year free agent, Harris played in 11 of the team's final 12 games, mainly on special teams, after being inactive four games with a fractured arm suffered in preseason. Played significant minutes against Cleveland when Fred Strickland was injured, making two tackles. Made a season-high three tackles against Tampa Bay when he played middle linebacker with Joe Kelly moving outside for injured George Koonce. Had 11 tackles on special teams.

COREY HARRIS

POS: DB, **HT:** 5-11, **WT:** 195, **COLLEGE:** Vanderbilt, **ACQ:** Waivers, 1992

A third-round pick by the Oilers in 1992, he was waived in the middle of that season and picked up by the Packers. Tied for team lead in special teams tackles (14) in 10 games. Would have led the NFL in kickoff return average in 1993, but knee injury left him short of minimum number to qualify. Played WR and some RB in 1993, catching two passes. Moved to defense and served as the Packers' nickel back in 1994, starting twice, and had career-high 38 tackles. Went to Seattle as restricted free agent in 1995. Green Bay got a No. 3 pick as compensation.

JACKIE HARRIS

POS: TE, **HT:** 6-4, **WT:** 248, **COLLEGE:** NE Louisiana, **ACQ:** 4th round, 1990

One of the best athletes to ever play the tight end position for the Packers, Harris shared time with Ed West his first two seasons. Took over the starting job early in 1992, then had knee troubles that cost him four games in his final season with the Packers before he signed with Tampa Bay as a free agent in 1994. Holds the Green Bay record for yards receiving in a game by a tight end with 128 against Denver in key win in 1993. Played in all 16 games as a rookie, with 12 catches. Finished with 24 catches and three TDs in 1991. Had 55 catches in 1992, one shy of Paul Coffman's team tight end record, and two TDs, then had a career-high 604 yards and four TDs with 42 catches in 1993. Also had injury problems his first seasons with the Buccaneers.

TIM HAUCK

POS: S, **HT:** 5-11, **WT:** 187, **COLLEGE:** Montana, **ACQ:** Plan B, 1991

Hauck played four solid seasons in Green Bay as a reserve safety and special teams standout. Backed up LeRoy Butler, starting three games, and served as the team's sixth defensive back. Finished with 40 tackles for the 1994 season, 16 on special teams. Never intercepted a pass in a regular-season game. Signed with Denver as a free agent in 1995.

WILLIAM HENDERSON

POS: FB, **HT:** 6-1½, **WT:** 248, **COLLEGE:** North Carolina, **ACQ:** 3rd round, 1995

Henderson got off to a slow start because of knee surgery after an injury in practice, missing the entire preseason and the first regular season game, but came back and displayed his blocking ability late in the season and in the playoffs. Made first start in season finale against Pittsburgh. Rushed for 35 yards on seven carries for the season and caught three passes. Considered by the Packers the best blocking back available in the 1995 draft.

CRAIG HENTRICH

POS: P, **HT:** 6-3, **WT:** 200, **COLLEGE:** Notre Dame, **ACQ:** FA, 1993

After spending the entire 1993 season on the practice squad, which proved how much the Packers thought of his potential. He beat out Bryan Wagner in 1994 and has been one of the NFL's top punters the past two seasons. Averaged 41.4 yards per punt as a rookie and 42.2 in 1995, while setting the Packers' all-time record with 24 and 26 punts inside the 20. Also stepped in when Chris Jacke was injured and made a 49-yard field goal, going 3-for-5 overall and making all five of his PATs. Has handled kickoff duties.

JOHNNY HOLLAND

POS: LB, **HT:** 6-2½, **WT:** 235, **COLLEGE:** Texas A&M, **ACQ:** 2nd round, 1987

Holland returned in 1993 after having neck fusion surgery. He started all 16 games in 1993 at right inside linebacker. He led the club with a career-high 145 tackles, 24 more

than his previous best. It was Holland's sixth straight 100-tackle season. He also led the team in tackles in the playoffs and had two fumble recoveries in 1993. In 1992, he suffered the first of two neck injuries that cut his career short. Was NFC Defensive Player of the Week for his 15-tackle, two-INT game Sept. 20 against Cincinnati. Played in all 16 games of 1991, tying for NFL lead with four fumble recoveries, and started all 16 games of 1989 and 1990. Was Packers Rookie of the Year in 1987, finishing fourth on team with 72 tackles and also intercepting two passes. After the 1993 season it was discovered Holland had developed a second herniated disk in his neck and after consultation with the Packers medical staff, he decided he didn't want to go through surgery again and announced his retirement. Holland amassed 766 tackles, nine interceptions and 13 fumble recoveries during his career, spanning 1987-93. Holland was named to Mike Holmgren's staff as a defensive assistant/quality control in 1995.

CHARLES HOPE

POS: G, **HT:** 6-3, **WT:** 303, **COLLEGE:** Central State, **ACQ:** FA, 1993

Hope spent two different stints on the practice squad in 1993, then got into six games in 1994 for the Packers, mainly on special teams.

PAUL HUTCHINS

POS: T, **HT:** 6-4½, **WT:** 335, **COLLEGE:** Western Mich., **ACQ:** FA, 1993

Hutchins played in all 16 games in 1994 with two starts to go along with action in one game in 1993. In short-yardage situations, Hutchins lined up up as an extra lineman in the Packers' unbalanced line. His first NFL start came in the 1994 season opener against Minnesota. Hutchins spent 1995 on injured reserve and was released after the season.

TUNCH ILKIN

POS: T, **HT:** 6-3, **WT:** 272, **COLLEGE:** Indiana State, **ACQ:** UFA, 1993

Signed as a free agent after Tootie Robbins left via free agency, this 14-year veteran had injury troubles in training camp, then Robbins was cut by the Saints and returned to take back the starting job. Ilkin was waived after five weeks of the 1993 season, then re-signed when Robbins got hurt for the season. Ilkin played in one game when Ken Ruettgers was hurt for four plays.

DARRYL INGRAM

POS: TE, **HT:** 6-3, **WT:** 245, **COLLEGE:** California, **ACQ:** FA, 1992

Ingram caught the only TD pass of his career as a rookie with Minnesota in 1989. Picked up by Packers as third tight end in 1992, playing in all 16 games, but never caught a pass. Was released in 1993, then re-signed in Week 12 when Jackie Harris got hurt and played in two games. Released again, then re-signed again for final two games when Harris was injured again. Never caught a pass with the Packers.

MARK INGRAM

POS: WR, **HT:** 5-11, **WT:** 194, **COLLEGE:** Michigan State, **ACQ:** FA, 1995

After a pair of six-TD years in Miami, Ingram came to Green Bay with high expectations, but had a subpar season with 39 catches, 469 yards and three TDs. The Packers didn't re-sign him after the season. Shared duties with Anthony Morgan opposite Robert Brooks. Had season highs of six catches and 77 yards in his first game as a Packer, the opening loss to St. Louis. Played six seasons with the New York Giants after being a first-round draft pick in 1987.

CHRIS JACKE

POS: K, **HT:** 6-0, **WT:** 200, **COLLEGE:** Texas El-Paso, **ACQ:** 6th round, 1989

The Packers' third all-time leading scorer, Jacke was 117 points behind Don Hutson's 823 and 54 behind Paul Hornung's 760 entering the 1996 season. Is in the top 10 all-time in field goal accuracy. Entering the 1995 playoffs, had made 152 of 197 field goals. Holds team record of 16 field goals of 50 yards or more, and has made an incredible 16 of 25 attempts from 50 and beyond in his career.

JOHNNIE JACKSON

POS: S, **HT:** 6-1, **WT:** 204, **COLLEGE:** Houston, **ACQ:** FA, 1992

Picked up when the Packers needed a safety for one week in December, 1992, when LeRoy Butler was suspended for a hit on QB Andre Ware of Detroit. He played in one game, made no tackles and was released when Butler returned.

KEITH JACKSON

POS: TE, **HT:** 6-2, **WT:** 258, **COLLEGE:** Oklahoma, **ACQ:** Trade, 1995

The Packers used a second-round pick for Jackson, also getting back a fourth-rounder they had traded to Miami for Mark Ingram. Jackson decided he didn't want to play and was replaced by Mark Chmura, who went on to the Pro Bowl. Jackson changed his mind and reported to the Packers Oct. 20, appearing in the final nine games with only 13 catches and one TD. Stepped up in the playoffs and was a key cog in the Packers' offense, returning to the form that sent him to five Pro Bowls. Had four catches for 101 yards and a TD against San Francisco and added a 24-yard TD and a 54-yard reception against Dallas. Signed a two-year deal with Packers in summer of 1996.

TRAVIS JERVEY

POS: RB, **HT:** 5-11½, **WT:** 225, **COLLEGE:** The Citadel, **ACQ:** 5th round, 1995

Jervey was an immediate surprise, displaying 4.3 speed in his first mini-camp and earning a spot on the roster. Played in the wishbone in college, resulting in a transition period as he learned a pro-style offense. Made 13 special teams tackles as a rookie and returned eight kickoffs (20.6 avg.). Never rushed or caught a pass from scrimmage.

KESHON JOHNSON

POS: CB, **HT:** 5-10, **WT:** 185, **COLLEGE:** Arizona, **ACQ:** Waivers, 1994

The Packers claimed Johnson off waivers from Chicago in the middle of the 1994 season and he played in seven of the team's final eight games. Had an interception against the Bears six weeks after they released him. Also recovered a fumble later in the season.

LESHON JOHNSON

POS: RB, **HT:** 5-11, **WT:** 200, **COLLEGE:** Northern Illinois, **ACQ:** 3rd round, 1994

Johnson occasionally displayed his great speed, but wasn't elusive enough to be the running back the Packers hoped he could turn into. Rushed for 99 yards on 26 carries as a rookie, including 43 on one play. Also caught 13 passes, including a 33-yarder. Season ended with a knee injury before playoffs. Came back in seventh week of 1995 season, rushed the ball twice in two weeks, spent four weeks on inactive list and was released. Picked up by Arizona but didn't touch the ball in two games.

REGGIE JOHNSON

POS: TE, **HT:** 6-2, **WT:** 256, **COLLEGE:** Florida State, **ACQ:** FA, 1994

Johnson was cut by Denver after three solid seasons, and was grabbed by the Packers, playing in nine of the team's final 10 games. Caught seven passes for 79 yards. He signed with Philadelphia for the 1995 season.

SEAN JONES

POS: DE, **HT:** 6-7, **WT:** 283, **COLLEGE:** Northeastern, **ACQ:** UFA, 1994

One of the NFL's premier pass-rushers for 11 seasons, Jones signed with Green Bay to be a bookend with Reggie White. Jones had 10½ sacks in 1994 and nine more in 1995. Also led Packers linemen with 51 tackles in 1995. Picked up his play when White was injured and had at least one sack in four of final five games. Scored his first TD of 12-year career against the Vikings when he recovered a Warren Moon fumble in the end zone. One of eight NFL players with more than 100 sacks. Was left unprotected in the '95 expansion draft but wasn't selected. A stockbroker and financial analyst in the off-season.

CHARLES JORDAN

POS: WR, **HT:** 5-10, **WT:** 183, **COLLEGE:** Long Beach City, **ACQ:** Trade, 1994

The Packers traded a fifth-rounder to the Raiders to acquire Jordan. He didn't catch a pass in 1994, but returned five kickoffs and impressed the team with his athletic ability. Played in six games in 1995, missing the last seven weeks with a knee injury, but caught two TD passes and was fifth in NFC in punt return average (10.1). Miami signed him to a free-agent contract prior to the 1996 season.

JOHN JURKOVIC

POS: DT, **HT:** 6-2, **WT:** 295, **COLLEGE:** Eastern Illinois, **ACQ:** FA, 1991

One of the most personable and popular players to ever put on a Packers uniform, Jurkovic worked his way from "never heard of him" to "Jurko!" in his five seasons in Green Bay before he went to Jacksonville as a free agent prior to the 1996 campaign. Spent some time on the Miami practice squad in 1990, was signed by Green Bay as a free agent in 1991, then was waived on the final cutdown. Joined practice squad and was called up to the majors when Shawn Patterson suffered a knee injury. Won the nose tackle job from Esera Tuaolo in 1992 and started 12 games, making 34 tackles with two sacks. Lost job to unrestricted free agent Bill Maas in 1993, then got it back when Maas got hurt and started final 12 games, finishing with 54 tackles and 5½ sacks. Gave up his 92 jersey to Reggie White in 1993. Was also the primary starter at nose tackle in 1994, finishing with 50 tackles but no sacks, and started 14 games in 1995 when he had 36 tackles but again no sacks. Known for his sense of humor, particularly on the WIXX morning radio program in Green Bay. Also made dozens of appearances for local charities and was Packers' 1995 nominee for Byron "Whizzer" White Humanitarian Award. Played in final 71 games as a Packer.

JOE KELLY

POS: LB, **HT:** 6-2, **WT:** 235, **COLLEGE:** Washington, **ACQ:** FA, 1995

Signed as a free agent in August, Kelly played in 13 games and made 11 tackles. Also had an interception, picking off Trent Dilfer. Played the first eight games on special teams when he suffered a shoulder injury and spent next three weeks inactive. Started four games at middle linebacker when Fred Strickland was injured, including the game against the Buccaneers when he made five tackles, stuffing Errict Rhett at the goal line to force a field goal. Shored up wing position on punts after Packers had two blocked early in season.

GEORGE KOONCE

POS: LB, **HT:** 6-1, **WT:** 243, **COLLEGE:** East Carolina, **ACQ:** FA, 1992

One of Ron Wolf's finest free-agent acquisitions, Koonce was cut by Atlanta in 1991, then led the World League in tackles in 1992. Led the Packers in preseason tackles in 1992, earning a spot on the roster, and went on to start 10 games and make 55 tackles. Started 15 games in 1993, but got hurt in final regular-season game and missed both playoff games. Finished second on team in tackles with 125, including 18 in a game against Chicago, then lead team in tackles in 1994 with 119. Moved to an outside LB position and finished fifth on team with 74 tackles in 1995 and had his first interception. Has 6½ career sacks.

BOB KUBERSKI

POS: NT, **HT:** 6-4½, **WT:** 300, **COLLEGE:** Navy, **ACQ:** 7th round, 1993

Was impressive in a 1993 training camp, fulfilled his service to the Navy in 1993 and 1994, was reinstated to the Packers roster in April of 1995. Played in nine games on special teams and in short-yardage situations and was inactive other six games. Finished the season with 11 tackles and two sacks, the first against former Packer Mark Brunell and the second against Neil O'Donnell in regular season finale.

MATT LABOUNTY
POS: DE, **HT:** 6-3½, **WT:** 278, **COLLEGE:** Oregon, **ACQ:** Waivers, 1993

A capable player who showed some good pass-rushing skills in his two-plus seasons with the Packers, LaBounty was traded to Seattle for safety Eugene Robinson prior to the 1996 season. LaBounty has a solid season backing up Reggie White in 1995, making two starts when White was hurt. He finished the season with 11 tackles and three sacks. Sprained ligament in his knee slowed early-season progress and he missed the first two games. Spent first season (1992) on the 49ers practice squad, then was waived six games into the 1993 season. Was impressive in early 1994 for Packers but missed season with back problems.

DORSEY LEVENS
POS: FB, **HT:** 6-1, **WT:** 240, **COLLEGE:** Georgia Tech, **ACQ:** 5th round, 1994

Levens won the starting fullback job in 1995 and saw action in 15 games, with 13 starts. A versatile player, Levens rushed 36 times for 120 yards and three touchdowns to rank third on the team, while finishing fourth on the Packers with 48 receptions for 434 yards and four touchdowns. Throughout the 1995 season, Levens moved to halfback for many goal-line and short-yardage situations to make room for William Henderson, who came in at fullback. The highlight of Levens' career came in his rookie season when he scored Green Bay's only touchdown in a 16-12 wild-card playoff win over Detroit in Lambeau Field on New Year's Eve 1994.

RON LEWIS
POS: WR, **HT:** 5-11, **WT:** 192, **COLLEGE:** Florida State, **ACQ:** FA, 1992

Lewis played in eight games as a rookie third-round pick with San Francisco in 1990, but hurt his back and missed a season and a half. Was waived in Week 5 of 1992 by the Niners and came to Packers, where he started four of final six games and caught 13 passes. Was waived in 1993, then re-signed and played in nine games that year. Caught seven passes but retired after Week 8 of 1994 season because football wasn't fun anymore.

BILL MAAS

POS: NT, **HT:** 6-5, **WT:** 282, **COLLEGE:** Pittsburgh, **ACQ:** UFA, 1993

The Packers first-ever signee in the free agent era, Maas was brought in to shore up the defensive line after averaging six sacks a season for the Chiefs in a nine-year career. He started three of the first four games in the 1993 season, then injured his Achilles' tendon and lost his starting spot to John Jurkovic. Finished his only season with the Packers with 13 tackles.

DON MAJKOWSKI

POS: QB, **HT:** 6-3, **WT:** 208, **COLLEGE:** Virginia, **ACQ:** 10th round, 1987

The Majik Man led the Packers to a magic season in 1989, when he led the league in passing yards with 4,318, threw for 27 TDs (including that reviewable Bear-beater to

Sterling Sharpe) and also rushed for 358 yards and five TDs. His 4,318 yards for a season is third in Packers history. Brett Favre surpassed his record of six 300-yard games in a career when Favre reached seven last year. Majkowski's 27 TDs in a season is fourth in Packers history. Started five games as a rookie and nine games in his second season. Suffered through injury-plagued seasons in 1991 and 1992, when he got hurt in Week 3 and never regained his starting position from Favre. Wasn't offered a free-agent contract by the Packers and went to Indianapolis in 1993. Spent two years with the Colts, starting six games, and spent 1995 as

the backup to Scott Mitchell in Detroit, completing 15 of 20 passes with one TD for a rating of 114.8.

TONY MANDARICH

POS: OT, **HT:** 6-5, **WT:** 286, **COLLEGE:** Michigan State, **ACQ:** 1st round, 1989

Considered by some the best offensive line prospect ever, the former Michigan State star came to Green Bay with high expectations and left humbled. Didn't break into the starting lineup until his second season. Had a decent 1991 season but suffered through injuries and a thyroid problem that put him on the reserve/non-football illness list for all of 1992 and hasn't played a down since. Had an unsuccessful tryout with Miami in 1995. Rejoined former Packers coach Lindy Infante in Indianapolis at the start of the 1996 season.

DAVE MCCLOUGHAN

POS: CB, **HT:** 6-1, **WT:** 185, **COLLEGE:** Colorado, **ACQ:** Trade, 1992

McCloughan appeared in five games in 1992 for Green Bay before being injured and missing the rest of the season. He never made a tackle for the Packers. Acquired from Indianapolis for a sixth-round pick, he was sent to Seattle for a sixth-round pick before the 1993 draft.

BUFORD MCGEE

POS: FB, **HT:** 6-4, **WT:** 205, **COLLEGE:** Mississippi, **ACQ:** FA, 1992

McGee was signed as a free agent and made the starting lineup, starting in three games and appearing in another until Harry Sydney took the starting role. McGee was waived.

LENNY MCGILL

POS: CB, **HT:** 6-1½, **WT:** 198, **COLLEGE:** Arizona State, **ACQ:** FA, 1994

Returning from a 1994 knee injury, McGill played in 15 games during 1995, making one start. McGill's primary role was as the Packers' nickel back, along with serving as Craig Newsome's backup. He finished the 1995 season with 27 tackles and one pass defensed. His bright spot of 1994 came when he picked off a Chris Miller pass in the end zone with 54 seconds remaining to seal the Packers' 24-17 victory over the Rams. McGill, who had two INTs with Green Bay, was traded to Atlanta in June '96 for RB Robert Baldwin.

GUY MCINTYRE

POS: G, **HT:** 6-3, **WT:** 290, **COLLEGE:** Georgia, **ACQ:** FA, 1994

McIntyre was brought in from San Francisco to plug the left guard position. He was the opening day starter in 1994, his only season as a Packer. A blood clot in his leg caused him to miss six games, but he returned to start the season's remaining games. McIntyre was part of the line that was instrumental in leading the Packers to 223 rushing yards in a win over the Bears in 1994. Following the 1994 season, he signed with Philadelphia.

PAUL MCJULIEN

POS: P, **HT:** 6-1, **WT:** 210, **COLLEGE:** Jackson State, **ACQ:** FA, 1991

McJulien was the Packers punter for a season and a half. In 1992, he averaged 38.5 yards per kick with a 30.2 net average and had two punts blocked, then was replaced by Bryan Wagner in Week 10.

JIM MCMAHON

POS: QB, **HT:** 6-1, **WT:** 195, **COLLEGE:** Brigham Young, **ACQ:** FA, 1995

Does it still look strange, Jim McMahon in a Packers uniform? Actually, it's rather comforting. After the Packers suffered injury and ineptness problems at backup quarterback, they signed the former Bear to provide veteran leadership behind Brett Favre. McMahon was on the active roster the final four games of the season, appearing only briefly and completing his only pass against Pittsburgh. Was re-signed for the 1996 season to prevent any more T.J. Rubley-type episodes.

STEVE MCMICHAEL

POS: DT, **HT:** 6-2, **WT:** 262, **COLLEGE:** Texas, **ACQ:** FA, 1994

Signed as a free agent from rival Chicago, Mongo played in each of the 16 games in 1994, including 14 starts at defensive tackle. McMichael played in an amazing 207 consecutive non-strike games in the regular season plus 12 postseason contents. He finished his only season as a Packer with 28 tackles, 2½ sacks and one fumble recovery.

DEXTER MCNABB

POS: FB, **HT:** 6-1½, **WT:** 245, **COLLEGE:** Florida, **ACQ:** 5th round, 1992

A capable performer, McNabb could never beat out fellow 1992 draft pick Edgar Bennett for the fullback job and was waived in 1994. Finished third in special teams tackles in each of his two seasons with 13. Forced a Curtis Conway fumble in 1993 that was recovered by the Packers and led to a game-tying TD. Finished Packers career with two rushes for 11 yards and never caught a pass.

MIKE MERRIWEATHER

POS: LB, **HT:** 6-2, **WT:** 230, **COLLEGE:** Pacific, **ACQ:** FA, 1994

Merriweather was signed by the Packers as a free agent on Jan. 4, 1994, to provide depth at linebacker following season-ending injuries to George Koonce and Keo Coleman. Merriweather played six seasons with Pittsburgh, four with Minnesota and one game with the Jets in 1994, prior to his stint with the Packers.

TERRY MICKENS

POS: WR, **HT:** 6-0½, **WT:** 198, **COLLEGE:** Florida A&M, **ACQ:** 5th round, 1994

The backup wide receiver saw plenty of playing time on special teams in 1995. He was used in short-yardage and goal-line situations due to his blocking skills. He also received playing time in the four-WR set. He saw action in all 16 games in 1995, catching three passes for 50 yards. In 1994, he had four receptions for 31 yards in 12 games. Mickens fininished 1995 with 15 special teams tackles, third on the team.

KEITH MILLARD

POS: DE, **HT:** 6-5, **WT:** 262, **COLLEGE:** Washington State, **ACQ:** FA, 1992
A serious knee injury cut short his career with Minnesota, though he made comeback attempts with three other teams. His Packers visit lasted three weeks. He appeared in two games, making three tackles and recovering a fumble, before asking for his release on Oct. 23, 1992. He later signed with the Eagles but never played near his former level.

ROLAND MITCHELL

POS: CB, **HT:** 5-11, **WT:** 195, **COLLEGE:** Texas Tech, **ACQ:** Plan B, 1991
Mitchell was signed by the Packers after a nondescript career with three teams, including Buffalo as a rookie in 1987, and worked his way into the starting role until a serious neck injury ended his career in 1994. Played backup at cornerback and strong safety in 1991 and led the special teams with 15 tackles. Blitzed on game's final play to force Indianapolis QB Jeff George into incompletion in 14-10 win over Colts. Took over as starter, replacing Vinnie Clark, midway through 1992 season. Had 50 tackles and two INTs, both in same game against Tampa Bay, the second a game-saver with 1:44 left in Week 11. Injured ankle and missed last game. Started all 16 games in 1993 with career-high 62 tackles and one INT. Suffered herniated disk when blocked by Vikings' Chris Hinton in 1994 opener and eventually retired.

RICH MORAN

POS: G, **HT:** 6-3, **WT:** 280, **COLLEGE:** San Diego St., **ACQ:** 3rd round, 1985
Moran was the starting left guard for much of his eight-year career in Green Bay, which ended with a knee injury. Played all 16 games as a rookie, starting at left guard for final nine games when Keith Uecker injured a knee. Suffered a knee injury himself on first play of 1986 season and played final four games as a reserve. Came back to start all 12 non-strike games in 1987, then all 16 in 1988 and 1989 before a contract holdout in 1990 cost him his starting position, assumed by Billy Ard. Regained starting spot in 1991, playing all 16 games, then suffered knee injury midway through 1992. Came back in early part of 1993 season, reinjured the knee after starting three games and never played again.

ANTHONY MORGAN

POS: WR, **HT:** 6-1, **WT:** 200, **COLLEGE:** Tennessee, **ACQ:** Waivers, 1993

After Morgan played his first two seasons with Chicago, catching two TDs in each, the Bears waived him and the Packers said, "Thank you." Saw action in only two games in 1993 for Green Bay, but played in all 16 in 1994, catching 28 passes and four TDs, then became a part-time starter in 1995, finishing with 31 catches and four more TDs. Started the Anthony Morgan Foundation, which works with homeless people and abandoned children in Chicago.

JIM MORRISSEY

POS: LB, **HT:** 6-3, **WT:** 232, **COLLEGE:** Michigan State, **ACQ:** FA, 1993

The former Chicago Bear was signed in the middle of the 1993 season and appeared in six regular-season games, mainly on special teams. He had five special teams tackles.

JOE MOTT

POS: LB, **HT:** 6-4, **WT:** 238, **COLLEGE:** Iowa, **ACQ:** FA, 1993

The former New York Jet was signed in December of 1993 and played in two games, recording two tackles.

RODERICK MULLEN

POS: CB, **HT:** 6-1, **WT:** 204, **COLLEGE:** Grambling, **ACQ:** FA, 1995

Signed off the Giants' practice squad in October, Mullen played mainly on special teams in the Packers' final eight games. Made four tackles on defense and three on special teams. Appeared in three games in the secondary.

TOM NEVILLE

POS: G, **HT:** 6-5, **WT:** 288, **COLLEGE:** Fresno State, **ACQ:** FA, 1986, 1992

The Packers picked up Neville in 1986 and he took over a starting role when Rich Moran injured a knee, starting final 15 games. Played as a passing-down reserve in 1987, then was waived by Packers in second week of 1988. Had stints with Detroit, San Francisco and Kansas City before returning to the Packers in 1992 when James Campen was put on IR. Waived again but brought back when Moran was hurt, again. Hurt Achilles' tendon and spent all of final season with Packers, 1993, on IR.

CRAIG NEWSOME

POS: CB, **HT:** 5-11½, **WT:** 188, **COLLEGE:** Arizona State, **ACQ:** 1st round, 1995

Walked into a starting position and immediately produced. Started all 16 games and finished fourth on the team with 75 tackles. Set a rookie record with 19 passes defensed, although he had only one interception. Best day was in regular season finale against Pittsburgh when he set career highs with 11 tackles and five passes defensed. A much more physical player than the Packers' previous No. 1 pick at defensive back (Terrell Buckley), had a solid playoff season, including solid tackling on Jerry Rice that kept him out of the end zone in the win against the 49ers.

BRIAN NOBLE

POS: LB, **HT:** 6-4, **WT:** 245, **COLLEGE:** Arizona State, **ACQ:** 5th round, 1985

A run-stuffing linebacker the Packers never really replaced, Noble had a fine nine-year career with Green Bay come to a close when he injured his right knee in the second game

of 1993 against Philadelphia. Made 13 tackles in his final game. Took over as starter for George Cumby in his second career game, was named Packers' Rookie of the Year and made most all-rookie teams, finishing third on team with 104 tackles. Led team in tackles in 1986 (113), 1987 (89), 1989 (138) and 1991 (121). Missed first four games of 1988 with holdout but still was third in tackles (98). Was second in tackles in 1990 (113) despite missing 2½ games with knee injury. Had contract and injury problems in 1992, his worst season with just 66 tackles. Finished career with 842 tackles, 14 sacks, three INTs, nine fumble recoveries and six forced fumbles. Named Packers' 1989 Man of the Year for local community involvement and can still be seen on preseason broadcasts and other TV shows, including an outdoors show on WBAY in Green Bay. Also has an interest in Pro Image sport/clothing shops.

DANNY NOONAN

POS: NT, **HT:** 6-4, **WT:** 270, **COLLEGE:** Nebraska, **ACQ:** Waivers, 1992

Noonan was released by Dallas and played in six games as a reserve for Green Bay, which had just released Esera Tuaolo and was in search of a backup nose tackle. Noonan had five tackles as a Packer before being released in favor of Alfred Oglesby.

226

ALFRED OGLESBY

POS: NT, **HT:** 6-4, **WT:** 285, **COLLEGE:** Houston, **ACQ:** FA, 1992

The day after Danny Noonan was released, the Packers picked up Oglesby and inserted him as John Jurkovic's backup. He played in seven games with the Packers, making seven tackles.

MUHAMMAD OLIVER

POS: CB, **HT:** 5-11, **WT:** 185, **COLLEGE:** Oregon, **ACQ:** FA, 1993

Oliver was picked up two weeks into the 1993 season after he was released by Kansas City and appeared in two games for the Packers, making nine tackles. He was released after Week 8 and was picked up by Miami. Also played as a rookie with Denver in 1992, and Washington with in 1995.

SHAWN PATTERSON

POS: DE, **HT:** 6-5, **WT:** 270, **COLLEGE:** Arizona State, **ACQ:** 2nd round, 1988

Patterson's six-year career was riddled with injuries, capped by a career-ending knee injury in 1993. Arrived with a flash in 1988, tying for second on the team with five sacks while starting four games. Started the first six games of 1989 before tearing the ACL in his left knee. Knee was rehabbed in time for 1990, but he pulled a hamstring and missed first six games, but had four sacks in final 11 games. Played first 11 games of 1991, recording 1½ sacks before spraining his right knee. Tore the ACL of his right knee in first preseason game of 1992. Worked his way back, again, for 1993 season and played in first eight games before tearing ACL in left knee in practice and retiring.

BRYCE PAUP

POS: LB, **HT:** 6-5, **WT:** 247, **COLLEGE:** Northern Iowa, **ACQ:** 6th round, 1990

One of the finest draft choices Tom Braatz made for the Packers, Paup played in only five games his rookie year because of a hand injury, then burst on the scene in 1991 with 7½ sacks and three forced fumbles as the Packers' "rover" linebacker. Was NFC Co-Defensive Player of the Week because of 4½ sacks against Tampa Bay, sacked Dan Marino twice the following week, forcing one fumble. Started 10 games in 1992 and played in all 16, losing LOLB starting role to George Koonce. Played mainly as designated pass rusher and finished second on team behind Tony Bennett with 6½ sacks. Started at four different positions in 1993 and had 11 sacks, an INT and two forced fumbles. Had three sacks in a Monday night loss at Kansas City and had 14 tackles in playoff loss to Cowboys. Named a starter for Pro Bowl after 7½ sacks, three INTs and 79 tackles in 1994. Was NFC Defensive Player of the Month in November. Returned one of the INTs for a TD. Left for Buffalo via free agency after the season and was named 1995 NFL Defensive Player of the Year because of two INTs and league-leading 17½ sacks.

BRUCE PICKENS
POS: CB, **HT:** 5-11, **WT:** 190, **COLLEGE:** Nebraska, **ACQ:** FA, 1993

The enigmatic Pickens, a first-round flop for Atlanta in 1991, spent five weeks in Green Bay and played in two games. He assisted on one tackle and was released after Week 13 of the 1993 season.

MIKE PRIOR
POS: S, **HT:** 6-0, **WT:** 208, **COLLEGE:** Illinois State, **ACQ:** UFA, 1993

The Packers let strong safety Chuck Cecil go to Arizona after the 1992 season, then signed Prior, a move that has paid off. The ex-Colt started first four games at free safety in 1993 before giving way to first-rounder George Teague. Finished with 36 tackles and one INT and also returned 13 punts for 105 yards. Played less in 1994 but led special teams with 17 tackles. In 1995, played in all 16 games for third straight year and started twice, finishing with 53 tackles, a sack, an INT, a forced fumble and four passes defensed. Had team-high nine tackles when replacing injured Teague in game against Tampa Bay. Had a sack and forced a key Jeff Blake fumble against Cincinnati.

TOOTIE ROBBINS
POS: T, **HT:** 6-5, **WT:** 315, **COLLEGE:** East Carolina, **ACQ:** FA, 1992

The Packers signed this huge veteran to play right tackle in 1992, and he proved worthy as the team ran behind him often in his 15 starts in 1992. After signing with the Saints as a free agent prior to the 1993 season, he was released by New Orleans and re-signed with the Packers. After would-be starter Joe Sims got injured, Robbins started the first four games at right tackle but injured his hip and missed a couple games. He then started seven more games but tore a triceps muscle and had surgery in December, missing the rest of the 1993 season. He never played again, with Sims becoming the starter.

T.J. RUBLEY

POS: QB, **HT:** 6-3, **WT:** 212, **COLLEGE:** Tulsa, **ACQ:** FA, 1995

A name that will live in infamy in Packers' lore, Rubley played his first three seasons with the Rams before joining the Packers and winning the job as third QB. Was forced into action against Vikings in a key game, when Brett Favre and Ty Detmer were both injured. Completed 4 of 6 passes for 39 yards to move team into territory for the winning field goal, then called an audible (from a QB sneak to a pass) and threw an interception. The Vikings drove, scored and won the game, and five weeks later, Rubley was released.

KEN RUETTGERS

POS: T, **HT:** 6-6, **WT:** 290, **COLLEGE:** USC, **ACQ:** 1st round, 1985

The Packers' best offensive lineman for the past decade, Ruettgers entered 1996 as the

starter at left tackle every season since 1986, starting in all 92 games he has appeared in during that span. Played in all 16 games as a rookie, then gained starting nod in second season, shutting out Lawrence Taylor in the season finale to deprive him of a new single-season sack record. Missed a game in 1988, then started 37 straight until missing five in 1990 after arthroscopic knee surgery. Missed 12 games of 1991 with a hamstring injury, then started all 16 games for three years until missing the 1995 opener, a game in which the Packers missed him dearly . He started the final 15 games in 1995. Ruettgers is poised to become

the team's longest continuing starter at 12 years, surpassing Larry McCarren's 11. Wrote the book *Home Field Advantage*, a collaboration with more than 50 other NFL players encouraging men to be role models, and has long been an active participant in charitable work, particularly near his home of Bakersfield, Calif.

HARVEY SALEM

POS: T, **HT:** 6-6, **WT:** 289, **COLLEGE:** California, **ACQ:** Waivers, 1992

Salem, then an 11-year veteran, was picked up on waivers from Denver and played in four games in 1992, starting one for the Packers.

BILL SCHROEDER

POS: WR, **HT:** 6-1½, **WT:** 198, **COLLEGE:** UW-La Crosse, **ACQ:** 6th round, 1993

A great athlete who was a 17-time track All-American at La Crosse and was also an accomplished decathlete, Schroeder didn't play football until his senior season with the Eagles but caught eight TD passes. The Eau Claire native was on the Packers practice squad his entire rookie season, but when Sterling Sharpe's career ended, Schroeder was put on the active roster for the playoffs, seeing action on special teams in both games. In 1995, he was traded to New England along with TE Jeff Wilner for C Mike Arthur.

STERLING SHARPE

POS: WR, **HT:** 6-1, **WT:** 207, **COLLEGE:** South Carolina, **ACQ:** 1st round, 1988

Although starting receiver Walter Stanley openly wondered why the Packers wanted another receiver when Sharpe was drafted, Sharpe rewrote the Packers and NFL record books in a brilliant seven-year career that came to an end at the close of the 1994 regu-

lar season because of a neck injury that is incompatible with playing in the NFL. He has since become an NFL analyst for ESPN. Sharpe had a decent rookie season (55 catches, 791 yards, one TD) before exploding to 90-1,423-13 in his second season. He set the all-time single-season mark of 108 catches in 1992, then broke his own record with 112 the following year. The record has fallen several times since. Scored three TDs in his final game, a 34-19 win at Tampa Bay on Dec. 24, 1994, to finish with 18 TDs for the season, one short of Jim Taylor's team record from 1962. Finished as the Packers' all-time leader with 595 catches (14th all-time in the NFL), second to James Lofton with 8,134 yards and third behind Don Hutson and Taylor with 66 TDs (one running). He's seventh on the team's all-time scoring list. Sharpe scored four TDs in a game twice and made the Pro Bowl five times.

WAYNE SIMMONS

POS: LB, **HT:** 6-2½, **WT:** 248, **COLLEGE:** Clemson, **ACQ:** 1st round, 1993

Packers fans were wondering if Simmons was going to live up to his first-round status when he busted out in the 1995 playoffs, dominating the 49ers with big plays, including causing a fumble on the first play of the game that was returned for a touchdown, and a sack of Steve Young. Started eight games as a rookie, making 39 tackles with one sack and two INTs, was chosen to several all-rookie teams. Missed first four games of 1994 with knee sprain and got stuck behind Pro Bowler Bryce Paup, finishing with only 14 tackles and no sacks or INTs. Was relatively quiet much of the 1995 season, making 91 tackles, second on the team, while starting all 16 games. Also had a career-high four sacks.

Return to Glory

JOE SIMS

POS: T, **HT:** 6-3, **WT:** 310, **COLLEGE:** Nebraska, **ACQ:** FA, 1992

Sims spent four seasons in Green Bay (1992-95), mainly at right tackle. After being released by Atlanta, Sims started 20 regular season games and two playoff games. A versatile player, he also filled in at left guard and left tackle due to injuries to Guy McIntyre and Ken Ruettgers. After leaving Green Bay after the 1994 season to sign a free agent deal with Philadelphia, Sims was released before the 1995 season began. He returned to Green Bay to start the first game at left tackle for Ruettgers. After sitting out two straight games on the inactive list, he was waived following the seventh game.

JOHN STEPHENS

POS: RB, **HT:** 6-1, **WT:** 215, **COLLEGE:** Northwestern St., **ACQ:** Trade, 1993

The Packers traded a fourth-round draft pick for Stephens, who rushed for 1,168 yards in his rookie season of 1988 for New England but had done little since. He didn't do anything for the Packers, rushing for 173 yards on 48 carries (3.6 average) in five weeks before he was traded to Atlanta and Darrell Thompson was inserted as the starter.

FRED STRICKLAND

POS: LB, **HT:** 6-2, **WT:** 250, **COLLEGE:** Purdue, **ACQ:** UFA, 1994

This veteran linebacker came to Green Bay as an unrestricted free agent to rejoin Packers defensive coordinator Fritz Shurmur, who liked Strickland's versatile skills when both were with the Rams for three years. Strickland started 14 games at middle linebacker in 1994 and 10 in 1995, when he missed a pair of games with a knee injury. Finished second on team in tackles in 1994 with 88 and had an INT and fumble recovery. Had 51 tackles in 1995, including a season-high nine against the Cowboys, helping prompt a free-agent offer from Dallas, where Strickland will play in 1996.

HARRY SYDNEY

POS: FB, **HT:** 6-0, **WT:** 217, **COLLEGE:** Kansas, **ACQ:** FA, 1992

Sydney, who was waived by San Francisco after training camp, was brought to Green Bay because of his knowledge of the "West Coast" offense. The fullback started 10 games in

1992, his only season as a player in Green Bay. Sydney hauled in 49 passes for 384 yards and rushed for 163 yards on 51 carries during the 1992 season. A three-year member of Mike Holmgren's coaching staff, Sydney enters his second season as running backs coach.

AARON TAYLOR
POS: G, **HT:** 6-4, **WT:** 305, **COLLEGE:** Notre Dame, **ACQ:** 1st round, 1994

This promising lineman, who won the Lombardi Award as the nation's top collegiate lineman as a senior, has struggled with knee problems in both of his years in the NFL. Tore the patellar tendon in his right knee in mini-camp as a rookie, ending his season on June 6. After a grueling rehab, he wasn't at 100 percent but earned a starting spot at left guard for the season opener. Gradually got stronger and was a key cog in the Packers' offense in 1995 when he injured the other knee in the first playoff game against Atlanta.

KITRICK TAYLOR
POS: WR, **HT:** 5-10, **WT:** 194, **COLLEGE:** Washington State, **ACQ:** Plan B, 1992

Taylor's only highlight in Green Bay came in one of the Packers' most memorable comebacks when he caught a 35-yard Brett Favre touchdown pass which provided a 24-23 victory over Cincinnati in 1992. Taylor only caught two passes for 63 yards in his season in Green Bay. Taylor was waived after the 10th game of the '92 season.

GEORGE TEAGUE
POS: S, **HT:** 6-1, **WT:** 195, **COLLEGE:** Alabama, **ACQ:** 1st round, 1993

General Manager Ron Wolf traded up to select Teague late in the first round of the 1993 draft hoping Teague could bring some big plays to the Packers secondary. Teague took  over the starting spot after four weeks, finishing the regular season with 36 tackles and one INT. Made one of the biggest plays in recent memory when he returned an Erik Kramer pass 101 yards in a playoff game for the key score in a 28-24 win, the longest INT return in NFL playoff history. A thyroid illness ruined his 1994 season, although he had 53 tackles and three INTs, starting every game. Started 41st straight game in 1995 before missing one with a toe injury. Had a career-high 57 tackles and two INTs in 1995, but the Packers went looking for more production and a better tackler and traded for Seattle safety Eugene Robinson prior to the 1996 season, then traded Teague to Atlanta for a draft choice to be determined.

JEFF THOMASON

POS: TE, **HT:** 6-4½, **WT:** 250, **COLLEGE:** Oregon, **ACQ:** FA, 1994, 1995

After spending two seasons with the Bengals, Thomason spent some time with the Packers in the 1994 preseason but was waived, then was re-signed and made the team in 1995 as a reserve tight end. Played in all 16 games, starting once in a two-tight end alignment, and caught three passes for 32 yards on the season. Had 15 special teams tackles, tied for fourth on the team, including four in one game.

DARRELL THOMPSON

POS: RB, **HT:** 6-0½, **WT:** 217, **COLLEGE:** Minnesota, **ACQ:** 1st round-B, 1990

The former No. 1 pick never reached his potential in Green Bay from 1990-94. Thompson's best year came in 1993, when he racked up 654 yards and three TDs on 169 carries, which ranked him 12th in the NFC. He tallied only two 100-yard games during his career, both coming in the 1993 season. His longest run from scrimmage was a 60-yard TD in a key late-season game against the Raiders. In 1994, Thompson subbed at halfback, but carried the ball only twice for -2 yards in the first four games and was released. He was brought back when the team became unhappy with Leshon Johnson, but didn't rush the ball in four weeks and was released again, after the 14th week of the season. Ranks 20th on all-time Packers list with 1,642 rushing yards.

KEITH TRAYLOR

POS: DT, **HT:** 6-2, **WT:** 290, **COLLEGE:** Central Oklahoma, **ACQ:** FA, 1993

Traylor was signed a couple weeks into the 1993 season, making four special teams tackles in five games before he was released by mid-season.

ESERA TUAOLO

POS: NT/DE, **HT:** 6-2, **WT:** 284, **COLLEGE:** Oregon State, **ACQ:** 2nd round, 1991

The defensive lineman who once sang the National Anthem before a Thursday Night Packers-Bears game, didn't make much of an impression on Ron Wolf or Mike Holmgren. After the fourth game of the 1992 season, Lindy Infante's second-round draft pick of the 1991 draft was waived. Later that season he signed with Minnesota.

DAVID VIAENE

POS: T, **HT:** 6-5, **WT:** 300, **COLLEGE:** Minnesota-Duluth, **ACQ:** Plan B, 1992

The Packers took a chance on this local boy from Kaukauna, Wis., who played two seasons with New England. Viaene was waived during the 1992 training camp, but was re-signed in time for rival Chicago in the eighth week of 1992, where he served as a backup tackle. Viaene was waived the following week.

BRYAN WAGNER

POS: P, **HT:** 6-2, **WT:** 200, **COLLEGE:** Cal State-Northridge, **ACQ:** FA, 1992

Wagner tied for sixth in the NFC in 1993 with a career-high 42.9-yard gross average on 74 punts – the highest gross average by a Packer punter since Ron Widby average 43.1 in 1973. He also had a 36.3 net average which was ninth in the NFC. It was the best net by a Packer punter since the league began compiling the stat in 1987. Wagner's highlight game came on Dec. 26, 1993, against the Raiders when he boomed a 51-yard punt and three punts inside the 20 in sub-zero temperatures. The two-year Packer (1992-93) was signed by the Packers as a free agent in early November to replace Paul McJulien, who had beaten him out earlier in training camp.

SAMMY WALKER

POS: CB, **HT:** 5-11, **WT:** 200, **COLLEGE:** Texas Tech, **ACQ:** FA, 1993

The Packers were Walker's third team after he was released by Pittsburgh and Kansas City. Appeared in eight games in 1993 with one start, making 12 tackles. He spent all of 1994 on injured reserve with a dislocated elbow and didn't make the team in 1995.

ED WEST

POS: TE, **HT:** 6-1, **WT:** 245, **COLLEGE:** Auburn, **ACQ:** FA, 1984

The crafty veteran, known as one of the NFL's best blocking tight ends, surprised opponents with his receiving abilities. West, who wore a Packer uniform from 1984-94, had his career bests in both receptions and receiving yards with 31 and 377, respectively, in 1994. His 202 career receptions ranked him 10th on the Packers all-time receiving list following the 1994 season. Only Paul Coffman (322 catches) has more career receptions among Green Bay tight ends. West is the 10th player in Packers history to catch 200 passes. He finished his Green Bay career

with 25 touchdown catches. Surprisingly, West had a 2-yard rushing touchdown in 1984 vs. Minnesota. He signed a free agent contract with Philadelphia after the 1994 season and spent 1995 with the Eagles.

ADRIAN WHITE
POS: S, **HT:** 6-0, **WT:** 205, **COLLEGE:** Florida, **ACQ:** Plan B, 1992
White spent the 1992 season in Green Bay. His only start of the season came in the fifth game at strong safety. As a Packer, White totaled nine tackles in '92. In April 1993, he was traded to New England for a seventh-round draft pick.

Reggie White-DE

REGGIE WHITE
POS: DE, **HT:** 6-5, **WT:** 300, **COLLEGE:** Tennessee, **ACQ:** UFA, 1993
Is there anything left to say? White turned around the Packers defense when he surprised the world and signed with Green Bay. The all-time leading sack leader since the league began counting in 1982 with 157, White was named to the NFL's 75th Anniversary Team in 1994. Made the Pro Bowl for the 10th straight time in 1995, a record for a defensive end. Overcame various injuries with miraculous recoveries to provide inspiration to Packers during 1995 season. Announced on Dec. 13 that he was having surgery for a hamstring inury, but changed his mind the next day, and played that Sunday in a key win over New Orleans. Missed the first non-strike game of his career (166 games) when he sat out Dec. 10 against Tampa Bay with the hamstring tear. Recovered from serious knee

injury to play in key win over Chicago. Had 12 sacks in 1995, third in the NFC and the 10th time in 11 NFL seaons he reached double-digits. Must be double- or triple-teamed or he will destroy an offense. Off-the-field exploits of this ordained minister are also well-documented. Spent much of 1996 trying to help rebuild churches burned in the South. Won the NFL Players' Association's Humanitarian Award in 1992.

DOUG WIDELL

POS: G, **HT:** 6-4, **WT:** 280, **COLLEGE:** Boston College, **ACQ:** Trade, 1993

Picked up in a preseason trade to bolster the offensive line, Widell wound up starting nine games at left guard when Frank Winters moved to center to replace the injured James Campen. Finished the year as the full-time starter when Rich Moran was also injured but wasn't resigned in 1994.

GABE WILKINS

POS: DT, **HT:** 6-4½, **WT:** 310, **COLLEGE:** Gardner-Webb, **ACQ:** 4th round, 1994

A talented lineman who earned a starting spot in his second season, Wilkins had sacks in three of the team's first four games in 1995 while starting the first seven games. Tore a medial collateral ligament and missed three games but played in final six games. Finished the season with 15 tackles. Played in 15 games as a rookie and made one sack.

BRIAN WILLIAMS

POS: LB, **HT:** 6-1½, **WT:** 240, **COLLEGE:** USC, **ACQ:** 3rd round, 1995

Williams played in 13 games as a rookie, backing up George Koonce at ROLB. Made six tackles on special teams. Recovered an onside kick to preserve 14-6 win over Giants.

KEVIN WILLIAMS

POS: RB, **HT:** 6-1, **WT:** 215, **COLLEGE:** UCLA, **ACQ:** FA, 1993

Williams was picked up early in the 1993 season as a rookie free agent after John Stephens was released, suiting up for three games, then being inactive the final eight weeks of the season. Was injured in 1994, spending first two weeks on injured reserve before being released.

Return to Glory

MARK WILLIAMS

POS: LB, **HT:** 6-3, **WT:** 240, **COLLEGE:** Ohio State, **ACQ:** FA, 1994

Williams was one of three rookie free agents to make the team in 1994. Played in all 16 games, finishing fourth in special teams tackles with 11. Had a pair of tackles in brief defensive appearances. Selected by Jacksonville in the '95 expansion draft.

JAMES WILLIS

POS: LB, **HT:** 6-1½, **WT:** 237, **COLLEGE:** Auburn, **ACQ:** 5th round, 1993

Injury troubles never allowed Willis to make a good run at a starting spot. Got his chance to play as a rookie when George Koonce was injured and played well, but then tore up his knee. Had two INTs in his second season, including a game-saver off the Vikings' Warren Moon with 1:52 left and the Packers clinging to a 16-10 lead. Was inactive first eight weeks of 1995 before being released to create a roster spot for TE Keith Jackson. Signed with Philadelphia one week later.

JEFF WILNER

POS: TE, **HT:** 6-4½, **WT:** 245, **COLLEGE:** Wesleyan (Ct.), **ACQ:** FA, 1994

Wilner became the first pro player in Wesleyan's 164-year history when he survived the final cut in 1994. He appeared in 11 games as a rookie, mainly on special teams and in short-yardage situations, while catching five passes. In 1995, Wilner lost the battle with Mike Bartrum to make the roster; he was traded to New England along with WR Bill Schroeder for C Mike Arthur. When New England released him, he rejoined the Packers when Bartrum suffered a broken arm. Wilner played in only two games, then was released.

MARCUS WILSON

POS: RB, **HT:** 6-1, **WT:** 215, **COLLEGE:** Virginia, **ACQ:** FA, 1992, 1994

During his four-year stay (1992-95) in Green Bay he was mainly a special teams star, pacing the Packers with 17 tackles on special teams in 1995, which tied him with his career-best (he also had 17 in 1993). He chalked up 52 career special teams tackles with the Green and Gold. He also forced two fumbles on special teams and recovered one in 1993. During his Green Bay career, he returned 11 kickoffs for 211 yards, a 19.2-yard average, with a 37-yarder his longest. On offense, Wilson rushed the ball six times for three yards and caught two passes for 18 yards, both in 1993. Wilson was injured a knee in the 1995 NFC Championship game at Dallas. He was not re-signed for the '96 season.

RAY WILSON

POS: S, **HT:** 6-1, **WT:** 204, **COLLEGE:** New Mexico, **ACQ:** FA, 1994

Wilson was signed to the Packers' practice squad in the middle of the 1994 season, then played in two of the team's final three games when safety Tim Hauck was injured. He made three special teams tackles.

FRANK WINTERS

POS: C, **HT:** 6-3, **WT:** 295, **COLLEGE:** Western Illinois, **ACQ:** Plan B, 1992

A versatile player on the offensive line, the durable Winters has played in all of Green Bay's games since joining the team in 1992. Winters has played both center and guard for the Packers and has been the starting center the past season and a half. He also has served as the team's long-snapper on kicks and as the backup on punts.

VINCE WORKMAN

POS: RB, **HT:** 5-10, **WT:** 193, **COLLEGE:** Ohio State, **ACQ:** 5th round, 1989

The player known as "Pookie" had his best year as a Packer in 1992, his last with Green Bay, when led the Pack with 631 yards rushing despite missing the last 6½ games because of a shoulder separation. He set a Packer record for running backs with 12 receptions in the 1992 season opener against Minnesota. He also tallied 47 receptions for 290 yards in 1992. Workman spent four seasons in Green Bay, 1989-92. He signed a free agent contract with Tampa Bay following the '92 season and spent two seasons with the Buccaneers. Played with both Carolina and Indianapolis in 1995.

LANCE ZENO

POS: C, **HT:** 6-4, **WT:** 279, **COLLEGE:** UCLA, **ACQ:** Waivers, 1993

Claimed off waivers from Tampa Bay in the middle of the 1993 season, Zeno played on special teams in five games that season, plus two more in the playoffs, but never played a down from scrimmage.

Top 10 lists

Rushers

NAME	ATT.	YDS.	AVG.
1. Jim Taylor, 1958-66	1,811	8,207	4.53
2. John Brockington 1971-77	1,293	5,024	3.89
3. Tony Canadeo, 1941-44;46-52	1,025	4,197	4.09
4. Clarke Hinkle, 1932-41	1,171	3,860	3.30
5. Gerry Ellis, 1980-86	836	3,826	4.58
6. Paul Hornung, 1957-62; 64-66	893	3,711	4.16
7. Donny Anderson, 1966-71	787	3,165	4.02
8. Eddie Lee Ivery, 1979-86	667	2,933	4.40
9. Edgar Bennett, 1992-95	714	2,454	3.44
10. Tobin Rote, 1950-56	419	2,205	5.26

Scorers

NAME	TD	PAT	FG	TP
1. Don Hutson, 1935-45	105	172	7	823
2. Paul Hornung, 1957-66	62	190	66	760
3. Chris Jacke, 1989-95	0	250	152	706
4. Jim Taylor, 1958-66	91	0	0	546
5. Chestor Marcol, 1972-80	1	155	120	521
6. Fred Cone, 1951-57	16	200	53	455
7. Sterling Sharpe, 1988-94	66	0	0	396
8. Ted Fritsch, 1942-50	35	62	36	380
9. Clarke Hinkle, 1932-41	43	30	28	372
10. Verne Lewellen, 1924-32	51	1	0	307

Receivers

NAME	NO.	YDS.	AVG.
1. Sterling Sharpe, 1988-94	595	8,134	13.67
2. James Lofton, 1978-86	530	9,656	18.22
3. Don Hutson, 1935-45	488	7,991	16.38
4. Boyd Dowler, 1959-69	448	6,918	15.44
5. Max McGee, 1954; 57-67	348	6,346	18.39
6. Paul Coffman, 1978-85	322	4,223	13.11
7. Bill Howton, 1952-58	303	5,581	18.42
8. Carroll Dale, 1965-72	275	5,422	19.72
9. Gerry Ellis, 1980-86	267	2,514	9.42
10. Edgar Bennett, 1992-95	211	1,744	8.27

Kickoff Returners

NAME	NO.	AVG.	LG
1. Steve Odom, 1974-79	179	23.04	t95
2. Al Carmichael, 1953-58	153	25.54	t106
3. Herb Adderley, 1961-69	120	25.67	t103
4. Travis Williams, 1967-70	77	26.73	t104
5. Tony Canadeo, 1941-44; 46-52	75	23.15	48
6. Dave Hampton, 1969-71	74	28.16	t101
7. Tom Moore, 1960-65	71	26.51	84
8. Harlan Huckleby, 1980-85	70	18.57	57
9. Corey Harris, 1992-94	68	23.31	65
10. Billy Grimes, 1950-52	67	23.94	47

Passers

NAME	ATT.	COMP.	YARDS	TD	INT
1. Bart Starr, 1956-71	3,149	1,808	24,718	152	138
2. Lynn Dickey, 1976-77; 79-85	2,831	1,592	21,369	133	151
3. Brett Favre, 1992-95	2,145	1,342	14,825	108	64
4. Tobin Rote, 1950-56	1,854	826	11,535	89	119
5. Don Majkowski, 1987-92	1,607	889	10,870	56	56
6. Randy Wright, 1984-88	1,119	602	7,106	31	57
7. Arnie Herber, 1932-40	1,006	410	6,749	64	90
8. David Whitehurst, 1977-83	980	504	6,205	28	51
9. Cecil Isbell, 1938-42	818	411	5,945	61	52
10. Babe Parilli, 1952-53; 57-58	602	258	3,983	31	61

Sacks (since 1982)

NAME	NO.
1. Tim Harris, 1986-90	55.0
2. Ezra Johnson, 1977-87	41.5
3. Tony Bennett, 1990-93	36.0
4. Reggie White, 1993-95	33.0
5. Bryce Paup, 1990-94	32.5
6. Robert Brown, 1982-92	25.5
t7. John Anderson, 1978-89	19.5
t7. Sean Jones, 1994-95	19.5
9. Mike Douglass, 1978-85	19.0
10. Alphonso Carreker, 84-88	18.5

Punters

NAME	NO.	AVG.
1. David Beverly, 1975-84	495	37.95
2. Don Bracken, 1985-90	368	39.68
3. Donny Anderson, 1966-71	315	39.62
4. Max McGee, 1954; 57-67	256	41.59
5. Earl (Jug) Girard, 1948-51	200	39.15
6. Dick Deschaine, 1955-57	181	42.62
7. Bucky Scribner, 1983-84	154	41.98
8. Craig Hentrich, 1994-95	146	41.72
9. Jack Jacobs, 1947-49	143	42.10
10. Don Chandler, 1965-67	135	41.92

Punt Returners

NAME	NO.	AVG.	LG
1. Willie Wood, 1960-71	187	7.44	t72
2. Phillip Epps, 1982-88	100	8.19	t90
3. Al Carmichael, 1953-58	100	7.53	52
4. Walter Stanley, 1985-88	87	8.28	t83
5. Johnnie Gray, 1975-84	85	7.72	24
6. Jeff Query, 1989-91	76	9.37	28
7. Elijah Pitts, 1961-69; 71	75	5.25	t65
8. Robert Brooks, 1992-95	67	8.79	t85
9. Steve Odom, 1974-79	64	8.89	t95
10. Billy Grimes, 1950-52	63	13.24	t85

About the authors

Author Kevin Isaacson is editorial director for Krause Publications' sports division. An award-winning sports editor and columnist for the *Green Bay Press-Gazette* from 1987-94, Isaacson observed firsthand the Packers' return to NFL prominence. *Return to Glory* reflects his intimate insights into the Packers' success in the 1990s. Isaacson, wife Michele and daughters Alex and Erin live in Green Bay.

Co-author Tom Kessenich is Packers beat reporter and award-winning sports writer for the *Oshkosh Northwestern*. A 1986 graduate of the University of Wisconsin, he has covered a variety of high school, college and professional sports. Kessenich has been reporting on the Packers since 1990.

Contributor Denis Dougherty is sports copy editor for the *Appleton Post-Crescent*. He served as sports editor and assistant sports editor of several Wisconsin newspapers, including the *Green Bay Press-Gazette* and *Oshkosh Northwestern*. Dougherty lives in Appleton, Wis., with wife Terri and children Kyle, Rachel and Emily.

Contributor Eric Goska is the author of *Packer Legends In Fact*, a comprehensive statistical guide to the Green Bay Packers. He has contributed to the *Green Bay Press-Gazette* coverage of the Packers for the past decade. Goska and wife Ann live in Green Bay.

Contributor Rocky Landsverk is associate editor of *Sports Collectors Digest*. He is a former sports reporter and columnist for the *Oshkosh Northwestern*. He lives in Waupaca, Wis., with wife Angie, daughter Marisa and son Michael.

Contributor Tom Hultman is associate editor of *Sports Collectors Digest*. He is a former sports editor of *The Kaukauna Times*. He and wife Laura live in Neenah, Wis..

Photos

Vernon Biever of Port Washington, Wis.
Michael Cramer and Jack Wallin of Pacific Trading Cards, Lynnwood, Wash.
Tony Inzerillo of Bensenville, Ill.
Scott Kelnhofer, Krause Publications, Iola, Wis.
Trading cards provided by Pacific Trading Cards, Lynnwood, Wash.

'Return to Glory' with the 1996 Packers!

How did Brett Favre, Reggie White & Co. bring the Pack back?

Return to Glory provides the intimate details behind Green Bay's return to NFL prominence.

Award-winning author Kevin Isaacson offers unique insight on Favre, White, Mike Holmgren, Sterling Sharpe and dozens of other players and team executives. Return to Glory is a must-read for any Packer fan.

See other side for ordering instructions!

Return to Glory with the '96 Packers!

And win two Skybox seats to the Packer/Viking game!

❏ **YES!** Enter my name in the drawing for the 2 **FREE** Packer Skybox tickets for the Viking-Packer game December 22, 1996.

NAME_____

ADDRESS_____

CITY_____ STATE_____

ZIP_____

Telephone _____

> You and a friend could watch the Packers' Dec. 22, 1996 game against the Minnesota Vikings from the warm comfort of a Lambeau Field Skybox.

All entries must be received by November 30, 1996. One entry per person. Must be 18 years old to enter. For a complete copy of the rules send a SASE to Krause Publications Return to Glory Rules, 700 E. State St., Iola, WI, 54990-0001.

❏ Please send me a **FREE** catalog of all Krause Publications books and periodicals.

❏ **YES!** Send me ___ copies of **Return to Glory** at $16.95 each.
(Shipping: $3.25 first book, $2 each additional. WI residents add 5.5% tax. IL residents add 7.75% tax.)

❏ Check or money order enclosed
❏ AMEX ❏ DISC ❏ VISA ❏ MasterCard

Card #_____

Exp date_____

Signature_____

Telephone #_____

Name_____

Address_____

City_____

State_____ ZIP_____

Return to:
Krause Book Dept KUB1
700 E. State St., Iola, WI
54990-0001

No purchase necessary

❏ Please send me a FREE
catalog of all Krause
Publications books and
periodicals.

PLACE
STAMP
HERE

KRAUSE PUBLICATIONS
700 E STATE ST
IOLA WI 54990-0001

IıIıIııIııIIIıııIıIııIIıııIIıııIIıııIIıııııIIIIıııIIııııIıII